WESTMORELAND

The Inevitable General

WESTMORELAND

The Inevitable General

BY ERNEST B. FURGURSON

with photographs

Little, Brown and Company   Boston   Toronto

Quotations from Rudyard Kipling's poems "Gentlemen-
Rankers" and "If" are reprinted by permission of Mr.
George Bambridge, Doubleday & Company, Inc., Methuen
& Co. Ltd. and Macmillan & Co. Ltd. "If" is from *Rewards
and Fairies* by Rudyard Kipling, Copyright 1910 by
Rudyard Kipling.

*Published simultaneously in Canada
by Little, Brown & Company (Canada) Limited*

PRINTED IN THE UNITED STATES OF AMERICA

PREFACE

Biography of any man in midcareer is a quicksilverish thing. When he is a general in midwar, the problem is compounded. For a scholarly biographer, this might be reason enough to wait until the subject is retired, or resting with honor at Arlington. But if a newspaperman were put off by having to write about men and things that might change tomorrow, he would find little to do.

I became acquainted with Westmoreland in 1965 in Saigon, and after my first reportorial tour in Vietnam encountered him every few months at some place where he and President Johnson were conferring—in Washington, Johnson City, Manila, Guam or points between. I was struck by the fact that my initial impression of his soldierly qualities held up over the months. I also was bothered vaguely by the fact that here was a man whose role compared to that of Eisenhower in Europe, MacArthur in the Pacific and later in Korea, yet none of us whose job it was to understand the leaders of our day knew much about Westmoreland before he arrived in Vietnam. I assumed that a great many Americans, whose sons and husbands had served under Westmoreland, or who cared to learn all they could about the most perplexing foreign problem the nation faced, also wanted to know more.

I suggested a book to the general. In a four-month exchange of conversation and correspondence with him and his chief of information, Colonel Rodger R. Bankson, they made it clear that Westmoreland sought no such publicity and only reluctantly had accepted the fact that his position made him a public figure in whom Americans had a justified interest. Even if he wanted to have a book written about him, no general fighting a war could spare the time to make a major contribution to it. Further, the Vietnam war is a continuing operation, and Westmoreland's records, motives and intentions in directing it will remain classified for some time to come. Thus, I undertook this project without initiative or encouragement on the general's part. It certainly is not a ghostwritten autobiography, nor is it in any sense an "authorized" biography.

It does not purport to be the inside story of his leadership in Vietnam, but rather is a reporter's account of where he came from, how he got there, what equipment he acquired along the way, and how it has applied to the unprecedented task he faced on arrival in Saigon.

Its main sources have been the recollections of dozens of those who have known him since his preschool days in South Carolina, supplemented by official and unofficial writings about him, placed against the background of his times. There is no escaping the fact that most of the people who have known him best are Army officers, who, if they were serving in Vietnam during the writing of this book, were under his command—and if they were serving anywhere else, they had a feeling that they might be under his command in the near future. This is not a circumstance contributory to a warts-and-all biography, and if the author's asides and interpolations often seem to take a contrary view, it is for the sake of balance.

No one agrees more than I with the tradition that distrust between press and government is normal and healthy, but this should not mean that we automatically disbelieve anything said by anyone connected with the administration or the armed forces. This leads me to confess that some of my best friends are military information officials, whose conflicting duty is to help inform the public while protecting both proper and improper secrets. Among those who have aided me with this book are Colonel Bankson; Lieutenant Colonel Robert A. Webb and Miss Anna Urband of the book and magazine section of the Office of the Assistant Secretary of Defense for Public Affairs, and officers and men at the Pentagon, West Point, Fort Campbell, Carlisle, Fort Bragg, Schofield Barracks, and in MACV.

I also wish to thank Mrs. Lois Aldridge, of the World War II Division, National Archives and Records Service; my friend and erstwhile colleague Henry L. Trewhitt of *Newsweek* for his comments while reading the manuscript; and *The Sun* for its consistently cooperative attitude. The many whose invaluable assistance was more substantive than procedural are mentioned in the source notes following the text.

Ernest B. Furgurson

Solomon's Gap, Maryland
February 1968

WESTMORELAND

The Inevitable General

1

Round Trip to Chu Lai

A doorbell sounded in the courtyard of the villa, and a dozen officers and men snapped to attention where they stood. There was quick activity around a door marked by a series of identity signs, the one on top reading "COMUS-MACV." Out that door, fresh from a long conversation with a visiting Senator from Michigan, the Commander, United States Military Assistance Command, Vietnam, walked past a bas relief of a Greek goddess with wands of grain, left over from French days in Saigon. Quickly greeting some of those awaiting him, he entered the back seat of a black Chrysler Newport with two radio antennae sticking out its roof, its headlights lidded with yellow dimout paint, and four silver stars mounted above its front bumper. An Air Force lieutenant colonel with a sheaf of paperwork slid in beside him, and the car moved past the sandbagged sentry post at the compound's entrance.

Plainclothes Vietnamese motorcycle policemen led the car north past halted traffic, out Rue Pasteur; behind it were three more plainclothesmen in a jeep, the muzzle of an automatic rifle pointing toward the roof between them. Another sedan trailed the jeep, carrying the commander's aide and sergeant major. Traffic policemen at corners blew whistles to halt the flow in all directions as the short motorcade passed, the men in the jeep waving aside slow gray United States Navy buses and little blue-and-yellow Renault taxis with doors held on by baling wire. A Vietnamese paratrooper on a motorbike, wearing camouflage fatigues, let go his handlebar to salute as he whizzed by in the opposite direction.

Past apartments abuilding, bare-bottomed children squatting alongside the curb, newly opened small hotels, quick wash laundries and scattered grimy bars, the Chrysler headed toward Tansonnhut airport, then turned right outside the airport through the towering gates of the Joint General Staff compound to a grassy field where two Huey helicopters waited. Their pilots cranked their turbines as the car approached. The commander handed the paperwork back to the lieutenant colonel as he stepped out of the car. Those remaining behind stood at attention, holding salutes as he buckled himself in and the rotor wash tugged at their caps. The chopper lifted, dipped its nose and started away, and as it did he snapped them a salute. Only then did they drop their arms and turn away from the stinging blast of the Huey's flapping blades.

General William C. Westmoreland looked down on stilted huts along the Saigon River, sampans with the red-striped yellow flag of South Vietnam painted protectively on their cabin roofs, buses edging along the Bien Hoa highway with passengers' bikes tied on top, dozens of new piers and warehouses, barracks and hospitals. He was en route to Di An, headquarters of the 1st Infantry Division, and another day flying the four-star flag before forces in the field.

At least three times a week, he tried to make flying trips to posts as close as Di An and as remote as the hills across which American Marines fought into the demilitarized zone, 440 miles from Saigon. The same helicopters that enable the Allies in Vietnam to use tactics which previously had been only theories also enabled their commander to become the most "visible" general who ever led a force of half a million soldiers. With short chopper flights stitching together longer jet hops between the airstrips freckling the country, he could touch every one of the country's four corps areas in a day, and often did so.

His purpose was multiple: to push the troops' morale upward by demonstrating his interest in them, to keep commanders and staffs alert and updated because they could not predict far ahead when he might show up and start asking questions, to keep feeding detailed data into his own remarkably retentive mind, and to make personal note of shortages or disagreements between headquarters and the field, problems that might bedevil a colonel for months but which could be dissolved by a single note or phone call from COMUSMACV.

Di An had come a long way from those days in 1965 when it was a tenuously held tent camp on the south edge of the Viet Cong's Zone D stronghold, beyond the Bien Hoa airport. There still were tents, but so were there permanent buildings, company streets, a modernistic 2nd Brigade headquarters across the road from a parade field where troops were drawn up for medal presentation and change of command ceremonies. Westmoreland rolled up in a jeep with Major General John H. Hay, Jr., division commander, and marched onto a concrete diamond-shaped reviewing stand to hear the same ruffles and flourishes that precede "Hail to the Chief," followed by the division band's "The Star-Spangled Banner."

It was Memorial Day, and the monsoon season was beginning. As the band struck the high notes four bars from the anthem's end, low wet clouds were scudding from the southwest under an upside-down half moon. Westmoreland stood solemnly, the first dots of sweat starting to stain the back of his starched jungle fatigues, which bore his combat infantryman's and paratrooper's badges over his left pocket, his Vietnamese paratrooper's wings over his right pocket, the MACV patch on his left sleeve and that of his Korean war command, the 187th Airborne Regimental Combat Team, on his right. Then he presented the Distinguished Service Cross to the lieutenant colonel who had commanded the brigade, an assignment normally given an officer one or two ranks senior.

The lieutenant colonel, as he turned over his command, told his brigade through loudspeakers that "this division has never looked for or sought any specific hooks or gimmicks . . . and if I have any advice to my successor it is to continue to adhere to the sound principles of infantry combat." Black smoke blossomed up from the jungle to the north, and flares dropped into it before the sound thumped across Di An. Westmoreland added his endorsement, almost as if undersigning the lieutenant colonel's transfer orders. Speaking slowly, he told the troops of their leader's "brilliant" performance. He slipped and called it the 1st Brigade rather than the 2nd, when stating with feeling, "Your hallmark has been adherence to fundamentals. I know of no better formula than this . . ." Coming from someone else, this could have been classified as the epitome of triteness from a man who could think of nothing else to say. But not from Westmoreland. From him, it was more like a statement of personal philosophy.

The band played "Auld Lang Syne." Westmoreland shook hands with the officers around him, slapping them on the arm as he did so. They moved into brigade headquarters, where two tables were covered with white cloths, with red flowers as end pieces, and young soldiers served coffee and iced tea. Westmoreland took coffee with cream, and moved about among the officers, spending many minutes with the Vietnamese general who commanded the area. Then his aide reminded Westmoreland of his schedule.

He headed for the jeep, boarded the chopper and flew across American bulldozers digging a trash dump beside a Buddhist cemetery, trucks lined up at a gravel quarry, farmers awaiting the monsoon rains. As the Huey pock-pocked along the landing strip at Bien Hoa, past F–100 SuperSabre fighter-bombers, F–102 Delta Dart interceptors, C–130 Hercules and CV–2 Caribou transports, the general fought back a yawn. A waiting Air Force officer drove him in a station wagon along another runway, past a procession of quadruple .50-caliber machine guns, 40-mm. anti-aircraft guns, forklift trucks carrying napalm bombs and dump trucks loaded with uniformed Vietnamese.

"What on earth is all this?" the general asked.

"VNAF day," said the Air Force officer. "Vietnamese Air Force Day is Thursday. They've been practicing their parade all week. Even wanted us to shut down the runway."

The general seemed astounded, but said only, "We can't shut down combat operations for anything like that."

Next to a small T–39 SabreLiner with four stars shining

beside its hatch, the station wagon halted. Shaking hands with the pilot, the general entered and sat before a work-table at the plane's rear. As the twin jets at the rear of the fuselage whined alive, he told his aide to get a message to Marshal Ky expressing his regret that he would not be able to attend the VNAF Day parade, that General Creighton Abrams would represent him, and explaining why. "Why" was that he had planned for weeks to make an overnight flight to Clark Air Force Base near Manila, to see his wife before she departed for a month-long vacation in the States.

Thrusting through the high clouds, the T–39 cut across the eastern ridges of the Central Highlands. The sergeant major, a veteran of twenty-two Army years named Harold L. McCoy, tried to nap. The aide, twenty-seven-year-old Captain Larry Budge, a Rhodes scholar who had been a company commander with the 1st Air Cavalry Division, pulled Jules Roy's *The Battle of Dienbienphu* from his briefcase. He already had read Bernard Fall's *Hell in a Very Small Place,* about the same French defeat, and it referred to Roy's book as the definitive work on Dienbien-phu. When he finished Roy, he was going to read Fall again. The general asked the aide for a scratch pad, and began making notes in a small, steady script that remained regular despite the jet's bumping through rainclouds passing Qui Nhon and letting down to Phu Cat.

Rolling to a halt off the green nonskid surface of the newly laid aluminum runway at Phu Cat, the pilot lowered the stairs and Westmoreland leaped out with a shout. "Jumping Jack! How are you?" He returned the salute of Major General John J. Tolson, commander of the 1st Cav, who had served with him two decades before in the 82nd Airborne Division. There apparently is not a United States Army unit as big as a battalion in which Westmoreland

14

does not know someone from out of his past. Thirty-six years is a long time, and out of it he can summon names or at least nicknames to go with faces familiar from West Point, Fort Sill, Schofield Barracks, Fort Bragg, North Africa, Sicily, England, France, Belgium, Germany, Fort Benning, Fort Leavenworth, Carlisle Barracks, Japan, Korea, the Pentagon, Harvard, Fort Campbell, Saigon or points between. It is a trait for which many a presidential candidate would forgo ten hours of free network time.

Captain Budge opened his briefcase again, and handed Westmoreland a pistol belt bearing a 9-mm. Browning automatic in a GI holster and a sheath knife with a handle of polished white bone. Westmoreland strapped it on, and aboard Tolson's Huey, the two generals were head to head over a map, with the 1st Cav commander pointing down past the chopper's flexible machine guns to features in his tactical area of operations.

Here, above the central eastward bulge of South Vietnam, the monsoon was past. The coastal plain, covered with water back to the mountains' edge in the rainy season, was dry now and busy along the nation's north-south aorta, Highway One. Following the road north, the Huey crossed Landing Zone (LZ) Crystal, where a regiment of the Army of the Republic of Vietnam (ARVN) 22nd Division was headquartered as it moved into the area cleared by the 1st Cav. It would provide protection to the Revolutionary Development (Rev Dev, or rural pacification) teams who would try to dig out the disguised Viet Cong soldiers and the villagers who supply, hide, propagandize for or openly sympathize with the Viet Cong. After that, theoretically, there would be peace and stability and the Americans and the ARVN could move on to other infested areas.

Westmoreland leaned to peer down when Tolson indicated a tin-roofed village of refugees from Viet Cong-held or disputed valleys back in the mountains, then an ARVN 155-mm. howitzer battery perched on a hilltop, commanding the plain. The chopper curved down to LZ Uplift, an oiled patch amid tents on a red dust hill, and the generals headed directly for a briefing by the staff of the 2nd Brigade of the 1st Cav.

Westmoreland listened closely as the intelligence officer described the enemy situation—which units were operating nearby; their strength, health, morale and weapons; how many prisoners were being taken; their routes of attack and withdrawal. "What kind of prisoners are these?" COMUS-MACV asked the young officer. They were mostly Viet Cong, the S–2 said, with a few from North Vietnamese Army (NVA) units and more who were NVA soldiers assigned to fill out decimated VC battalions.

The operations officer (S–3) took the telescoping pointer then, to brief on his own brigade and other friendly units, including accounts of how the brigade had been using not only its own choppers but Navy landing craft to come in on unfriendly villages from the sea, often in the dark of morning. It had sifted those villages not once but repeatedly, the S–3 said, and each time had taken more prisoners, found more "civil defender" types.

Westmoreland commended this persistence, and after further questions listened to the civil affairs officer (S–5). In peacetime, S–5 is a billet seldom filled; in wartime his job in friendly or potentially friendly territory is to try to win the population to the American side, and in enemy territory to administer military government. This S–5 was strong on two programs: psychological warfare and civilian police work. In recent days, three Lambretta three-wheeled minitrucks had been blown up by enemy mines on roads nearby. The S–5 had a Vietnamese employee tape an account of the incidents each time, and within hours afterward these records about the Viet Cong killings were blared by loudspeaker down to the population along the plain. Within days, enough leaflets, with photographs of the victims, were dropped to provide each village with half a dozen copies. Next, the S–5 told about an experiment underway in cooperation with the National Police Field Force, in which a 120-man company of police was assigned to work with an American brigade. Broken down into platoons and six-man patrol squads, these units comb villages in areas newly occupied by friendly forces, doing a much slower, more knowledgeable job than American troops could do. They were armed with "blacklists" of known Viet Cong, and interrogated villagers at length about their comings and goings. Westmoreland, recently assigned to take over the American advisory role in the lagging pacification effort, listened and questioned intently.

The S–5 told him, too, how persons in the refugee camps who had relatives remaining in Viet Cong areas in the mountains had been sent back to their homes to proselyte, and were bringing back to the coastal refugee camps many converts.

"That's a damn good idea," said COMUSMACV, and those around him seemed surprised at his choice of words.

Off again, Westmoreland flew across the Bong Son plain, paralleling the An Lao valley, both scenes of vicious, prolonged fighting in the 1st Cav's Operations White Wing and Masher a year before. One, then a series of hamlets, whose dozen or so huts were burned flat, passed beneath. Next stop, Landing Zone Two Bits, two miles west of Bong Son along the Song Liang River. The Huey wound down onto an asphalt pad, on a spot bearing the yellow shield and black horse's head of the 1st Cav, and the warning, "CG Only."

COMUSMACV had no more than dismounted when he asked, "Where's Sergeant Major Pearce?" Immediately, there appeared a smiling soldier with a handsome mouth of teeth who threw the general a highball salute and sang, "All the way, sir!" He had been a corporal in Westmoreland's 504th Parachute Infantry Regiment twenty-one years earlier, and since paratroopers, unlike some other bearers of arms who also consider themselves special, carry with them through the years the mumbo jumbo that is intended to build esprit in training, he had given his old commander the second part of the chant that goes, "Airborne . . . all the way!" Westmoreland inquired about Pearce's recent wound —"It was in the buttocks, wasn't it?" "Nossir, it was in the back and leg." One of the other soldiers nearby said it was too bad Pearce's paratrooper days seemed to be over. "Nossir, I'm going back on jump status," Pearce said, and everyone believed him.

Lunch was waiting beneath a long tent. Roast beef Army style, well-done with gravy; potatoes; a vegetable; an endless supply of red Kool-Aid, to satisfy a thirst the general quenched with cold soft drinks at least half a dozen times in the long day; chocolate ice cream and raisin cookies. As Westmoreland and the 1st Cav staff ate, one officer told about the young woman captured in the hills who had proven to be a well-trained Communist political cadre member. She answered questions by asking questions right back, he said, and when he had no more questions she gave him a speech on her political beliefs. "It was like listening to a long-playing record," he said. Somebody asked how old she was. "Twenty-six." Was she good-looking? Pause. "Depends on how long you've been out here." The chaplain leading, everybody chuckled except COMUS-MACV. So the chuckling died quickly, and he asked whether the ARVN had been showing any enthusiasm for civic action. Not much, was the gist of the answer. Prod them, he said.

Sergeant Major Pearce waylaid the general en route to the chopper. "All the way, sir," he challenged. "All the way, Pearce," the general gave the countersign.

As he flew toward LZ English, the colonel commanding the 1st Cav's 1st Brigade (who had been a lieutenant under Westmoreland in 1946) told him he had just received approval of a Distinguished Service Cross for one of his soldiers. Would the general present the medal? Of course he would, and the brigade had anticipated this, because a small formation already was drawn up awaiting him.

Front and center stood a skinny red-haired ridge-runner named Hatterson, a machine gunner who had gone on a rampage against VC fortified positions despite his own two wounds. It was the kind of performance that has won many a soldier a Medal of Honor. The general stood at attention facing the young soldier as the adjutant read the citation. The soldier, his pistol sagging off a hip hardly big enough to hold up his web belt, looked the general in the eye throughout. As he took the medal from its box and pinned it to the gunner's fatigues, the general talked quietly to him, and only the corporal heard the words of congratulation, for a departing helicopter drowned them out for those standing close by.

The ceremony over, the general noticed a sharp Negro lieutenant he had known when he was West Point superintendent. Shaking hands, he started into the briefing tent and spotted a captain with a plastic bottle of insect repellent stuck into the rubber band tightening the camouflage cover

19

on his helmet. He shook hands with him, too. He had ridden the Army mule at football games in the early '60's.

The S–2 and S–3 of the 1st Brigade told of the unit's efforts to clean out Sa Huynh, an inverted hook of a peninsula surrounding a salt lake, where the mountains push close to the sea. When they were done, Westmoreland stood before maps in the briefing tent and gave them a short discourse on Sa Huynh. He told them the area had been an enemy stronghold for twenty years, that here the VC could get fish, salt and rice, and across only that front range of mountains lay the An Lao valley and the Ho Chi Minh trail, plugging those back-toted foods into the VC's nationwide supply system. In addition, it had been relatively untouched because it lay along the I and II Corps border, in a strip where neither corps commander had wanted to intrude on the other's jurisdiction. It was almost as if he had prepared his little speech in advance. He concluded with a restatement of how important Sa Huynh was to the enemy, and thus how important it was for the 1st Brigade to clean it out. The staff, which had stood at attention to hear him, remained there as he headed out of the tent.

Along the CP (command post) street, as at every stop he had made, soldiers wielding cameras waited to take a shot of him as he passed. Inevitably they were confused about whether to snap first, then salute, or vice versa. One had a tripod set up, and for this one the general paused a second to pose beside one of the MP's assigned to escort him.

B–52 tracks, carpets of hundreds of holes fifty feet across and thirty feet deep, each ripped out of the jungle by a 750-pound bomb, ran up a streambed used by the VC as an assembly area and supply route from Sa Huynh. The general's chopper curved over the peninsula, over gashes in the cliffs at its tip, where a destroyer's five-inch guns had been called in on caves presumably used by the enemy. Close by along Highway One, safe in the daytime, soldiers sloshed in a river, washing the red grime off their two-and-a-half-ton trucks.

Down again at Duc Pho, Westmoreland got a detailed briefing on the operations of the 1st Brigade, 101st Airborne Division, a division he had commanded only seven years earlier. At midafternoon, the weight of the coastal heat pressed down onto the canvas. More cold soda pop, but here there were no fans like those rigged at most of the general's earlier stops. Westmoreland leaned forward to listen.

Sweat ran down the long scar that has wrinkled the left side of his face since an automobile accident when he was eleven. It was not yet near the end of a day crammed with dozens of names that can blur together in a tired mind until all Vietnamese places sound the same; crammed with battalion numbers, prisoner of war statistics, rice tonnages, unit strengths, police techniques, battle plans. The general flexed his jaw muscles, as if willing himself to concentrate. The sound of outgoing artillery fire gently rippled the tent's sloping roof. Then he stood to deliver again, almost word for word, the talk about fish, salt and rice which he had applied earlier to Sa Huynh.

Duc Pho airfield, built in twenty-five days, fled beneath the helicopter. A forward air controller in a low-flying Bird Dog circled above sudden puffs of gray smoke as artillery rounds crept between two long hill fingers. Westmoreland studied a translation of a captured VC intelligence report, assessing the helicopter-borne troops who had moved into

the enemy's Binh Dinh–Quang Ngai stronghold. Emphasizing that the Americans already had been defeated several
times since their arrival, it concluded nevertheless that they
were stubborn, and would continue to attack even after
taking heavy casualties.

Sharing the document with him was Major General William B. Rosson, an officer with one of the most brilliant
reputations in the country. He had been MACV chief of
staff in Saigon before taking field command of Task Force
Oregon, and later would win a third star and broader responsibilities. The task force was Westmoreland's way of
unifying command of three Army brigades sent north into
"Marineland," the I Corps area which had been the nearly
exclusive domain of the III Marine Amphibious Force and
two Vietnamese divisions until the NVA invasion across the
demilitarized zone demanded the shift of major Marine
strength north along the border.

The first sign of Mo Duc is tin roofs, above mud and
bamboo huts sheltering eighteen thousand refugees from
the hills, who have multiplied the population of that tiny
district town in Quang Ngai province. Alongside them is a
triangular fort like the Special Forces outposts that are
spotted in enemy and marginal sections all over South Vietnam. From the chopper pad the generals jeeped through the
gate of the district headquarters, another fort with log walls
and barbed wire.

A squad of Popular Force troops was in line, flanked by
local policemen and three girls in wispy *ao dais* who presented Westmoreland with a bouquet of red lilies. He made
a point of stopping to chat with the squad leader through an
interpreter. The corporal held his salute, his wrist bent in
unconscious violation of the rules of military courtesy as

22

taught in American basic courses, as Westmoreland asked about his background. He had been decorated three times, wounded twice. The general said, "Tell him I congratulate him on his military record." Without speaking, the corporal held the salute, quivering, as the general briskly returned it.

Two splendid girls from the centerfold of *Playboy* hung on the walls of the subsector adviser's office. He was a major with a bald spot, a tall American who ran down the less than assuring situation in Mo Duc district. Forty-four of its fifty-eight hamlets were controlled by the VC. The men who worked the rice fields by day disappeared when American troops came into the area. Road minings were frequent, the latest only a thousand yards down Highway One from the headquarters. The regional force units along the highway had commanders of divergent personalities. The one on the northern end, where the VC regularly used a trail as a supply route into the hills, was reluctant to tangle with the enemy. The one in the south had been more eager, lending troops to try to cut that route, until one of his platoons had been wiped out as it waited in ambush there. Since then, he had been less willing to carry part of his neighboring officer's burden. The supplies were moving unhindered, for American troops were not available in Mo Duc.

COMUSMACV shot a few crisp questions at the major. He reminded him that Mo Duc had "psywar" importance because it was the home district of Pham Van Dong, the North Vietnamese premier, and other leaders of the Hanoi government. Then he asked the Vietnamese district chief about enemy activity in MR–5, which is VC nomenclature for the mountainous inland area of Quang Ngai and nearby provinces. The chief did not understand him, and though the general repeated his question thrice, enunciating it slowly for the interpreter, he finally changed the subject and promised the chief that by the end of the summer a new airstrip would be completed for Mo Duc.

Another soft drink. Another jeep ride to the helicopter pad, where the general spotted an Australian military adviser, floppy fatigue hat and massive belt buckle setting him off from Americans in comparable jungle uniform. The Aussie took his picture as he advanced, then Westmoreland asked him the automatic questions about morale, food, mail, and as he headed for his chopper the Aussie snapped him a magnificent palm-forward salute. The general was suppressing a grin as he climbed aboard and whirled away.

He and Rosson put on headsets to confer on the chopper's intercommunications system as they puttered over the Song Be River, where bamboo fish traps patterned the water with V's, and over the hills south of Chu Lai where American Marines had fought for almost two years before being dispatched north along the DMZ. At Chu Lai, half a mile from the fighter runway, was headquarters of Rosson's Task Force Oregon.

The hawk-nosed Rosson sat alongside Westmoreland as officers of the 1st Brigade, 101st Airborne; 196th Light Infantry Brigade; and 3rd Brigade, 25th Infantry Division filled them in on their kill scores and other statistics since they moved into southern I Corps to replace the Marines. A civil affairs officer related how the friendly side was broadcasting Vietnamese folk music, with propaganda commercials, toward nearby villages in the evening after civilians had completed dinner and were waiting for bedtime—in prime time. Rosson said two of the tunes they used were "Come Back to Central Vietnam" and "Moon over Chu Lai," and they were "bringing them in in droves." This reminded Westmoreland of a tale told by Tran Van Do, Saigon's foreign minister, about the sentimental importance of flute music in the days before it took a role in psychological warfare.

The officers dealt with the problem of the 3rd Brigade, 25th Division's operating far from its parent unit, and whether it should be redesignated a separate brigade. The brigade commander, clearly desirous of having a separate command, nevertheless was leery of changing his unit designation. His battalions were developing some esprit and it would not do to change their numbers arbitrarily overnight, he said. In addition, they had a strong attachment to the taro leaf patch of the 25th, the "Tropic Lightning" division. Well, what about making it the 325th Brigade, Westmoreland asked—would that be close enough to its current designation? He promised to see about it on returning to Saigon.

A tall, sweating Negro shot baskets alone on a court beside the chopper pad, but mechanics atop helicopters, soldiers beside and under them stood at attention, saluting in a whirl of sand, as the generals lifted off, then dropped onto a taxiway beside the T–39 waiting at the Chu Lai fighter strip.

Westmoreland looked, as he saluted farewell to Rosson, as if it were early morning. The sweat of midday had faded; he was as well-pressed as he had been while receiving the Senator back in Saigon. He unstrapped his pistol belt, handed it to his aide, and while the T–39 sped past A–6 Intruders, A–4 Skyhawks, F–4 Phantoms and an EC–121

Constellation radar picket plane, he dug from his fatigue pocket the notes he had made during the day. Before the SabreLiner was airborne, he was at work again.

CIDG (Civilian Irregular Defense Group) troops would not move into a camp newly prepared for them because they were reluctant to pack up their families and move back into the mountains. Intelligence reports. Personnel. Weapons. Morale. Command jurisdiction.

In an hour, the T–39 was letting down again at Tansonnhut. The lieutenant colonel, loaded with papers, was waiting.

Perhaps six hundred times in more than four years, Westmoreland has spent those days afield, each day ten or a dozen separate helicopter and airplane hops. They are not all upcountry, but in every direction. They are to hills newly captured, to hospitals filled with freshly wounded, to muddy clearings where Special Forces camps are being built in enemy territory, to landing ships tied up in the My Tho River, floating base of the Riverine force that probes up the canals of the Mekong Delta.

There was the day the general spent flitting from one headquarters to another, in the critical provinces surrounding Saigon. He talked to American advisers and the Vietnamese province chiefs who were their "counterparts," and his urgent message that day was the need to work to win over the population. At Bao Tri, Tan An, Ba Ria, he covered the routine subjects in order, then gave emphasis to civic action by returning to it, asking for details on local programs, underlining the degree of his own interest so that no junior military man listening could fail to understand what he had better be doing if he had not started already. Win the friendship of the population, build schools and markets, open roads, protect harvests, issue pills, soap and inoculations. And then, near the end of that day, his Huey touched down on the strip at Go Cong, inland from the bay south of Saigon. As it did, the escorting Huey gunship directly overhead suddenly let go one 2.75-inch rocket, totally accidentally, because of a short circuit in its firing mechanism. The missile sped into the center of the town and exploded. A few minutes later, at province headquarters, an officer reported to the general that the round had killed a Vietnamese child playing outside its home and wounded three other civilians. Westmoreland's self-control never wavered, but for a moment there was an expression, a tightening of the lips, that spoke of the irony of this particular accident on this particular day.

There were other days, some when the general produced his stock portfolio or newspaper clippings about the war from his briefcase for review in flight. More than once, there were conversations about the value of the Vietnam experience to American military men. "I bet that Russian Army is jealous as hell. Our troops are here getting all this experience, we're learning about guerrilla warfare, helicopters, vertical envelopment, close artillery support . . . Those Russian generals would love to be here . . . Any true professional wants to march to the sound of gunfire."

The visible vignettes all say something about Westmoreland's character, but they do not fit into a simple pattern, in fact are often contradictory. A President who quite literally risks his own future on the correctness of the general's judgment, a diplomat, a Senator, a Marine general—all men dedicated to eventual American success in Vietnam—will base their assessments of him on different midnight conversations, reports, committee testimony, operations orders. Another man may feel he caught the most concise

27

possible insight the day his boots left a hunk of black delta gumbo on the beige carpet of the general's office, and COMUSMACV, leader of the greatest, most complex field army of our generation, leaned over wordlessly, almost formally, eight embroidered stars gleaming, and picked up the mud and deposited it with care in his wastebasket.

2

South Carolina

1914–1931

Spartanburg lies along the line where the rivers roil down
out of the Blue Ridge toward Charleston and the sea.
Angling gently northeast to southwest, this Piedmont has
been hospitable to those who came inland first—rich in cotton and tobacco for enough generations for those first families to have the land, money and education to retain their
gentried status. It lasted through The War, through Reconstruction, and into the industrialization that began in the
late 1800's and has accelerated since World War II. Beginning in the 1880's, the Piedmont, with its strong streams
and labor quick to grab the chance to abandon hardscrab-
ble farms, became the new heart of the American textile
industry. From Virginia down into Georgia the mills sprang
up, often financed by Yankee money and managed by men
who either were born into or were imported and quickly
joined the plantation-banker-lawyer class that ran those

towns and counties by assumption. Mostly, they were men with English names who went to the Episcopal church; the men—and women—at the looms in the red brick mills were mostly the Scotch-Irish who worshiped in the frame Baptist or Pentecostal Holiness churches. Thus it was in Spartanburg, and up and down the line of the Southern Railway, in Danville, Greensboro, Charlotte, Greenville, on into Seneca, Toccoa and Gainesville.

Not many families preceded the Westmorelands into inland South Carolina. They had come from England early, too. The first of them to arrive in Virginia was Richard Neville, who sailed there with that name in 1650, but died as Richard Westmoreland. He is said to have been the son of Ralph Neville, the eighth earl of Westmoreland, whose line was traceable directly back to another Ralph Neville, the first earl, one of the most powerful men in England in the late 1300's and early 1400's. Some of the family's genealogists maintain that the title was passed down directly until the sixth earl was deprived of it by Elizabeth I. He and his son and grandson insisted the title was still theirs, and when the latter Ralph Neville decided to come to the colony he announced that in the New World he would use his father's rightful title as his own family name.

The version most commonly accepted by the South Carolina Westmorelands is that three brothers, John, Robert and Thomas, came to America in the 1740's, with John settling in Pennsylvania, Robert in Virginia and Thomas in South Carolina. It was Thomas who came to the Enoree River, near Van Patton's Shoals, and marked off with a hatchet six hundred acres of land, to which he obtained a grant from King George. The story is that Thomas later died of a rattlesnake's bite, but not before he had implanted

Childs Westmoreland shortly after be-coming an Eagle Scout, summer 1929.

At the start of his military career: Westmoreland before a sally port at The Citadel, Charleston, 1931.

Westmoreland as a West Point cadet, en route to becoming first captain of his class.

Second Lieutenant Westmoreland aboard Pollyann, Fort Sill, 1938.

Lieutenant Colonel Westmoreland with Brigadier General Reese M. Howell, 9th Infantry Division artillery commander, Barton Stacey, England, 1944.

*Westmoreland as a thirty-year-old colonel,
chief of staff of the 9th Division, 1945.*

*Colonel Westmoreland receiving the Legion of Honor
from French General Louis-Marie Koeltz, April 1945.*

Newlyweds Colonel Westmoreland and the former Katherine Stevens Van Deusen, Fayetteville, May 1947.

the family in what is now southwestern Spartanburg and upper Laurens counties, South Carolina.

Only after the Revolution did Spartanburg get its name: the backwoods volunteers who joined in 1775 to oppose the Tories of the Piedmont called themselves the Spartan Regiment, and the county and town later sought to perpetuate their pride in the regiment's formation.

There was no military tradition among those early Westmorelands, and in fact there still was no serious one when the family's most famous soldier chose that career more than 150 years later. Thomas Westmoreland "served the cause of the Revolution by furnishing supplies for Continental use," according to one researcher; his grandson, also Thomas, was a soldier, but he was only twenty when the war was over. The fighting itself never touched the family at home; the battle of King's Mountain, where the redoubtable redcoat Major Patrick Ferguson was killed, was the most famous clash nearby, and the battle of Cowpens, eighteen miles away, was the closest.

Between the Revolution and the Civil War, the family spread thickly but not widely outward from its base along the Enoree, and developed a strong interest in the career of medicine. Two generations before the Civil War, it produced a pair of physicians, Willis and William, who organized the Atlanta Medical College, later the medical department of Emory College. They had a brother, Dennis, who did his healing nearer home, as a horseback doctor just across the Enoree from the old estate.

By the time the Civil War sparked fire at Fort Sumter, 205 miles southeast of Spartanburg, there were enough Westmorelands so that at least ten are traceable in the county's service records. One died of wounds at the Wil-

31

derness, one at Petersburg, one at Antietam, another at home, one in a Yankee prison, another was wounded on the Rappahannock. Most were privates. James Riley Westmoreland, another brother of the doctors, served in Wade Hampton's brigade of South Carolina cavalry; so did his son, Dr. John A., who took over Dennis's home and country practice and had a son, James Ripley Westmoreland, in 1876.

This youngster was not to make it a third successive generation of physicians; his father sent him to The Citadel, the Military College of South Carolina, at Charleston. Here might have begun the military tradition one could expect to produce a four-star general in one more generation, but this Westmoreland never saw a day of active service after his graduation in 1900. He entered college late, working several years to help his brothers in medical school. And his graduation was postponed further when "Rip," as he was called at The Citadel, was expelled for misconduct while ranking high in his class. He and his classmates found another student guilty of "something dishonorable" and dispensed vigilante-style justice, thus were kicked out. But he was allowed to return later, after making up his examinations. While he never made use of his military commission, he had absorbed a Citadel spirit that made him the school's most active booster for many years, and earned him the title of "colonel" without any honorary ties to Kentucky.

"Rip" might have chosen to take his commission and use it as a way out of South Carolina into a world that could hold attraction for an assertive young man. There was the post-Spanish-American War push of "gunboat diplomacy," and if he had been able to go on to study law, he could have taken part in the resurgence of Southern politics. He had to make a decision, and apparently recognized it when he did: he could go out into the world, or he could stay at home, meet the responsibilities that followed his father's death, and aim frankly at business success.

He became a businessman. Out of college, he went with the Central National Bank of Spartanburg, and later organized a bank at Woodruff, South Carolina. He was thirty-seven, established, a no-nonsense man who knew what he wanted when he focused on a tiny, gentle girl from Columbia named Eugenia Talley Childs.

The Childses were prominent in the state capital, eminently solvent and with historical lines at least to match the Westmorelands. As Eugenia ("Mimi") remembered shortly before her death in 1967, her grandfather had run a cotton mill near Lincolnton, North Carolina, before the Civil War (she called it the War Between the States, of course), and then he came to Columbia with the Saluda cotton mill. His oldest son was only sixteen, too young to go off to war, but he insisted, and finally got on his white pony and rode the 127 miles back to Lincolnton to join the outfit into which his cousin already had volunteered. The boy was John Ebin Childs, and he never came back. He was killed at Chickamauga. His still younger brother, W. G. Childs, went to Virginia Military Institute just after the war, and graduated in 1870 on the Lexington campus adjacent to Washington College, where Robert E. Lee died as president the same year. But this was no professional soldier, either, and he swore he would never send one of his sons to VMI because the Valley of Virginia was too hot in summer, even for a South Carolinian. But other branches of Eugenia Childs's family included many officers as well as physicians, and one prominent combination—Robert Wilson Gibbes, C.S.A., surgeon general of South Carolina.

W. G. Childs used his father's solid textile position to

branch out, as builder of the Columbia, Newberry and Laurens Railroad, founder of the Bank of Columbia and interested party in a series of the state's major concerns. He had much in common with the man courting his daughter, who married her in 1913 and took her back to the upper Piedmont, where he, too, was joining the region's heavy concentration in textiles.

Westmoreland was restless, still wanting to push ahead, but most of the world seemed calm that year and the following spring, awaiting unknowingly what lay just ahead in Europe.

On March 26, 1914, for example, the Spartanburg *Journal* gave front-page space to the news of United States troops' driving Mexican soldiers back across the Rio Grande, and the defeat of Mexican rebels at Torreón. The most prominent display related to affairs across the Atlantic was a set of boiler-plate portraits of the main figures in the Ulster crisis. There was more attention to what was happening at home, and in ladies' fashions and other soft consumer goods.

Herbert D. Hemenway, of the National Society for Broader Education, lectured with stereopticon slides at the Spartanburg County courthouse, on the problems of beautifying grounds surrounding the home. A lengthy account of his talk was offered near an advertisement: "Ladies! Darken your hair! Grandma's Sage Tea and Sulfur Recipe and nobody will know!" There was intelligence from New York on fashions: ". . . on the best of clerical and civic authority it is claimed the dresses worn by the American woman have achieved a crescendo of naughtiness—slits, transparencies and other sartorial elisions or revelations . . ." Some blame this on French designers, the neutral correspondent reported, while the French blame it on women who take their designs and "go overboard." Suitably restricted to a back page among the feed and seed ads was a notice that Clarke's Happy Valley corn whisky was available at $2.50 a gallon.

Few people in Spartanburg remember anything the *Journal* printed that day, but many are aware now that Mrs. Westmoreland gave birth that midnight to her first child. A country doctor named Blake officiated at the Westmoreland cottage at Saxon, a village three miles west of Spartanburg, where the father had become a cotton mill official. Westmoreland called in a Presbyterian pastor to baptize the boy, taking it for granted without asking his wife that his own denomination would be the proper one. But without his knowing it, Mimi had sent for the Episcopal rector, Dr. W. H. K. Pendleton, and they both arrived at the same time. The two ministers talked it over with the father, and decided Mrs. Westmoreland's wishes should be respected. As the rector's wife told it fifty-three years later, "The Presbyterian minister was a Christian gentleman, so he stepped aside." It was an uncharacteristic instance of anyone's preference prevailing over Westmoreland's, and it was to be important in later years both to himself and to the boy, who thus was christened William Childs Westmoreland.

The family's stay in Saxon was short. Westmoreland, with more incentive now than ever, accepted an offer to become local manager of Pacolet Mills, one of the county's major textile plants, on the Pacolet River about twelve miles on the other side of town. So he and Mimi and the boy, whom she insisted on calling Childs, moved in April 1915 to Victor Park. This was the residential section for Pacolet Mills officials, named for Victor Montgomery, then head of the family that had led the buildup of the industry in the area thirty years earlier. They lived there in a big two-story shingle house, with a broad front porch shaded by oaks and maples. Out back was a cabin where a Negro couple lived who served the Westmorelands much as they might have done half a century before.

Down the hill along the muddy river were the brick mills, and across a narrow bridge the village of duplex houses for the doffers, loomfixers and sweepers who worked in those days for the same low wages prevailing throughout the industry in the South. Miss Belle Fuller, who came there as the mill nurse in 1916, recalled that there were no side-walks or paved streets, and when she complained to Victor Montgomery, he gave her a horse on which she rode around the slippery red hills of the village every day. Westmoreland, she remembered, was "stern and businesslike" even then, but this did not prevent her from developing a special affection for the manager's son.

Obviously many others in the village did, too. He was the sort of handsome, serious little boy for whom his parents liked to buy soldier suits, and who clearly liked to wear them. The family albums are rich with photographs of him posing here and there, saluting, on one occasion on the steps outside the mill clinic where Miss Fuller had her office. World War I suggested some of this play, and Mimi admitted years later that she feared it would last long enough for him to have to go.

While Childs was much too young to go off to war, his father was too old, and displeased by the fact. When he made inquiries, he was offered a major's leaves—but for duty in procurement and quartermaster assignments in this country. He sneered at the suggestion, maintaining that he was doing that sort of thing right there at Pacolet Mills, and

36

that if he could not have an opportunity for combat, he would just stay at home.

Through most of his preschool days, Childs was the only focus for his parents' devotion. Then his mother gave birth to a daughter, Margaret Rush, but there was no question that the boy remained number one. He was sent to grammar school at Pacolet, two miles up the road. Most of the pupils there were children of the mill workers. Childs made friends with them, and at home he was allowed to play with the "mill boys," but Margaret was forbidden to socialize with them. Summers, Westmoreland would load the family into his air-cooled Franklin (he was a Franklin fan, and kept one long after they had disappeared on most Main Streets) and make trips to Myrtle Beach, or on Sunday afternoons drive west for picnics in the mountains.

There also was Sunday visiting with the families of Dr. Boykin Lyles, Mayor Ben Hill Brown and Conrad Cleveland, and with others among the acknowledged upper class of the little city. But the first order of Sabbath business always was services at the Episcopal Church of the Advent, to which Westmoreland transferred from the Presbyterian church when Childs was about eight. One of Childs's Sunday school teachers was James F. Byrnes, then a Congressman and later to be, among many other things, a Senator who was able to give the boy an important boost. The elders of the church liked to stand around outside and talk about affairs of the world before going home to Sunday dinner, and Westmoreland, who often wore a bow tie and boutonniere on such dressy occasions, was one of them in substance even before he matched them in age.

Seeing a need to be filled, he had founded the Employees Savings Bank at Pacolet Mills, and in his wife's words, "It was a gold mine." The bank provided much of the money he invested shrewdly and regularly in a variety of stocks, and his judgment was consistent enough to enable him to give his family, and especially his growing boy, more advantages than the dependents of a mill official might have expected.

As Childs grew, he got his "fair number" of spankings, but despite his disciplinarian father he had his irrepressible moments. There is a photograph of him atop the family garage, twirling a lasso. His sister recalled that "he used to give us heart attacks." He showed a self-control unusual for his age when he was nine and two of his constant play-mates, Jonathan and Samuel, sons of the bookkeeper at the company store, drowned in the river together with their father and baby brother. Childs's mother wept, but she said later he was "a soldier to the limit," and did not let her see him shed a tear.

A more physical stoicism was required of him when, a couple of years later, he was riding in the front of the car as his father drove down toward the mill. Margaret was in the back, playing with her dolls, when the car turned and was struck head-on by a grocery truck. The boy's head crashed through the windshield, and he acquired a wound down his left cheek and under his jaw which left a scar noticeable the rest of his life.

Childs by now was completing grammar school at Pacolet and switching to Spartanburg High School. He also became old enough to join the Boy Scouts, and with his father's encouragement he became a member of the Church of the Advent's Troop 1. Every Tuesday evening, West-moreland drove him in to meetings at the troop's log hut on the church grounds. But such encouragement was superfluous as soon as the boy hit his stride in the Scouts. His flair for uniforms, acceptance of discipline, love of competition and self-confidence all were fed and flowered. He was no sooner a Tenderfoot than he was off on what one of his fellow Scouts called his "drive" to become an Eagle. By the time the year was out, he had become a First Class, which in the hierarchy of scouting is roughly equivalent to becoming a commissioned officer.

He also became a patrol leader, responsible for about eight boys in a troop of thirty or forty; and troop scribe, or secretary. He took to leadership naturally, perhaps too presumptuously in the eyes of some of his contemporaries. There was the occasion when one of the boys in his patrol balked at an order. Childs picked him up bodily and dumped him in a mountain creek.

Childs's mother sewed on his troop and patrol insignia and his merit badges, and he insisted that they be perfectly spaced and aligned. His father saw to it that he had every item of equipment he needed, because "he was so ambitious for him," Margaret remembers. Camping was his favorite activity, but it covered a whole field of scout skills, and among them Childs had his particular areas of interest. Indian lore was among them. On his front porch he had two big Indian stone bowls, and he hunted and swapped for an arrowhead collection. He learned the details of tribal dances, and had himself a costume with loincloth, moccasins and headdress.

Summer weeks were spent at the Rotary camp at Lake Lanier, in the Smokies in North Carolina, and at the Episcopal Camp Canuga. There was a plentitude of fascinating snakes in the mountains, including rattlers, moccasins, copperheads and king snakes. One year the patrol put a king and a rattler together, and the king proceeded to swallow its poisonous opponent. The boys took stage-by-stage photographs of the eighteen-hour process. Knot tying was one of Childs's specialities, too. His mother remembers that he used to take a length of rope to bed at night when he was practicing for a test, and for years there was an instructive knot board mounted in the Troop 1 hut, as prepared by Childs Westmoreland.

Around Spartanburg, the boys often hiked to the Meadows, a stream-cut pasture and pine forest about two miles east of town, and many of them used the fourteen-mile round trip to Conrad Cleveland, Jr.'s farm to satisfy the hiking requirement on their way to becoming First Class. That route passed by the old foundations of buildings that had been Camp Wadsworth during World War I. Some of the barracks had been converted into tenant houses.

One of Childs's close friends was Wardlaw Hammond, who is now a successful physician with a home on a lake built in the Meadows. He and Childs decided to earn the cycling merit badge, which requires among other things a fifty-mile bike trip. They borrowed bicycles and pedaled twenty-six miles to Union, South Carolina, had lunch, headed home, and were sore for days after their unaccustomed but successful exercise.

Scouting gave Childs a new reason for a physical fitness consciousness that had been pushed by his father since grade school. Westmoreland had him up and running three or four laps around Victor Park in the mornings before breakfast, and Childs went out for the track team at Pacolet school before transferring to Spartanburg. He was serious, sometimes imaginative, about self-discipline. Once he fancied he had flat feet, so he did a lot of extra running and his friends watched him walk around at an awkward gait with his toes scrunched up until the fancy passed. Any of them who went to spend the night with Childs at Pacolet were sure to be subjected to sleeping under pounds of blankets outside on the porch, no matter what the weather, because he craved that healthy fresh air. Outside the house, Childs had a gym bar and basketball backboard. He drafted Margaret to toss the ball to him as he drove in for layup shots, and to pass a football to him over and over.

Despite this willingness to practice, he never was to become a star on any of Spartanburg High's major teams. One reason was his living out of town, which made staying after school for practice inconvenient. He was on both the basketball and gymnastics teams, though, and before he was fifteen had developed into a lanky but broad-shouldered boy with considerable athletic versatility.

Any boy who went out for sports at Spartanburg High came into contact with Hubert R. Dobson, a Furman graduate whose nickname was "Red." Lieutenant General Joseph H. Moore, now inspector general of the Air Force, then one of Childs's classmates, called Dobson "one of the finest men that young men were ever under the influence of . . ." Dobson not only coached football, soccer and other sports, but also taught Sunday school and played banjo in raccoon-coat style. Moore says that Dobson "got me through that period when you learn to smoke. I wouldn't have dared." Dobson never allowed his football teams to call time out; when the other side did, the Spartanburg boys could go down on one knee to rest, but any who sat or flopped were jerked out of the game. He was the kind of leader young Westmoreland understood.

By the summer of 1929, Childs was completing his requirements for Eagle Scout: twenty-one merit badges, some of them very demanding, which guaranteed their winner a broad variety of outdoor skills and citizenship training. And early that same summer, there arose an opportunity few were able to realize in those days. That was to attend a world Scout jamboree abroad, and in this case to combine it with a Scout's version of the grand tour of Europe.

Other Scouts in South Carolina were as accomplished as Childs. Others were from families just as financially comfortable. But his father saw to it that he made the trip. It was a seventy-day excursion, costing $395. Westmoreland gladly made the expenses available, but there was another detail without which the trip could not begin in proper form. Childs had passed all his Eagle requirements, but there had been no local Court of Honor, the formal occasion on which promotions and merit badges are awarded with ceremony. Special arrangements were made to hold an individual award ceremony for Childs at Savannah, from which he sailed as an Eagle with ten Georgia Scouts for New York.

At New York, the group boarded the steamer *Belgenland* and headed for Cherbourg. Childs's notes in his album meticulously record that the ship displaced 27,000 tons. In France, they saw the Arc de Triomphe and the grave of the Unknown Soldier, and toured the battlefield at Belleau Wood. After a week in Paris, they headed for Switzerland, where Childs was photographed "climbing an Alp," as his own caption has it. They boated down the Rhine, and visited Heidelberg, where German students were impressed and deferential because they thought the still livid streak along Childs's cheek was a dueling scar. He did nothing to discourage them. The Americans continued on to Belgium and The Hague before turning back to England.

Their destination was Birkenhead, where about fifty thousand Scouts from seventy-four countries were gathering. It was the third time since the Boy Scouts were organized in 1910 that boys from every direction had assembled in such a reunion.

Boys from each country were organized into troops, thus tossed in with others they never had met before. In Childs's unit were not only the Southerners he traveled with, but others from Pennsylvania, California and such non-Rebel, thus Yankee, states. Their camp was pitched across the road from the Yugoslavs and near the Indians, Chileans, Swedes, Maltese and Germans. Language was not as much of a barrier as it would have been to a delegation of grown-up tourists; the boys used sign language. Childs picked up a few phrases in several other languages, although he never was able to unlimber his tongue enough to become a linguist.

Childs noticed the English newspapers, and thought it "a funny thing" that all the advertisements were on page one. "The English boys and I each thought the other country was funny," he reported soberly on his return, "but we talked it over and decided one was best for America and one was best for England." Predictably, he was interested in the other boys' uniforms, which did not differ from the Americans' except that the Indians wore turbans, the Scots kilts.

Each day started with a flag-raising ceremony, when the banners of all seventy-four countries went up simultaneously. In the afternoons, delegations took turns staging national pageants. The United States did a grammar-school-ish one about its history, beginning with Columbus, in which Dan Beard, the father of American Scouting, retained his familiar white beard in his role as a red Indian chief. Five Scouts played Indians, too, but somehow Childs was not one of them. He was on the rope-making and knot-tying team.

"Did it rain? Well, I guess it did," Childs said. "But it didn't dampen our spirits," he insisted. The most impressive event for the young South Carolinian was the visit of the Prince of Wales, soon to become King Edward VIII, who wore shorts and knee stockings as part of his own Scout uniform as he inspected the boys in camp.

Jamboree over, Childs's group toured Scotland for ten days before sailing from Liverpool aboard the *Albertin*. In New York, they met James E. West, the chief Scout executive, who received them as the important travelers they were and treated them to a picnic at Coney Island.

Back in Spartanburg, the *Herald* sent an interviewer to talk with Childs, and the lady reporter was impressed by him. She wrote that he was "the same quiet dignified boy" who had left in early summer, but that she could see "added understanding in his eyes." The paper covered his journey in half a page on Sunday morning, and included a photograph of him in uniform complete with merit badge sash, hand on one hip, with the caption, "Spartanburg's Own."

The "added understanding" discerned by the interviewer was in fact a totally new awareness on Childs's part of the fact that there was more to the world than small-town, textile-official life in the South Carolina Piedmont. It seems doubtful that he could have been so conscious at the age of fifteen, but in later years he was to consider his trip to the jamboree a turning point in his life. He not only discovered the attractions of different places and people, but got his first idea that his father's type of success would never satisfy him—and some guidance on how he might substitute for it another kind. This came from a group of midshipmen from

Annapolis, whom he met in Europe and with whom he discussed academy life. It appealed to him, and from that trip dated a decisive divergence between his own ambitions and those of his mother, who wanted him to become a doctor like so many respectable Childses who had gone before. To a lesser degree, it also conflicted with those of his father, who envisioned Childs as the lawyer he himself would have liked to be.

There was no need for a showdown yet, however. There remained two more years of high school. They were idyllic ones for Childs, although much of the world was in deepening trouble. On the day it reported his return from Europe, the paper carried accounts of labor violence in North Carolina cotton mills, as well as the Graf Zeppelin's exciting return to Germany. Within six more weeks, there came "Black Friday," and the country plummeted into depression. But it affected Childs little; his father's bank was among the very few in the area which did not fail, and the strikes that spilled blood around the mills at Gastonia and Danville swirled only lightly past Pacolet.

Young Westmoreland by then was driving himself and Margaret back and forth to school every day in a green Chevrolet bought for him by his father. They came into Spartanburg along a road bordered by scrub pine, red oak, sweet gum and tulip poplar, eroded red clay fields overrun by Queen Anne's lace and plowed ones where Negro tenants followed mule-drawn plows to produce enough cotton to surpass subsistence. Childs had little direct contact with this part of his environment. His father's business was with the predominantly white employees of the mill, and of course the Church of the Advent and Spartanburg High School were totally segregated.

Within the high school, there were the inevitable

"bunches," based on economics and neighborhoods. Joe Moore (he was "Harold" then), for example, repaired refrigerators and was a lifeguard to earn spending money and keep up a long line of Model T jalopies. To him, an important pastime was "dragging" Main Street, hoping to attract a following carload of girls, and rolling out to LaMott's drive-in barbecue on West Main Street, or to Rainbow Lake, spoken of by the teen-agers as "going to the waterworks." Childs, though he had his own car, was a little too proper to be a major participant in these diversions. On Friday evenings, he and his closer friends often went to parties given by girls who lived in the shaded section of expansive homes known as Converse Heights, along with Jimmy Byrnes and Donald Russell, later another South Carolina governor.

Childs played the field among the girls of Spartanburg High. He liked them, but never became serious about any one of them. Virginia Barnwell had dances at her house about once a month, as other girls took turns playing hostess, and couples did the shag to "Three Little Words" and "South" from a wind-up record player. As ever, it was the girls who knew the dance steps, and they taught the boys. Childs always showed up well-dressed, his dark hair parted sharply just left of center, his shoes shined totally unlike those of most boys his age. He sometimes dated Elizabeth Lyles, and Elisabeth Jennings had a thoroughly gossiped crush on him. Both were appealing brunettes, Elizabeth later being voted best-dressed and Elisabeth most popular girl in the senior class. But there were others; one of Childs's friends recalls that he seemed to guard himself from becoming too involved, as if looking to something vague that lay ahead.

When Childs was not earning more merit badges, dancing, acting as business manager of the yearbook, practicing sports, functioning as vice president of the Literary (debating) Society or talking at great length about his adventures abroad, he was compiling a better-than-average scholastic record. In the ninth grade, he scored mostly in the 90's; in the tenth, geometry was his best subject; in the eleventh, which then was senior year, he brought home 90's in physics, American history and algebra, and high 80's in English and French. His senior year average was a commendable 91.25—a tie with his close friend, Wardlaw Hammond.

One of the best remembered of his teachers was Mrs. Emma Evans, who tried to inspire a love for Latin in a corner room which was surrounded by busts of noble Romans but distractingly overlooked the athletic field. Childs did well in Latin, for his orderly mind took the grammar in stride. But he dropped it in his last year, in order to take American history. Because of his balky tongue, he had trouble with French. Neither was he an accurate speller. Ben Hill Brown, Jr., now a senior diplomat, recalls that Childs demonstrated once how "ingenuity can overcome handicaps." He desperately needed a good grade on an English composition, something he seldom won because he was marked down for bad spelling. But "he accomplished it," because "his composition took the form of exchanges of letters between two poorly educated mountaineers, neither of whom could spell."

His application, his handsomeness, his breadth of interests combined to make Childs a natural candidate for president of his class. There was no campaigning and hullabaloo as there often is for such student elections now. The Class of 1931 met in assembly one morning and quickly voted to make Childs Westmoreland its president.

Elizabeth Lyles was vice president, and Elisabeth Jennings secretary. The senior class history published in the 1931 yearbook *The Scribbler* refers to that year's "very capable officers," and the class prophecy fantasizes in part: " . . . the chorus girls filed in, one by one, led by Elisabeth Jennings, dancing the new specialty number called the Pacolet. As she danced into the circle, she threw a rose to Childs Westmoreland, prominent explorer, who had just finished a trip around the world on a bicycle." Co-author of the prophecy was Lib Lyles. A sidelight to those final weeks was the commencement debate, between Childs and William L. Ball, Jr., who is now a Baptist pastor in Spartanburg. Their subject was "Resolved: That the government should censor moving pictures." Billy Ball won, as might be expected for the son of a preacher, destined to become a preacher himself, but both he and Westmoreland insist today that they cannot remember who took which side of the question.

As usual, part of the final weeks in June was swapping yearbooks around, inscribing mushy sentiments and pat compliments above fancy autographs, beside the photograph of himself which the signer found most glamorous. The class president chose the one which introduced him in that office, wearing a serious expression suitable for men of affairs. And, as if the name he had used through his first seventeen years was becoming too childish, he signed himself "Childs 'Rip' Westmoreland."

There was some significance in that autograph. His father, after all, was "Rip," and the boy was about to embark on a period when he would be more than ever his father's son—though living away from home for the first time. He was going to The Citadel.

His high school record and his family's means could

have sent him to almost any college he chose. But for the father, there was little question about where his only son would go to college. This was so much an accepted fact that Childs already had prevailed on Wardlaw Hammond and Conrad Cleveland to plan to go there, too.

Going to The Citadel was a perfectly acceptable way of gaining one's premedical or prelaw background, if one wanted to approach it that way; it also was a perfectly acceptable way of preparing for a career that would take a young man out of South Carolina and into the world.

Thus, one evening in September, Wardlaw Hammond came down to Pacolet to spend the night with the Westmorelands. Mimi Westmoreland prepared a turkey for dinner, for it was the eve of a big event. The boys retired with instructions from Mr. Westmoreland to be up and ready to leave at five o'clock sharp. They slept restlessly, then dawdled and were not ready until 5:02. Childs's father was temporarily grumpy about that, but it did not last long. He packed them into his car, along with Margaret, who was going to drop off for a visit with relatives in Columbia, and headed for Charleston to enroll his son in the school he had revered so long.

3

First Rat, First Captain

1931–1936

Palmettos edge the parade ground of the Military College of South Carolina. Barracks with crenelated walls and sally ports overlook the flat, tidal Ashley River as it "joins the Cooper to form the Atlantic Ocean," the way Charlestonians tell it. The cadets who sweat in formation are almost all Southern boys; The Citadel has a tradition it likes to compare to that of the Virginia Military Institute.

The school's original quarters were not so classical. They had been a tobacco inspection station at the port of Charleston until a Negro named Denmark Vesey led an uprising in 1822. His effort failed, of course. After it thirty-five slaves were executed, and many others sent out of Charleston with a warning that they would be killed if they came back. The South Carolina legislature, anxious to prevent any further such threats to the established order, turned the tobacco station into an arsenal and guardhouse for the militia. It filled this role for two decades before South Carolina's leaders decided their state should keep up with Virginia by creating a local counterpart to VMI, which was founded in 1839.

Thus The Citadel came into being in 1842, and produced small classes of young officers until the spring of 1861. Then, South Carolina seceded and the Union soldiers at Fort Sumter in the harbor refused to strike their flag. A vessel named *Star of the West,* flying the Stars and Stripes, tried to reinforce the besieged fort. Cadets from The Citadel, handling guns emplaced at Cummings Point on Morris Island, turned back the ship. They were the first shots of the war.

In the spring of 1862, a company of cadets who refused to stay in school while their brothers were fighting went into the Confederate Army as a unit. It fought at John's Island, then with the Sixth South Carolina Cavalry in the Valley of Virginia, and later at Congaree Creek and Bentonville as Sherman drove north. Those cadets who remained in Charleston in December 1864 were sent to reinforce troops holding the Charleston-Savannah Railroad. When the war ended, there was no Citadel until Reconstruction began to loosen, but then there was a stronger sentiment than ever that the reincarnated school live on to perpetuate the memory of such men as Wade Hampton and Barnard Bee. This ultra-Southernness prevailed while The Citadel produced first-rate officers for World War I, and still dominated the school's atmosphere when James R. Westmoreland, former president of the association of graduates and chairman of the board of visitors, drove up with his boy that midday in September 1931.

When he left Pacolet that morning, the boy had been Childs. When his father returned to Pacolet without him, the young man was "Rip," as his father had been at The Citadel beginning thirty-five years before. The school was not new to Rip, because his father had taken him there several times to football games or reunions. Thus he started with more than one advantage. For his fellow freshmen— "rats"—the spontaneous hazing and calculated ignominy of the coming weeks were worsened by their unfamiliar setting.

On arrival, the rats of the eventual Class of 1935 were issued a single uniform—one wool shirt and one pair of wool trousers. The temperature hung near one hundred degrees, and the uniform was sopping in no time, so repeatedly had to be hung up to dry, putting its owner out of business for a while.

There is ample evidence that the new students did not mind these drying-out breaks; when mobile they were detailed to act as porters for the arriving upperclassmen, and each of them answered to orders from their seniors which invariably were shouted, echoing back off the long concrete walls of the barracks, and invariably began with the same two words, as in "Mr. Damn Westmoreland!" or "Mr. Damn Cleveland!" Regulations required them to wear their hats whenever they left their rooms, even to go to the toilet. As soon as all the cadets were checked in, each rat was assigned as valet to an upperclassman, and had to turn down his bedding, handle his laundry, polish his brass and, on cold winter mornings, warm the toilet seat for him.

At first, Rip roomed with Hammond, but then the cadets were separated into companies by height, and the solid, chunky Hammond went one way while Westmoreland, pushing six feet, was billeted with Hayne Glover, a lanky business administration major from Greenville, which is just down the road from Spartanburg. Rip was assigned to the freshman artillery section, and his room was in Murray Barracks with the rest of the student gunners. They learned basic artillery fundamentals, using 3-inch anti-aircraft and 155-mm. coast artillery guns. The latter had tracking gear, and students used it to follow ships in the river, servicing the pieces in drill after drill, no doubt imagining that the freighters they pretended to sink were christened *Star of the West*.

After the first week, each cadet's most pampered possession was a 1903 Springfield rifle—the model which then was still standard issue in the Army. They were required to clean it as seriously as they pressed their uniforms. Each room had a series of wooden shelves, where every uniform and personal item had to be folded in its assigned spot for Saturday morning inspections. Cadets had to stay inside The Citadel from retreat on Sunday till after the Friday parade, then be ready for the weekly Saturday inspection on the parade field and in their barracks. Competition between companies was motivated not only by pride but also by the spankings received by rats of the losing units—with brooms, coat hangers and even the flat of swords.

At The Citadel, whose administrators were responsible to a state legislature which even today keeps its citizens in a semidry situation, alcohol was forbidden. Drinking was supposed to mean automatic expulsion for any cadet. Chicken wire was rigged over the sally ports of the barracks to keep cadets from sneaking themselves out or whisky in. Graduates still tell about how Colonel John W. Lang, the mustached, ultimately military commandant in those days, traced a student one weekend through cocktails, through picking up his date, back to a fancy ball, and there confronted him with his sin.

The idea of the insults and restrictions was, as it is in

so many military organizations, to crush a young man as completely as possible before starting to rebuild him in the mold of the parent institution. Westmoreland's friends swear that the process never produced in them the slightest consideration of quitting and going to some gentler school. And certainly it never entered the mind of Rip himself. Not only had he begun to work, rather than play, at being a soldier, but the discipline and temperance were just the sort of things he had imposed on himself as a Scout and high school leader. In addition to that, he was the son of "Mr. Citadel," and rather than assuming that this would make things easier for him, he seemed to think it obliged him to work harder.

Examples were being set for him by men ranked by the cadets with the great soldiers of all time. Most omnipresent was the bristling Colonel Lang, a former counterintelligence officer, but most omnipotent was General Charles P. Summerall, who had retired in March 1931 after four years as Army chief of staff, the eighth man in American history to be promoted to full general.

Summerall by then was sixty-four, portly and more distant than when he had commanded the 1st Infantry Division and V Corps during World War I. He arrived at The Citadel with Rip's class, and from the start the cadets trembled when the general was near. He conducted regular chapel services, and those who heard him aptly called him a "George Washington-type speaker."

But he had the misfortune to arrive at a time of depression which straitened the school's budget. He squeezed all he could out of the rare South Carolina tax dollar that came his way. Cadets were required to take water-saving showers —wet down, turn it off, soap up, turn it on and rinse—as if they were on a troopship at sea, and only one light at a time was allowed in a barracks room. Despite this effort, what one graduate called the "backwoods legislature" accused him that winter of mismanagement of the school's meager funds. Summerall made another chapel speech, declaring with dignity that he would resign rather than have his honor impugned. The cadets, against all regulations, organized a petition, and since all of them signed it, disciplinary action against them was impossible. They implored Summerall to stay, and he did.

When he announced his decision, there was a celebration to match that after a football victory over the University of South Carolina. On March 4, the cadet regiment formed to do honors to the superintendent. The band struck up the "Artillery Song," and the regimental commander stepped up to Summerall to wish him a happy birthday. The general appeared in full uniform with decks of ribbons, as if surprised, and accepted the cadets' salute. The superintendent's birthday review since has become a tradition at The Citadel.

Rip not only did not object to the rigors of Citadel life, but he quickly became a helping hand to some of the boys who were less militarily inclined. From the first, he had a confidence built on his extensive time away from home at Scout camps and in Europe, and on the familiarity with The Citadel which had rubbed off his father. Though he was a rat, too, other seventeen-year-olds were turning to him for advice even before the rough first six weeks were over. His father contributed further toward Rip's self-management by opening a checking account for him as soon as he went away, and the boy was making decisions for himself and liking it.

Predictably, since he liked it he was good at it. He played basketball, coached some of his friends in math, and managed to average 83.12 academically, with 4.24 of a possible 5 in conduct, which he could have rated only by passing up the temptation to join some of the shenanigans organized by the "bolsheviks." These were senior students who had never managed to rise above private, who had nothing much to lose so occasionally upset the peace of Charleston by flinging garbage cans down from the arches of the barracks all at once, with a great clang, or by slingshooting explosive "torpedoes" across from the artillery to the infantry barracks. After each such outburst, the entire regiment was ordered to fall out and march through the streets of the city for a few hours as punishment.

Westmoreland's grades placed him thirty-third among 169 members of the rat class. This was not outstanding but his almost instant recognition by his peers and his instructors as a "prototype military man" was unusual enough to be remembered by most of them today. Of the rat class, ninety-six cadets were selected to become corporals in their sophomore year. This was an honor, though it came to more than half those eligible. It rewarded neither academic nor athletic ability, but qualities like military bearing, command presence and performance on the drill field. Rip was number one on the promotion list.

Robert M. Hitt, Jr., the same "Red" Hitt who was later to become editor of the Charleston *Evening Post,* placed ninety-seventh on that list. He lived with his disappointment until one day in spring, when an announcement was made at mess that Hitt was moving up to ninety-six, because the first man on the list had been accepted at West Point.

When he had enrolled at The Citadel, Westmoreland vaguely agreed with his father's idea that it would be a suitable preliminary to Yale Law School. But he still had in the back of his mind that conversation with the Annapolis midshipmen in Europe, and the fascination of faraway places. Now he had found out that he not only enjoyed the military life that might provide a route to that kind of life, but that he was good at it. He asked his father to see Jimmy Byrnes, then Senator from South Carolina, about an appointment to the naval academy. The elder Westmoreland, perhaps a little piqued about his son's apparent decision against becoming a lawyer, told the boy that he knew Byrnes as well as he did, so he could ask him himself.

Byrnes had said many times to Childs, as they stood about talking after church in Spartanburg, "Just let me know when you're ready for that appointment, young man." But he did not expect young Westmoreland to take him up on it; his father had told the Senator that The Citadel offered a military man everything "except the numbers" (meaning West Pointers' automatic priority on each year's list of new lieutenants), and "the numbers don't guarantee anything, anyway." Byrnes recalled that the boy wrote to him, and when he followed up by coming to talk to him, the Senator convinced Westmoreland that the Army, rather than the Navy, would offer him the broader education and just as much chance for adventure. After hearing a high recommendation from officers at The Citadel, he appointed Westmoreland—first as second alternate, then first alternate, and when the primary selection did not make it, Westmoreland did.

By that September, the end of the summer during which already established military men were called on to disperse the Bonus Marchers in Washington, and Franklin Roosevelt was nominated in Chicago, Rip was eighteen. He traveled to West Point alone, by train to New York City, then by Hudson River Day Line up past the Palisades, through

Haverstraw Bay toward Storm King Mountain and the gorge of the Hudson. Aboard the boat, he met another incoming cadet, Robert Fergusson, a Chicagoan who later was to become commanding general of American forces in Berlin. The two stood together to watch the old gray battlements come into view on that rocky ledge above the river's western bank. They remembered it well.

But if the view and the climate were different, and checking into West Point an inevitable thrill, the experience was not as new for young Westmoreland as for most of his classmates. He was exchanging the title of "rat" for that of "plebe," but the atmosphere, the techniques, the commands and the uniform were very much the same. Upperclassmen recognized his experience, and harassed him more than most others. But anyone who had endured rat status for a year and come out as number one rat had learned not only how to dress and respond to hazing, but also that a carefully controlled degree of self-assertion within tight freshman discipline makes its impression on the officers and upperclassmen who must assess the beginners.

Thus he was noticed promptly. One of his fellow plebes remembers now that "Westy was such a distinctive-looking fellow, the type you'd look at a second time, good-looking, with a commanding way. Even then he seemed more mature, yet very friendly, wasn't a bit conceited, didn't pop off about what he was going to be." "Westy" had become his new nickname, because cadets were known by their last names only, and there was no "Rip" Westmoreland who had preceded him here. And while he may not have popped off about "what he was going to be," his classmates talked about it. "Everybody was inquisitive about this Westmoreland they'd heard so much about . . . It was our first impression that he would wind up as first captain." The first captain of the cadet corps is the senior who holds highest rank by virtue of his leadership qualities, not necessarily his scholarship.

Scholarship was not a serious problem for Westy in that plebe year, however, for much of the academic side also was an approximate though tougher repetition of courses at The Citadel. He was not the only cadet repeating freshman courses; in that depression class, there were many other transfers and several college graduates who were turning to the Army because they could not find decent jobs elsewhere. The average age of the plebes in 1931 was about 20.5 years.

Westy managed to place well up in the first quarter of his plebe class, standing 71st among 328. Math continued to be his best subject; he placed 62nd in it. He was 71st in French, 103rd in tactics, 74th in conduct, and had a total of 36 demerits. But in English he placed only 172nd, and rougher months were ahead. His sister still is able to joke that the greatest problem he ever faced in his career was passing English at West Point.

The compilation of grades led to commencement, where those ending their plebe year could draw inspiration from the fact that most of the first classmen who had broken them in at the academy were certifiable second lieutenants, and where in 1933 they drew extra inspiration from the fact that the commencement speaker was one of the most flamboyantly brilliant soldiers who ever graduated from West Point. Douglas A. MacArthur at that point was chief of staff of the Army, a title to which only the most confident cadet might secretly aspire as the capstone of his career. While MacArthur had eighteen more years of triumph and controversy ahead of him, he already had been a cadet whose record was memorized at the academy, a decorated brigadier general at the age of thirty-eight, the youngest superintendent in West Point's history, and, just that spring, the general on the white horse who scattered the Bonus Marchers away from Anacostia Flats. His message that day was to the graduating class, but no one there could have been more impressed by the general himself than West-moreland. His admiration continued past MacArthur's death.

That summer the rising sophomores (yearlings) went to camp. It did not mean traveling far—they lived in tents with screen walls and wooden floors, pitched from the edge of the parade ground out onto the cliffs overlooking the Hudson. But for Westy, that summer was a takeoff point in the intense competition at the academy.

Selected new yearlings were appointed as acting cor-porals for the camp period only, and among them a few were designated as officers. Westy was picked as acting commander of one of the six companies, and part of the time had a chance to act as regimental commander. His reputation broadened, and one of those who watched him most closely was the senior tactical officer for the summer camp, a Lieutenant Colonel Omar N. Bradley.

As a yearling in 1933–1934, Westmoreland began to branch out into extracurricular activities, including athlet-ics. As in high school, he never became a varsity star, but he played soccer and basketball, went out for track and tried his horsemanship in the pentathlon. He was still a nonsmoker and nondrinker, choices clearly linked to his Boy Scout days.

With an early show of a sense of drama and tradition that was to be conspicuous in his later career, Westy got the idea during this period that West Point's setting was not quite historic enough. "It appeared to me that the military academy should be located on a victorious battlefield, and one seemed to be at Saratoga, which was the site of our first great American victory . . ." he recalled afterward. "Beautiful country up there." Only years later, when he prepared to make a speech at the Saratoga battlefield, did his research convince him that the academy should not be known as Saratoga rather than West Point.

Then, "it was suddenly revealed to me that the Founding Fathers were very wise in selecting the site, and that the reason was far more profound than the one I had conceived. Because during the period 1778 to 1780, West Point was perhaps the most important fortified area in America . . . as a result of the strong fortifications that were constructed here, West Point served a strategic role during our struggle for independence without a shot's being fired or without blood being shed. So actually West Point . . . is profoundly symbolic of a sound philosophy of national defense . . ." He was satisfied then, in 1964, but in the long meantime he had the feeling that his judgment may have been better than that of George Washington, who recommended in 1799 that the academy be established where it is.

Westy's life outside class included serving as a Sunday school teacher and chapel usher, and later he went out for the business side of the *Howitzer,* his class yearbook, and took on a series of offices that came with prominence in his class.

A cadet with energy found time to spread himself this broadly on the West Point reservation because he had almost no time off it. Christmas leave was the only free period worth noting before a class's second summer. There were no radios in barracks, and lowerclassmen could not even go out for a stroll around Highland Falls, the town outside the

61

gates. There was, of course, the annual Army-Navy game at Franklin Field in Philadelphia, and plebes had to be able to shout out the number of days before the next one on demand of anyone senior to them. Most of Westy's years at the academy, Army won. The whole cadet corps also went to New York annually to confront Notre Dame.

But these exciting points were rare, and the tight restriction of cadet life made all of them look forward to the few weekends they were allowed out as they gathered seniority. Some used their weekends to party in New York City, and others, including Westmoreland, often went to visit the homes of their nearby classmates. Almost all managed to get home at Christmas, and when Westy did, some of his South Carolina contemporaries were annoyed by what they considered a put-on Yankee accent acquired by the erstwhile Childs Westmoreland.

The summer between sophomore and junior year was cleared for furlough, and those months of 1934 were the last such extended period Westmoreland was to spend with his family and friends in the Piedmont and the mountains. It was a nostalgic summer, and he spent much of it as he had spent the years of his early teens. Westy and some of his friends, including one or more who had stayed in his class at The Citadel, so were a year ahead of him now, signed on as counselors at a camp run by their old high school coach Red Dobson. As ever, Westmoreland was looking ahead: he used to paddle his canoe through a culvert to an abandoned neck of the lake and sit there shouting parade-ground commands out over the ridges, startling crows and woodcocks as he perfected and deepened the staccato shouts on which a disproportionate part of the assessment of a cadet is based. He took along a friend, a Citadel man, to offer constructive criticism.

One of the innovations the cadets found on returning that fall was that young lady dance instructors had been imported to help the future officers acquire a social grace considered mandatory in the peacetime Army. There was one blonde and one golden redhead, both in their early twenties, and Lieutenant Colonel Simon Bolivar Buckner, commandant at the academy, concluded that he was "highly gratified at the experiment." "It's caused a sort of renaissance," he said. "A lot of the boys who qualified in previous classes when they had male instructors have applied to take the course again. I guess they're beginning to realize their deficiencies." One of the girls maintained that their pupils worked hard, but had a lot to learn. "The trouble is, they don't concentrate on the lesson," the other said. "They're all so anxious to tell you the story of their lives." They got the impression that the boys felt that the less they learned at each lesson, the more lessons there would be.

Westy had done the shag and other steps taught by the girls on Friday nights back in Converse Heights, and he went through the requisite lessons in one-two-three, one-two-three ballroom movement at the academy. But he did it mainly out of duty; he was screwing down his ambition again on the objective of being number one, without acquiring a reputation as a "file boner," who would lick boots or cut corners to get ahead.

When Westy began his junior, or second class, year, Buckner changed the rank system among cadets, creating conflicting requirements for tact and forcefulness among those who benefited. Previously, cadet rank had been concentrated in the senior class. Buckner altered this to retain all the officers in that first class, but decreed that the sergeants be second classmen and corporals be yearlings. Westy was made first sergeant of his Company C. Several other classmates had these company level assignments, and two ranked higher as regimental sergeant major and supply sergeant.

Those first classmen who remained cadet privates resented having to follow orders from men below them in the academy's traditional seniority system. Westmoreland was not inclined to pass up the responsibility that went with his chevrons, and if he had been he would have "caught hell from Buckner and the tactical officers," a classmate recalls. But he handled the situation with maturity, and there was less friction in Company C than in most of the other units. He showed a stubbornness that was to remain one of his characteristics, strong enough even then to annoy some of those who had to work closely with him. But it was the quiet kind, not accompanied by overacting.

As the academic year ended, the corps gathered to say farewell to its senior members, and to hear a voice that had dominated the rest of the country during their years at the academy, but had dealt with forces from which many of them had been insulated. The great depression had little effect on them while they were cadets; they had limited time for newspapers, their courses included almost nothing related directly to what was happening in 1935, and without radios in their barracks, most of them had never heard a "fireside chat." So when Franklin D. Roosevelt came to the academy as commencement speaker, he was much less familiar to his listeners than he might have been to an audience of pick wielders or stockbrokers.

The President told the cadets that he favored "partial restoration" of a national defense that had waned with post-World War I optimism and depression economies. His position was tied both to affairs abroad, in Germany, China, Ethiopia and Spain, and to stubborn unemployment at home. "On some occasions in our history we have reduced our army to a level unjustified by a due regard for our own safety. It was in the conviction that we had again drifted too far in that direction that I have recently approved acts of the Congress to accomplish a partial restoration of the army's enlisted strength and increasing the enrollment of cadets in the United States Military Academy," he said. The cadets sent cheers rolling across the Hudson.

In the mid-1930's, they were fortunate young men. Few Americans could afford college then, and of those few, many could not find commensurate jobs when they graduated. More than a third of the Class of 1936 had been eliminated in its first two years at West Point; of the 328 who survived the plebe year, only 276 were to graduate. Most classes of the period cut 35 or 40 per cent of their strength in four years. Retention of an individual cadet depended on his own academic and military standing, of course, but the number to be eliminated depended on national policy, on the number of lieutenants' vacancies available. Graduation from West Point was the principal way to enter the Army with a commission then; only a few honor graduates of the ROTC were accepted as regulars, and most of them went on to inactive reserve duty. Thus Roosevelt's message meant a great deal to those cadets whose survival at West Point was not yet guaranteed.

In Westy's personal recollections, however, the day had to be most memorable for another reason. That evening, the corps gathered in the dining hall before the evening meal to hear its orders of the day, which on commencement day included the announcement of "makes" for the coming year. They were the commandant's appointments, based on recommendations by the tactical officers, of cadet corps military ranks. They were based not only on what the students had learned about the theory and practice of handling men in battle and the minute skills of the parade field, but also on their possession of personal conduct exemplifying the West Pointer. On the basis of what they had seen in the past year, the tactical officers chose Westmoreland for the top-most position in the corps, that of first captain.

It was the fulfillment of one ambition, but it brought with it new and heavier duties. Westmoreland's first major job as first captain was to lead the class as it went on a summer trip to posts down the East Coast, representing selected branches of the Army. It would turn out to be an excursion that was more outright fun than any strictly military experience of the class's student life. But some serious talk was demanded early in the outing, and Westmoreland played a role in it.

Benjamin O. Davis, Jr., son of the first Negro general in the United States Army, was a member of the Class of 1936. A few other Negroes had been cadets, but he was to become the first to graduate. He had been subjected to a disproportionate amount of hazing as a plebe, but stuck it out. As the class sailed south from New York aboard the troop transport USS *Chateau Thierry,* there was concern that there might be unpleasantness when the ship reached Savannah. A delegation of prominent Georgia Negroes was waiting there to greet Davis. At sea, Westmoreland and the regular officers quietly lectured the cadets to prevent any embarrassing incident on landing. There was none.

At sea and ashore, Westy was on familiar ground again. He was a veteran of transoceanic travel, and could act as his classmates' guide through the ports he had transited as a Scout. For all of them, the trip provided "a tremendous feeling of freedom, of relaxation away from the reservation." It was "quite a lark," not least because they were first classmen themselves at last, and could look forward to giving more than they received of orders and discipline.

Once ashore in Savannah, the class boarded trucks and set out across the country roads of Georgia toward Fort Benning, home of the Infantry School. The trucks stirred clouds of red dust. Once the convoy stopped alongside a watermelon field, and suddenly the field turned gray with cadet uniforms. A farmer came yelling out of the house adjacent, and while the cadets' first impulse was to sprint away, he was merely telling them he had a whole cellar of cold melons for sale. Though they were cheap, and each cadet had five dollars for the two-week trip, few had any change. The farmer prospered that day, and as the column headed west again, a glorious battle with red dust-covered watermelon rinds took place back and forth among the bumping trucks.

If he tried, Westy did not succeed in stifling that outburst of high spirits. But he was in charge as the cadets loaded and unloaded, came and went under the eyes of the real soldiers at Benning and elsewhere. The infantrymen in Georgia put on an exciting show for the young men, who were stuffed with theory and eager to see some of their knowledge put into practice. They saw a dummy tank, towed on a zigzag course, "punctured like a potato grinder" by new 1-pounder and 6-pounder antitank guns. The new M-3 Christie tank performed for them. Planes laid smoke-screens, camouflaged machine guns stuttered, scout cars and Thompson submachine guns were unlimbered, and sharpshooters from the cadet ranks were allowed to test-fire the new Garand rifle. A-8 attack planes bombed from low altitude, and there was practice in firing blanks at strafing aircraft.

The hope of each post was to convince the cadets that

its branch of the Army was the most rewarding or adventurous, thus attracting the best selection of new officers. The class had had its field artillery familiarization with the lighter pieces at West Point; it went to Fort Monroe, Virginia, to see the coast artillery. Huge, thick-tubed, soon to be outmoded mortars, long-reaching rifles in fortified positions and mobile 155-mm. pieces traversed and boomed at a cadet's tug on the lanyard. New ordnance was inspected at Aberdeen Proving Ground, Maryland. But the exhibition that caught Westy's imagination was the later one at Mitchel Field, Long Island, where the Army Air Crops performed.

It revved up Keystone bombers, fabric-covered biplanes with their radial engines suspended between the wings, and O–48 observation planes, and gave the cadets a few minutes "stick time" in each. There also were snappy little P–36 fighters, with streamlined spats on their nonretractable landing gear, and the new AT–6 advanced trainers. Westmoreland decided he wanted to become an aviator. It was not a new interest; back in South Carolina, he had liked to go to the airport to inspect visiting craft, and when he posed once in his Scout uniform beside a rickety two-winger on the dirt taxi strip, it might already have occurred to him that flying would be a dashing way of seeing the world. By 1935, it seemed that one simple decision could make it all come true.

Back at the academy, Westy turned to an academic schedule that was tougher than ever before, partly because of the usual intensification from year to year and partly because he was carrying such an extremely heavy extracurricular load. Not only was he first captain, at the head of a staff including adjutant, supply officer and supply sergeant, and Sunday school superintendent, and *Howitzer* advertising manager; he was also chairman of the board of governors of the First Class Club, vice president of his class, and chairman of the academy's honor committee.

The honor system operates at many American schools, sometimes effectively, primarily for prevention of academic cheating. At West Point, it solemnly underlies every part of cadet life. The honor committee is the cadet tribunal which sits in judgment on violators. It does not concern itself with offenses against academy regulations as such; they are handled by the tactical department, and the usual sentence is a specified number of demerits. But when a cadet is involved in cheating, lying or otherwise breaking trust in class, in barracks or elsewhere, he must face the honor committee. If he has reported himself for the violation, he can escape with a heavy penalty of demerits. If someone else has to report him, he is expelled from the academy. The honor committee's recommendations are the basis for these decisions, and the only recourse from such a decision is appeal to court martial. Such appeals are not normally successful. The system imposes heavy, adult responsibilities on the members of the committee. Westmoreland more than once was called on to recommend the expulsion of a fellow cadet.

As first captain, Westy shared special quarters with two fellow members of the regimental staff. He and Stephen Holderness, the adjutant, and Leonard Shea, the supply officer, were assigned to a tower room in the "8½ division," at one corner of the old central barracks. It was cramped, but it had an inspiring view across the plain to the north, it made possible the unheard-of luxury of sharing a bath among only three cadets, and it was almost—not quite—inspectionproof. One of the prerogatives of attaining the regimental staff was that the tactical officers usually skipped over its quarters, on the assumption that they would be in perfect order. Occasionally, however, they bothered to check on their assumption. The tower room also had a nearby door used only by the staff, giving it direct access to the parade ground, saving seconds that would have been used winding down the stairs to exit through the common sally ports.

Seconds were precious. With Holderness and Shea, Westy worked out a close timetable for taking turns shaving and helping each other dress in a hurry. The latter involved, in part, wrapping a thirty-eight-foot red sash about the waist—neatly. Because Westy thought the use of under-classmen for such aid was too much like hazing, the three top-ranking cadets did it for each other. In their tight quarters, the result, without a system, could have been like a Marx Brothers closet scene. But it usually worked.

When they knew they had to change uniforms fast between classes and formations, the three laid out their gear on their desks so they could rush in and don it in an orderly way. One spring day they did so and fell out for a parade. They were in formation, Westy had just taken the adjutant's report, and they prepared to draw swords on Shea's order when Shea realized Westy did not have a sword. He whispered this news to Westmoreland, who said under his breath, "What can we do?" Shea advised him to go through the motions as if everything were normal, and proceeded to give the commands, "Prepare to draw . . . Ready . . . Draw!" Westy made the same movements the other cadet officers did, holding his breath all the while, and if anybody else noticed the absence of his sword, they never said so.

As regimental staff, this group had much more contact than the average cadet with the regular officers who ran the military side of the academy. They looked up to Buckner, who invited them to his home to discuss changes in cadet policies. He was a direct, stern man, exuding strength of character, later to die at Okinawa. Major Willard Holbrook, master of the sword, was remembered for his personal instruction to the staff and cadet officers in command and ceremony. Westy, as honor committee chairman, also worked often with Bradley, who was on the battalion board of regular officers who considered violations of academy regulations.

Another privilege of making the staff was permission to keep lights on an extra half hour after other cadets, partly making up for the time they had to put into staff work. Westmoreland used some of this extra time for doing business chores for the *Howitzer,* and during that first class year was asked if he would pose for a picture to be used in promotion for the yearbook. He did, and his profile, beneath hat and shako, was portrayed alongside that of Anita Colby, reigning cover girl of that day. This brought on cracks about the first captain's being "body beautiful," but he survived it, even when the same painting ran on the cover of *Cosmopolitan* magazine the following summer.

His classmates used some of those extra half hours for typical undergraduate bull sessions, but Westy seldom joined them. He was never adept at small talk. When he took part, it was essentially about business—quizzing Shea about Army life, since he was an officer's son, or expressing repeatedly his curiosity about whether a young officer should get married. The consensus was that one should not; a lieutenant's pay of $125 a month did not go far, and wives and families were proven to be demanding of time that could be more profitably devoted to duty. Westmoreland did not seem to have any special candidate in mind, anyway.

71

Most of Westy's after-hours time went into study, however. As his military and extracurricular role had expanded, his academic standing had slipped. The plague of English had been lifted after his sophomore year, but Spanish had replaced French, and it dragged his average down. In his final year, his worst subject was economics and government, a combined course in which he placed in the bottom tenth. His most impressive improvement had been in tactics, which after all is the most basic of military subjects. Starting at 103rd in his class as a plebe, when the course was new to him, he had come up to 54th as a yearling, and ranked eighth in each of his last two years. But his scholastic standing in class had gone from 71 of 328 in his first year to 107 of 296, then 117 of 280 and finally 151 of 276 as a first classman, averaging out to an overall standing of 112th. There was no reason for this to depress him, however, for he had been an exemplary first captain, and this was enough to recommend him for any next step. But the nightly grind of study had done what mere competition had never managed before—it frustrated Westmoreland in something he wanted badly. It caused his eye muscles to malfunction just slightly enough so that he failed the Air Corps physical examination.

Near the end of their final year, cadets were allowed to pick their branch of the Army. But they took turns by their standing in class, and since vacancies in most branches were limited, those in the top fractions had a good chance of getting their first choice, while those far below seldom did. Most of the leading students chose the engineers, considered the most intellectual branch. When Westmoreland could not pass the Air Corps physical, he turned toward the field artillery. He was interested by what he had learned in class about Confederate use of guns at Fort Sumter and after—by John Pelham, and by Stonewall Jackson's employment of the weapons attached to his "foot cavalry." Major General William D. Connor, the academy superintendent, convinced Shea that the artillery was a challenging mixture of mental and physical service, and Shea's subsequent conversation reinforced Westy's opinion. So when the 112th man in the class made his choice, it was the field artillery. If he had placed a few numbers lower, there would have been no artillery vacancies left.

But a cadet does not have to place high academically to be prominent in the final week at West Point. It is the first captain who leads the regiment on the parade ground, and he who receives the Pershing Sword, symbol of surpassing all his fellow cadets in military proficiency. Before his mother and father and what seemed to be the eyes of the world, Westy took these honors, and heard General John J. Pershing himself address the departing Class of 1936. Westy was so busy with his duties that he did not bother to invite a date to the graduation hop, but he arranged a date for Margaret with one of his classmates.

For the new Lieutenant Westmoreland, there was a bonus. Among his additional chores during that year had been escorting visiting dignitaries about the academy, and among them had been the Alfaro family, most conspicuous political lineage in Ecuador. Several Alfaro sons had been West Point cadets. In appreciation for the hospitality, the family invited Westmoreland and a few other outstanding cadets to Ecuador as guests of the government.

The Spanish he had studied as a first classman was hardly enough to enable Westy to see the country without a guide, but that mattered little, for the proud young officers

73

were made to feel as if just graduating made them heroes. The Quito newspapers ran long articles about where they came from, what they looked like and what they said.

Back home after two months, Westy headed at once for Michigan to pick up at the factory a new Oldsmobile, a graduation gift from his father. He drove it back to Spartanburg, arriving with sixteen cents in his pocket. Then he visited with the home folks and prepared to take a longer drive.

Ambitious young men are prodded partly by a curiosity about themselves, a need to find out whether they are as good as others on a level beyond their peers. Westmoreland had satisfied himself that he could excel in Scouting, in high school, at The Citadel and at West Point. Now he was moving out of the years of boyhood and preparation. He was a professional soldier, called on to compete with and lead other professionals. As the summer of 1936 ended, he loaded his foot lockers into his new car and drove west to report to Fort Sill, Oklahoma, where American officers learn the trade of the field artillery.

4

Learning the Trade

1936–1939

No matter how eager the soldier, life in the United States Army in 1936 went at a gentlemanly jog. There were some in the upper ranks of the War Department who concerned themselves with developments across the oceans because it was their duty. But for the many, the prospect seemed peace. There was polo for young officers, and they were expected to help organize Sunday morning pink-coat hunts, keep immaculate sets of whites for dances at the club in the summer, and make themselves available for social tasks which were monitored carefully by those who signed their periodic efficiency reports. It was an army of only 166,114, of only 12,902 officers, so that with time, one could expect to know personally or by reputation a respectable percentage of his fellow officers, especially within his own branch or specialty.

Most days, however, even then, some work came before

play. Fort Sill offered an interesting challenge to anyone who, disappointed at not making the Air Corps, seemed to have decided that the most desirable short-term goal was to become the best field artillery lieutenant in the Army. The late Thirties were years of quick evolution in weaponry— not revolution, as with the later arrival of nuclear warheads and intercontinental missiles, but accelerated perfection of tools and techniques that already had served with bloody efficiency in one World War. The American Army still was using small arms of that earlier era—the 1903 rifle, the 1911 pistol (which remains standard issue today), and machine guns and automatic rifles modeled in 1916–1919. Faster aircraft and tanks were being designed. With an army that never had fired an American-built artillery piece during the war in Europe, the United States still depended heavily on equipment constructed either in France or by French patterns. But by 1936 new light artillery, which would double the range of the old, was promised. It would bring obvious tactical advances, accompanied by problems. Solutions to those problems were being devised there on the rolling prairie of central Oklahoma.

A new lieutenant arriving at Sill would not be assigned to the one-year formal course at the artillery school. That came later, when he was a first lieutenant or captain. Those with fresh gold bars were ordered to the school troops, where they learned by doing in on-the-job training with the batteries which showed the officers in school how it should be done. One officer who spent many years at Sill considers assignment to school troops an "extremely valuable experi- ence," because there an officer got more maneuvering and firing than anywhere else in an army whose ammunition expenditure was tightly limited by a depression budget. Those troops not only demonstrated artillery drill for student officers, but they carried out all the army's experiments in artillery tactical and technical doctrine. "There you could see all the trends of the future."

Westmoreland was assigned to the 18th Field Artillery, a school troops regiment. The outfit had won the Croix de Guerre for its action at the Marne in 1918, then served at Sill since 1922. Its post-World War II history notes that "many officers associated [with the 18th during the Thirties] have since acquired greatly higher rank and are filling positions of great responsibility in the army. Also, it was during the school troops period that the 18th became so well known to all artillery officers, for there was scarcely one who did not at some time or other attend the Field Artillery School and come in close contact with the unit . . ."

Because the 18th was supposed to be a model unit, any officer on its rolls was expected promptly to become an artillery expert. It ran an indoctrination course for newcomers, and a man like Westmoreland, who needed no prodding to improve himself, combined this help with study of the manuals to bring himself to the regimental standard without delay. Then he was in the field as a battery officer, trotting alongside 1898-model French 75's drawn by six horses, plotting barrages under hot canvas, learning through repetition the drill which had to become unthinking habit.

It was during those first months out of West Point that Lieutenant Westmoreland confided to one of his classmates that he did not think he was particularly well qualified to function as a platoon leader, but he really believed he would make "a damn fine regimental commander."

The captain who was his first battery commander at Fort Sill felt no obligation to help the young officer skip those intermediate ranks, however. Westmoreland said this captain was "so dumb he had failed the basic course at the Field Artillery School . . . had a reputation for not being too bright, a nice fellow but a mediocre officer, and he inherited me as a battery executive. He was so incompetent that the first sergeant and I (the first sergeant was a great big man known as Bullhead MacCullough, and he was a good, strong first sergeant), the two of us arrived in the battery and I must say we did a good job of it.

"The captain appreciated this when he made out my efficiency report. He brought me in the office one day, where he sat most of the time fiddling with minor problems while we solved the big ones. He showed me my efficiency report. I looked at it and it was a very, very poor report, so I just handed it back to him and I said, 'Captain, thank you very much.'

"I was about to depart when he said, 'Lieutenant, I think you deserve a much better report than this, but when I was a second lieutenant this was as good as I received.' So then I said, 'Captain, if this is the basis of your making out my efficiency report, I officially request that you make out no report, since you have to use that type of fallacious objectivity.' And he said, 'Well, I'll see the battalion commander about this.' "

When Westmoreland told the story twenty-eight years later, he ended with, "I'll make a long story short: the efficiency report stood . . ."

Picture a twenty-two-year-old officer with single gold bars on his collar, with more experience in the Boy Scouts than in the Army, standing before a salty captain who already had resigned himself to the limitations on his military career and reading him off about his "fallacious objectivity." It conjures up a young Ronald Reagan impatiently trying to alert a sloppy cavalry general to the fact that the Indians are coming. But if it sounded like play-acting, it was a role for which Westmoreland was typecast.

When it happened at Fort Sill, he had not yet decided to stick with the Army all his life; his investment had been brief, so he had little to lose. But the same sort of thing was to happen later, during World War II, in the postwar years and in Korea. He said modestly that over the years he hoped he had lived down that first efficiency report. There is nothing that demonstrates that either it or any of the later instances, when he was of higher rank and had committed himself to the Army, made the slightest negative difference to his career. Quite the contrary. He moved at Sill from battery officer to battery executive officer to assistant battalion communications officer.

All of Westmoreland's relations with his seniors at Sill were not so rough. On social occasions, for example, he understood and later passed on "the old adage that chaperones are there to watch their young daughters dance with the new lieutenants. Speak to them because elders are very flattered when a young person comes up and pays his respects, and this is a matter of courtesy. Don't hesitate to get up and speak to your commanding officer at a social formation, and his wife. I mean this not as a matter of bootlicking, it's a matter of common courtesy . . ."

A young man with this forthcoming attitude was popular at the club. Westmoreland became whip of the Fort Sill hunt, and led riders across the Oklahoma fences of a Sunday. One such day, he saw a group trying to keep up with a mount ridden by a tiny nine-year-old girl, her pigtails flying out behind like a Spad pilot's scarf. Her name was Katherine Van Deusen. Her father was a Vermonter who had been commissioned in the cavalry out of the West Point

Class of 1909, and had become well known as one of the Army's best horseman. At that time Frederick Van Deusen was executive officer of Fort Sill.

Katherine was called "Kitsy." She was smitten with Westy, with a nine-year-old's passion that sent her galloping after his horse at every subsequent hunt at Sill. Westmoreland, however, had his more mature interests. He thought Kitsy was cute, but like a little sister. He concentrated harder on Melly Hatch, another "Army brat" who was closer to his age.

For the first time, he was infatuated enough with one girl to consider marrying her. But there seemed no urgency to the question until he received orders sending him four thousand miles away from Fort Sill, to Schofield Barracks, Hawaii. At this same period, as his first hitch as an officer came to an end, he also had to make up his mind whether he was going to stay in the Army. He decided without hesitation in favor of the Army and, since Melly had other plans, against marriage. The way it worked out, Melly married a mutual friend, and Kitsy Van Deusen was a member of the wedding. When Westy learned of this, he told Kitsy it was a shame she would help marry off his girl friend that way—and Kitsy replied with confidence, "Don't worry, just wait a few years and then I'll marry you."

So Westmoreland sailed for Hawaii. Even for a man who had seen the great sights of Europe and traveled to South America, Hawaii was a romantic and, in those prewar, pre-jet days, a far more exotic place than today. It was the sort of destination that called at least one young lieutenant up on deck before dawn, while his ship lay waiting for the morning tide, to find Oahu silhouetted to the north, and on the trade wind the scent of flowers reaching those five miles out to sea. Whether Westmoreland also got this seductive first impression or not, he had to be taken in by the twenty-four mile drive from Honolulu to Schofield Barracks, out around the northern end of Pearl Harbor and up the valley northeast, past sugar cane and eucalyptus and bougainvillea, between mountains where seeing two rainbows at once is a common experience.

There, Schofield was spread out at a one-thousand-foot elevation, looking out its plateau toward Kahuku, the island's northernmost point, and off to the west to Kolekole Pass, through which Mitsubishis and Nagasakis with red spheres on their wings were to swoop on a Sunday morning thirty months later.

Schofield was the home of the Hawaiian Division, so named for its location rather than its personnel. In those days native Hawaiians were called "gooks" by the soldiers. (Today the word does not exist there, and elsewhere is limited primarily to description of an Asian enemy, as the North Koreans or the Viet Cong.) Only a few Hawaiians were in the division. There was little open contact between soldiers from the mainland and the Hawaiians, except at night, when many of the enlisted men shacked up with girls in Honolulu. This was frowned on officially, but not halted.

It was still a distinctly peacetime outfit when Westmoreland arrived, with most of its top sergeants veterans of twenty-five years service or more, with frequent retirements, with companies that might muster ninety-seven men against a tabled two hundred. Its most noticeable activity was parading, and it was proud of how its troops, wearing uniforms of different colors, wheeled on the parade field in front of the officers' club and formed a giant taro leaf, the insignia of the Hawaiian Division.

Westmoreland was assigned to the 8th Field Artillery, a

regiment armed with British three-pounders which by then were towed by tractors. The unit's nickname had been simply "the Gunners," but later was switched to "the Automatic 8th."

As usual, Westmoreland jumped in enthusiastically. Even when he was that young, his reputation preceded him. Major General Charles D. Herron, commander of the Hawaiian Department, knew he was coming. And it was not long before the general knew the lieutenant in person, for Westmoreland still believed that "old adage" about being attentive both to commanding officers and their daughters. Herron's daughter was a slim brunette nicknamed Jimmie, and although she, too, later married another officer and mutual friend, she saw a lot of Westy in those days.

The usual training day ran from 8 to 11:30 A.M., with the afternoons scheduled for sports and large-scale cleanup details. The artillery would roll out along the rough red volcanic earth roads, up and down irregular gulches to McCarthy Flats, where it fired and drilled, drilled and fired into impact areas on the slopes below Mount Kaala, highest peak on the island. Cloud shadows shifted and dappled the mountainsides, adding to the difficulty of range estimation. The infantry ran the ridges right and left.

Westmoreland was broadening his artillery experience. Promoted to first lieutenant in June 1939, he moved into staff assignments within the battalion—S–1, responsible for personnel and their problems of pay, morale and records, then S–3, in charge of plans, operations and training.

Usually, by the time the sun was high, the battalion's officers could shed their boots and breeches, Sam Browne belts, sabers and campaign hats, and turn to more comfortable pursuits—which nevertheless could be classified as militarily desirable because they helped keep the Army in good shape. Westmoreland was just as interested in sports as ever, but often someone seeking him for tennis would be told he was still working.

Westmoreland's battalion commander told him forthrightly that he had no liking for West Point men, and when Westmoreland made captain in October 1940 and wanted to take over a firing battery after a period as S–3, the commander refused to let him leave the battalion staff. So Westmoreland was serving as both S–3 and battery commander, and on top of that working on an ingenious project of his own. He was devising a logarithmic fire direction control system for the mechanical solution of artillery problems.

Laboriously, he figured charts that would produce firing data based on such variables as range, powder charge and even the weather. He instructed the lieutenants and corporals of his battery in the method, ordered some extra ammunition and invited the colonel down to see a demonstration. The colonel picked the targets, and the battery laid its fire on them. Impressed, the colonel asked Westmoreland to write a report on his system and send it to the *Field Artillery Journal* and the artillery school. The school wrote back that it appreciated the young captain's initiative, but that researchers at Fort Sill had just come up with a similar system, using slide rules instead of charts.

Many evening hours that might have gone into social life had been poured into that fire direction control system. But Westmoreland had not become a wallflower. He and the other young officers would take their dates on beach parties, sometimes on the white Waikiki sand at Fort De-Russy, sometimes on the smooth-pebbled shore of Waimanalo Bay alongside Bellows Field, on the windward side, and sometimes at Waianae, over Kolekole Pass from Schofield. Westy, who would try anything physical once, experimented with surfing at Waikiki. There was tennis, which Westy took up late, but to which he later clung more faithfully than to other more time-consuming sports. He used to drive over to the courts in Honolulu, where a classmate, Richard Ripple, was stationed at Fort Shafter.

With Ripple and Jimmie Herron, who had come out to join her family after college, and their collection of friends, Westy also rode as enthusiastically as he had at Fort Sill. He took jaunts with General Herron, and made the Schofield polo team. All artillery officers rode then, and Westy was "crazy about horses." Once, when his sister Margaret came to Hawaii to visit him, he played on the post team against the Oahu civilian outfit. He took Margaret to parties among the polo set, too, at the homes of such old island families as the Dillinghams. And before her departure, Margaret went riding once with Ripple, and fell and broke her back.

Westy did not have a Boy Scout troop, as he had at Fort Sill, but he was active at the YMCA, and coached a basketball team. He also was required to attend the only service school he ever undertook in his Army career—cooks and bakers school at Schofield. He did not intend to become a cook or baker, of course, but company-grade officers were sent there to qualify them better to provision their units and inspect their kitchens. And he came close to failing this apparently simple training effort because of his course paper. The instructor did not like its subject: "The Potential Use of Mother's Milk as a Food for Troops in the Field." His wife is convinced to this day that he chose this uncharacteristically offbeat approach to provide himself an excuse for pseudoserious discussions with a cute dietitian at the post hospital.

The cute dietitian was one of many, however, for with the exception of his nearly decisive friendship with Melly Hatch, he still was playing the field. He was always ready when one of the post girls called and said, "Oh, Lieutenant, we're having a party and would you mind picking up so-and-so on your way?" But he balked when they asked him to bring the same girl too often. He was asked often, for he was polite, confident, a good dancer in the newly popular Latin American steps as well as the one-two-three he learned before and after West Point. If his careful approach to a highball or two was even noted, it is not remembered by his Hawaii friends today.

They do remember his "beautiful manners," and the strictness with which he supervised Margaret when she came to visit. He laid down the law about who she could go out with and when she had to be in. This may be traceable to the discipline exercised back in Spartanburg by their father. But despite his courtesy and his South Carolina roots, Westy was not a professionally Southern young officer. His drawl had started to fade when he went away to school, and while any perceptive listener could tell then or now that he was from somewhere in the South, his accent was hard to classify by exact geography. One of his former admirers considers that socially, he was "more the perfect officer than the Southern gentleman as regards manners."

He liked to talk about almost everything, but if he chose the subject it was likely to be his work. A conversation about his basketball team might turn to how he had given one man an angry but careful kick, and got results from it. And from there, he would go on to just how such a calculated action could be used to best effect. "He was fascinated by how to deal with people," a friend says, and in fact this long fascination is what gives many watchers the impression that his flashes of sternness, his pats on the back sometimes lack spontaneity.

He talked about horses, too. In one important respect, riding in Hawaii had come to resemble riding in Oklahoma. Kitsy Van Deusen was there again, now twelve or thirteen years old, still big-eyed, long-haired, affectionate and an expert horsewoman. Her father was at Schofield as commanding officer of the 12th Field Artillery, sister outfit to the 8th.

Colonel Van Deusen and still higher officers, specifically General Herron, got hints as 1940 wore on that their commands soon might see more than half-day drills and intra-unit athletic competition. The general had a dispatch in midyear saying a Japanese attack on Hawaii was "possible." With no sudden sense of urgency, officers' uniforms were changed from boots and breeches to more businesslike straight trousers and leggings. The soldiers spent more time in their blue denim fatigues than before, and more time in the hills and jungles draping the mountains around Schofield. The coast artillery and anti-aircraft batteries around Honolulu and the airfields started holding practice alerts. Herron ordered the planes at Wheeler Field, immediately adjacent to Schofield, dispersed and camouflaged. (Though later, after he departed in the last prewar months, the Air Corps's fear of sabotage by local Japanese-Americans prevailed, and the craft were parked in bunches to be easily guarded.)

But those who were junior officers there recall little awareness of emergency at their level. Westmoreland paid attention to what was happening but was concerned less with the estimates of the intelligence branch than his own clinging desire to be an aviator. His concentration on the artillery job at hand had not wiped the idea out of his mind.

86

Thus he paid to take commercial flying lessons in Hawaii, and went to Hickam Field for another examination like the one he had flunked before leaving West Point. His eyes let him down again. But the doctor held out hope: if Westmoreland would exercise his eye muscles, he probably could pass a later examination.

Westy's friends knew that his broad interests might surprise them now and then. There was the time when he arrived half an hour late for a party, and when asked why, disclosed that he had driven past some farmers planting pineapple, and stopped to watch long enough to find out exactly how it was done. But when they found him occasionally in a corner at parties, sitting quietly staring at the end of his outstretched thumb, crossing and uncrossing his eyes, they wondered. He was following the doctor's recommendation, of course. Putting a red pin on the end of his toothbrush and crossing his eyes twenty times every time he brushed his teeth was not enough. He had to manage a little extra practice, and he never has been above a little showmanship. Finally, he thought he was ready, and applied for assignment to flight school once again. This time, the answer was that he had served only one year of a scheduled two-year tour outside the country, and could not be switched to the Air Corps before the full tour was up.

By the time his transfer was due, however, it was May 1941. The Japanese were consolidating their occupation of Indo-China and preparing bolder moves, and the Germans were driving arms of a great pincer through the Balkans and North Africa.

Captain Westmoreland's orders arrived, sending him not to Randolph Field, Texas, but to Fort Bragg, North Carolina, only 150 miles from home. He was not being sent to flying school, but to the newly reforming 9th Infantry

Division. Clearly, the Army needed him as he was. And, he thought to himself, with five years service as an artillery officer I can be of some help immediately, while in the air I would be a neophyte, no better a pilot than somebody just drafted out of civilian life.

As he rolled back across country toward familiar places and people, the imminence of war was obvious as it never had been on the bridle trails or even at McCarthy Flats in the perfumed mountains of Oahu. At Fort Bragg, it was overwhelming.

5

"Sergeant, There's a War On"

1939–1942

★

Fort Bragg in 1941 "damn near exploded."

It stretched over miles of sandy soil and pine woods on the northwest edge of Fayetteville, a tobacco town which in the census the year before had recorded 17,413 citizens. By mid-1941 the soldiers at the post outnumbered them three to one. But the growth was not all military personnel; unskilled labor arrived by the thousands. Scores of trailer and tent camps fringed the reservation. Many newcomers brought clapboards, tin or tarpaper with them and erected their own huts. A family lived in an abandoned school bus. Some Fayettevillians found it profitable to rent their homes at high prices and move to another town where rents were low. All the huts and trailers were not confined to family living, either. Country girls still poor from the lingering depression flocked there and did their own business. Downtown, hot doggeries multiplied. The smell of hamburgers and onions hung over the shopping streets where soldiers shouldered their way, inspecting the window-shopping young ladies. Some restaurants had to lock their doors and admit customers only in shifts.

On the post, one million board feet of lumber were going into construction every day, mostly for standard two-story barracks. Westbrook Pegler paid a visit and did a column praising the accomplishment of so much by non-union labor. Bulldozers moved in through the sand and converted pine woods to blacktop roads and company streets in two or three days. While the barracks were building, troops lived in tents on mosquito- and fly-infested sand. Their immediate task was to swing brush hooks to clear the way for more tents, then buildings. Their nearest shower was likely to be a three-mile walk, to an old CCC camp.

President Roosevelt, who knew better than most the cause for all the rush, came down to inspect progress in early spring. Commanding officers carefully hid away the logs on wheels which they used for most of their artillery training, and instead lined the roads with the few real weapons they had received. Many other officers thought this a mistake, maintaining that Fort Bragg should have "done like the Navy," and let the commander-in-chief see its worst side, thus improving the appropriations atmosphere.

When Westmoreland reported for duty in May 1941, the 9th Infantry Division already had been reincarnated for nine months. It was a unit with tradition, based on the records of its three infantry regiments—the 39th, 47th and 60th—in the Aisne-Marne, St. Mihiel and Meuse-Argonne fighting of World War I. Those regiments were the maneuver elements of this modern 9th Division, but in the spring of 1941 there was little reason for esprit de corps. Most of the division's officers and NCO's had been summoned from posts all over the Army to make soldiers of raw draftees who swarmed into the division. Then when the best new men developed into NCO's themselves, they were stripped away and sent out as cadre personnel for still other units being formed daily. The 9th, like most other American Army divisions, had a long way to go merely to approach readiness for war.

Westmoreland was assigned to the 34th Field Artillery Battalion, one of four artillery units organic to the infantry division. He arrived on a breezeless, sultry day at the battalion headquarters on Fort Bragg's McPherson Road. Others in the unit recall that the battalion then was much like the weather—"inept, indifferent and just going through the motions." Westmoreland was assigned as S–3, the one job outside of commanding officer itself from which an individual could most affect an outfit's readiness status.

Without hesitation, he did so. The battalion's training schedule was revised so drastically that "it was more like a surgical operation" than an adjustment in routine. "The only things unchanged were reveille and retreat," one of its veterans remembers. Westmoreland, the physical fitness bug, the well-conditioned athlete from Hawaii, soon had the battalion's draftees starting the morning with a two-mile hike and run, sandwiching an hour of calisthenics between combat exercises and classes, and ending the day after evening chow with an hour and a half of intra-unit sports.

The 34th tightened up, and not just physically. Perhaps because they were just too tired to get into trouble after hours, its men recorded the lowest delinquency rate of the four division artillery battalions.

Westmoreland was barely on the division's rolls when the 60th Combat Team (the 60th Infantry plus the 34th and 60th Field Artillery Battalions) headed for Bowling Green, Virginia, in a 741-vehicle convoy for two-day maneuvers at what is now Camp A. P. Hill. It competed in the field against the 44th (National Guard) Division, out-pointed it, returned to Bragg without denting a fender, then went directly into the pine woods for more maneuvers. At the end of June, bolstered by praise for its units' work in Virginia, the 9th began its first division-level war games, which in that busy summer melted into the biggest peace-time maneuvers in American history in early fall.

In the 34th, Westmoreland and his fellow officers (he was the only one from West Point) were confronted by the hardware problem faced by all American artillerymen of that day. After learning his trade on French 75's at Fort Sill and moving through the battery grades working with British three-pounders at Schofield Barracks, Westmoreland now had to organize the employment of a dozen 155-mm. howitzers built on a French 1918 model, improved only with high-speed axles and pneumatic tires. Each weighed four and a half tons, was towed by a five-ton truck at no more than thirty-five miles an hour, and eventually its nine-man squad would be able to put its ninety-five-pound pro-jectiles on target at an extreme range of seven miles. It was an inferior weapon by 1941 standards.

To employ it in the Carolina maneuvers, the 34th used Westmoreland's own fire direction system. It was the first time the method had been employed in war games, and it was brilliantly successful. The battalion "soon ran out of targets," and was cited after the exercises by the II Corps commander as the artillery battalion with the highest point total awarded by umpires in the entire games.

There were maneuvers in June, July, August and Sep-tember. Westy managed to take a short time off in August to go to Washington, where he was best man for his class-mate Richard "Rip" Ripple when he wed Jimmie Herron, one of their carefree bunch from Hawaii, in the garden of the Herrons' Bethesda home. Westy disclosed his continu-ing interest in the Air Corps when he cornered another of his roommates at the reception, and quizzed the flying offi-cer in great detail. The aviator said Westmoreland knew more about the Army's airplanes than he did.

The division by then was "training madly," and as a division, rather than a mere cadre-training source for other new units. Maneuvers were planned again throughout the fall, and their highlight was a mass paratrooper attack against an objective near the Pee Dee River in eastern South Carolina in late November. The attack was "repulsed" by troops on the ground, but it had attracted much attention. Those maneuvers ended November 28, and the artillery battalions were back at Bragg by December 2.

The following Saturday, there was a dance at the offi-cers' club. It was more of an event than such a dance might have been a few months before, at Schofield Barracks. The division's busy training schedule kept its officers in the field so much there had been less time for partying than in the peacetime Army whose disappearance they were rushing. Westmoreland, still playing the field, was constantly being introduced to young ladies whose sisters or cousins hoped the promising young captain would be impressed enough to decide to settle down. For that dance, Westy had a date with Sally Payne, a Greensboro girl whose twin sister al-ready was married. It was a pleasant dance, but not one that either of them would have remembered forever, except for the drive back to Greensboro the next day. As did mil-lions of other Americans, Westmoreland listened to the radio as he drove along the ninety-mile route to Sally's home town. When the news of Pearl Harbor was broadcast, he put the pedal on the floorboard, raced to Greensboro, unceremoniously dropped Sally off and sped back to Bragg.

Nobody knew any more there than in any civilian home about what the Japanese or Germans might do next. The post's infantry units were ordered out to guard waterworks, bridges and factories. There were blackouts and emergency drills. When the uncertainty of the situation passed, training resumed with new purpose. In January and February of 1942, the division and its units practiced quick railroad embarkations. Washington decided to designate the 9th a motorized division, and half-tracks and other mechanized equipment started to arrive, but then in March it was re-designated an amphibious division.

Westmoreland, sixteen months a captain, was promoted to major on February 1. Two months later, he became commanding officer of the 34th Field Artillery Battalion.

This was the role, command, to which he had aspired as a boy, and would aspire later as a general officer. All the staff and communications jobs, all the familiarization with weapons and drill in displacement and fire control, were preparation for command of an artillery battalion. One of those who worked with him then, who remains quite frankly a Westmoreland admirer, described him as a twenty-eight-year-old battalion commander:

"The picture of robust health and strength—the stalwart posture, thrust chest, the stiff back, the impressive shoulders . . . His power of concentration—he looked straight into your eyes, penetratingly as a laser beam, did not move a muscle, was oblivious to everyone but you . . . His determination—written all over his mouth and chin and in his one or two quick chopping nods . . . His charm—

deep-set twinkling brown eyes topping a generous smile from ear to ear . . . He was a commanding figure."

When Westmoreland took command of the 34th, the 9th Division was trying busily to conform to its assigned role of amphibious landing force. Its troops were learning how to scramble up and down nets draped on mockup gunwales at McFadyen's Pond outside Fayetteville. In units, they were practicing moving on and off ships—out of Norfolk and up the Chesapeake Bay to Solomon's Island, at the mouth of the Patuxent River, and in and out of New River, where the Marines had been developing amphibious doctrine on the Carolina coast between the wars.

At first, the 34th Field Artillery Battalion did not take full part in this training, because the Marines and Navy had perfected neither techniques nor equipment for handling 155-mm. howitzers like those assigned to the battalion. But the battalion was not loafing. If it was not afloat offshore, it was likely to be in the forests around Fayetteville. Those woods were so heavily used by soldiers that for months there was a standing order that slit trenches would not actually be dug, they would merely be simulated by string or log markers. For the sake of realism and developing calluses, this order was lifted, and on the first day the 34th was allowed to dig, Westmoreland believed the artillerymen had not dug deep enough. He kept them out far into the night, learning by doing this essential art of the combat soldier. Less than a year later, more than four thousand miles away, one of the troops who bitched mightily that night came up to Westmoreland's executive officer and thanked him for the lesson thus taught.

Another soldier remembers the edginess that sometimes set in as the 34th prepared for that forthcoming trip. He was a radio operator and part-time musician, and once when he was far away in a syncopated land, tapping his hands on his transmitter during a field exercise, he was brought back to the pine woods by Westmoreland's voice: "Sergeant, there's a war on."

When the battalion began participating in amphibious training, Westmoreland went to New River one spring day and returned to find that a new executive officer had been assigned to him. He was an Illinois National Guardsman named Otto Kerner, Jr., who two decades later was to become governor of his state. On conditioning hikes out of Bragg, Westmoreland and Kerner would stand by the road and watch the battalion march past, then run up past the moving column, march with it awhile, stop, watch it pass, run up again and finally get ahead at the end so they could review the troops as they filed past into their barracks area. The morale effect of the outfit's two senior officers dog-trotting while the men moved at route step was noticeable.

So was another Westmoreland gesture, made as the battalion fell out to begin its first twenty-mile hike. No sooner had "Forward, march!" rung out than Westmoreland moved over to the sergeant major, a man in his fifties, weighing well over two hundred pounds, and quietly ordered him to return to the barracks. The sergeant major told a friend later that he knew he could not have marched over five miles at his age and in his condition, but that he had no intention of asking to be excused from the hike. He would have marched until he dropped, and he believed the resulting humiliation would have made him unwilling ever to face the battalion again. The commanding officer spared him that humiliation, and the sergeant major said he was "forever grateful" to him.

Westmoreland's solicitude for individual soldiers of his unit, not merely for the 34th Field Artillery Battalion as such, was unusual for an ambitious officer at such an early age. It is typical for officers to realize only when they are mature, perhaps middle-aged, and have much less contact with individual private soldiers, that they could have achieved as much, moved as fast, and been respected more as lieutenants and captains if they had been less haughty and more soft-spoken. Some leaders are born with an instinct to handle themselves this way; most learn it at an age they consider too late. Westmoreland used this technique as if he were born to it, yet there always was a totally conscious air about him. He studied leadership as if it were tactics.

A chaplain who served with him at Bragg and abroad recalls that "he was genuinely interested in his men, in their welfare and living conditions, and would make surprise visits to places where the likes of an officer were never seen for quick checkups . . . He was very much concerned with the attitude of the men and did everything possible to uplift their morale. He knew everyone by name and catalogued in his mind some personal history about each. It became a familiar occurrence to hear him ask, 'How's your Dad's grocery store coming along, Corporal?' or 'Are you going to resume postgraduate work when you're back in civilian life, Sergeant?'

"He was a meticulous dresser, changed uniforms every day, looked as sharp and smart at night as in the morning. He deplored sloppy dress, not so much because of its hygienic and aesthetic aspects as because he reasoned it was a manifestation of an indifferent, sloppy attitude. He would often say that by his dress you can tell if a man has a positive or negative attitude. He wanted alert, positive-minded soldiers in his command, and his training policies and pronouncements were dictated toward that end. He believed it vital to train the mind as well as the body, and to that end programmed throughout the battalion general exercises in mental gymnastics and special classes in para-environmental situations, surroundings and influence . . ."

For a professional officer, life at Bragg or anywhere in the United States was a frustrating affair in early 1942. Personally, a man like Westmoreland was as thoroughly prepared for combat as any general could ask. But the citizen soldiers who poured into the Army by the hundreds of thousands during those months were not; many had never fired a rifle nor seen a 155-mm. howitzer. The frustration of the professionals was partly, but only partly, relieved as they watched draftees turn into soldiers while Bataan and Corregidor fell and the Germans pushed east toward the Volga and the Nile.

It was understandable if Westmoreland's mind strayed elsewhere as the 34th drilled and sharpened. Harry S. Truman, then chairman of the Senate Preparedness Sub-committee, came down to Bragg one day, and it was the 34th which was chosen to stage an artillery shoot while he watched from an observation post. Amphibious training for the battalion quickened, much of it on ships out of Norfolk to Cove Point, up the Chesapeake in Maryland. Westmoreland, thinking of matters more flamboyant than loading and unloading four-and-a-half-ton howitzers from ship to shore, and closer to what was happening in the world than the choppy crosscurrents of Hampton Roads, decided he wanted to become a paratrooper.

Developing alongside the 9th Division at Bragg was the nucleus of American airborne capability. Westmoreland had become friends with one of its prime movers, James M. Gavin, then a colonel and operations officer of the airborne command. Gavin's enthusiasm had been catching. Westmoreland earlier had envied two lieutenants from his own West Point class who were picked to travel about from post to post, demonstrating jumps and spreading the airborne gospel. And he had seen the mass drop in South Carolina in previous fall's maneuvers. It was not piloting, but it involved flying, and he was convinced that it was the coming specialty, with great tactical potential, and he wanted to hitch his career to it.

In mid-1942, Kerner was assigned as a liaison officer with the Marine Corps at Cove Point. Westmoreland, with the 34th back at Bragg, sent by Kerner a message to Brigadier General S. LeRoy Irwin, commanding officer of 9th Division artillery, and as such Westmoreland's direct superior. Irwin, already present at Cove Point, was both popular and efficient, and would move far as the war ground on. Kerner told Irwin that Westmoreland would like his approval for a transfer to the airborne troops. Irwin wanted to know why Westmoreland could not wait to tell him in person, but Kerner said Westmoreland was very concerned that he get the request to the general as quickly as possible. Irwin, inadequately informed about Westmoreland's reasons, not wanting to be rushed and not wanting to lose an outstanding battalion commander, abruptly said no.

Westmoreland had been offered command of the first airborne artillery battalion, and the opportunity to organize and train it from the beginning. He remembers getting approval eventually, passing the necessary physical tests and preparing to make the transfer when Washington ordered all 9th Division field grade officers frozen in their units. The explanation offered then was that an emergency situation was feared in the Caribbean area. When that anticipated crisis did not develop, another, concrete assignment for the division did, and Westmoreland once again remained in the field artillery. In late September, less than eight months after making major, he was promoted to lieutenant colonel, the proper rank for a battalion commander in the tables of organization.

Early in September, a warning order for division movement was issued by the commanding general, Major General Manton S. Eddy. In a steady rain on September 17, the first unit of the division to head overseas—the 39th Infantry Regiment—departed from Fort Bragg for Fort Dix, New Jersey, en route to Scotland, then Ireland. Eddy addressed each of the combat teams as it packed up, telling them that "the regiments of this division will soon have the opportunity to make history," and that the entire division would reassemble somewhere before the end of the year. In mid-October, the 47th and 60th Infantry headed for Norfolk and further, final amphibious practice, and on October 23 they slipped out of Hampton Roads as part of the Western Task Force of Operation Torch. The 39th Infantry was assigned to the operation's Eastern Task Force. The 34th Field Artillery Battalion was left behind at Fort Bragg, and it was not until the morning of November 8 that the artillerymen found out that the rest of their division was spearheading the American invasion of North Africa.

Westmoreland and his battalion continued training, reading in the Fayetteville papers, as any civilian could do, about the progress of the division's infantry units through submarine screens, harbor defenses at Algiers, Safi and Port Lyautey, and the tortured, heavily censored political efforts to convince the French that they should not continue to resist. The best the cannoneers could do was carry out their training schedule while remembering Eddy's promise of a full-division reunion before the end of 1942.

In the late, raw fall, most of the battalion became seasick on still more amphibious exercises off Norfolk. But when they returned to Bragg again, there was enough excitement to cause them to forget that their next move would involve their most extended time afloat. Working furiously, they crated their equipment and boarded trains for Fort Dix, and from there continued to New York. They sailed in mid-December aboard the USS *Monterey*, which in peacetime had been a passenger vessel of the Matson Lines. They would catch up with the rest of the division in time for the rendezvous predicted by General Eddy.

6

Casablanca to Bizerte

1942–1943

The voyage was tense. That was the year when German submarines were sinking Allied ships faster than they could be replaced. But it was not until the convoy approached the coast of Africa that the submarines started hunting it. One attack was launched before the ships passed south of Gibraltar, another soon after. As the convoy drew close to Casablanca, its destination, the U-boats scored their first torpedo hit on one of its vessels. Some nervousness on the part of the Navy thus was predictable when the ships drew into Casablanca, past the sunken French battleship *Jean Bart*, on Christmas Eve 1942.

Westmoreland, conscious that it was the first Christmas away from home for many of his men, struck a bargain with the Navy. He offered his troops' labor to clean up the *Monterey* after the voyage if, in turn, the ship would feed the battalion Christmas dinner aboard the following day.

When the ship's captain approved, the artillerymen turned to and, perhaps anticipating turkey, had the vessel swabbed and neat by midnight. But at 2 A.M. higher authorities were alarmed by a report of an imminent enemy air attack, and the soldiers were ordered ashore immediately. They had to unload all their equipment in the dark, groping their way to a field behind the Casablanca lighthouse. They went ashore with loaded weapons, not knowing the mood of the French factions in the city, and pitched pup tents in the blackout. Next day, Kerner toured the area in the only available truck, looking for food for the troops. The 34th Field Artillery Battalion finally had a Christmas dinner of C rations scrounged from a unit down the road, but its soldiers directed their special holiday swearing at the United States Navy, rather than their commanding officer.

The first problems of the battalion ashore were intramural or man-to-man between American soldiers and Arab civilians, not organized military actions. Westmoreland's troops, days at sea, wanted excitement. Some of them thought a good drunk after the long dry voyage would be a good start in that direction, and they started buying bad Arab wine and bringing it into the camp. Some other soldiers who did their drinking outside the tent area had been robbed, stripped and murdered in side streets of the city.

Kerner thought the outfit could contain this trouble by taking orders for legitimate wine and letting the troops enjoy it while blowing off steam in their own camp—behind a triple guard, with the first sergeants in charge. He suggested this to Westmoreland, who at first said absolutely not, this is Army property and no alcohol is allowed. But, reminded of what already had happened despite orders to the contrary, he later listened to his executive officer's proposal that he simply busy himself elsewhere so he would not

103

know regulations were being violated. So for a few days wine was brought in, the troops held their own well-policed and organized drinking sessions, and then the novelty wore off and battalion life returned to normal. Westmoreland ordered establishment of a "buddy system," comparable to that used during swimming hours at a Boy Scout camp. Each soldier was assigned to stick with one other, no matter where he went or what he did while on liberty, and to be responsible to bring him back if he got drunk or combative. Disciplinary problems were held down this way.

The German air raid that never came on Christmas Eve came New Year's Eve instead. The bombers hit Casablanca for the first time, and some of those who ducked assumed they came from nearby Spain, because they carried such heavy loads. It was the first time under fire of any kind for the 34th, and its reaction was typical of any unit.

Its soldiers, still living in tents behind the lighthouse where they were pestered by sand and scorpions, feared a white water bag in the company street would be visible to the aviators, so one of them went off to tell his lieutenant about it. In his excitement, he went into the lieutenant's tent with a flashlight, violating blackout orders, and the lieutenant angrily told him to report to the colonel. Westmoreland, aware that it was New Year's Eve, accepted the man's explanation that it was all an accident, and told him not to do it again. The battalion's first casualty was a soldier killed by his own tentmate, who apparently thought in the dark that he was a German paratrooper.

In mid-January, the 34th moved out of Casablanca to the cork forest outside Port Lyautey, about a hundred miles northeast. There the division was bivouacked all together, and the artillerymen spent most of their time teaching the Free French how to use the French-model howitzers. There was USO-style entertainment, too, and Westmoreland got himself photographed with Martha Raye, the ubiquitous comedienne who was to tickle his troops in another war on another continent two decades later.

Most of the other units of the 9th Division already had been blooded. The infantry regiments in combat against the French in the November landings had been accompanied by the three 105-mm. howitzer battalions. But the 34th still was a virgin outfit when it shifted eastward another three hundred miles, from the cork forest in Morocco to the town of Tlemcen, just inside the Algerian border, on February 10 and 11.

This eastward move followed British, American and coordinating French units trying to beat the Germans to the ports of Tunis and Bizerte in Tunisia. The entire landing had been conceived as one arm of a pincer that would close on the enemy in Tunisia, expelling him from Africa. In Egypt, Lieutenant General Sir Bernard Montgomery's Eighth Army had halted Field Marshal Erwin Rommel's Afrika Korps and was forcing it back through Libya. Rommel hoped to withdraw, consolidate with Germans in Tunisia and hold the vital ports while striking westward at the new Allied threat from Morocco and Algeria.

The Allies were slowed by terrain, transport shortages and wet, cold weather, and the Germans around the ports dug in solidly. General Dwight D. Eisenhower, commanding in the west, saw an opportunity in southern Tunisia. He remained cautious, holding strong forces, including the 9th Infantry Division, back in Morocco to guard against German moves through Spain or Spanish Morocco. But he decided to send United States forces into the hills and valleys around Tebessa, Algeria, near the Tunisian frontier,

105

with orders to prepare to drive on to Tunisia's east coast. Yet, as January ended, it was the Germans who were taking the initiative there in southern Tunisia.

They struck through the Eastern Dorsal, one of two mountain ranges that separated the German-held east coast from the Allies' interior. Scattered American and French units could not hold them back. Supported by strafing and dive-bombing, the enemy pressed ahead.

Rommel, in disfavor with higher Axis headquarters, reacted quickly to this success. Turning his eye westward, he saw a chance to deal the Allies at least a demoralizing tactical defeat, perhaps a strategic blow that would kick them out of Tunisia, and in either event a boost to his damaged prestige. He gained permission to continue the attack on through the Western Dorsal, with the alternatives of smashing the valuable Tebessa buildup or swinging up to the north coast, cutting off the Allies there and forcing their pullback into Algeria.

His tanks and planes hammered into the Western Dorsal, eventually concentrating their weight through a pass beyond the village of Kasserine. Wildly assorted American and British units—engineers, tank destroyers, artillery and infantry—dribbled forward, resisted, slowed him, then were overrun or outflanked and defeated. The situation for the Allies was critical as mid-February passed. In their first major ground battle across the Atlantic, United States forces had been beaten soundly.

Kasserine Pass belonged to the enemy. The roads through it branched west toward Tebessa and north toward the coast. The northern fork ran through the village of Thala, on the hard rock desert, three minor ridges away from the pass. The only blocking force was a brigade of outgunned British tanks under Brigadier Charles A. L. Dunphie on the second of those ridges, and a battalion of the British 5th Leicesters digging a final defensive line on the third. If the Germans broke through that line, the road to the north would lay open, and the Allies probably would have to retreat from Tunisia.

As Rommel's thrust developed, Eisenhower sought reinforcements. The United States 9th Infantry Division, with four fresh artillery battalions just about to start maneuvers on the desert below Tlemcen, was among the first he spotted. General Irwin, the division artillery commander, was ordered on the morning of February 17 to rush three battalions and two cannon companies to Tebessa.

Irwin was not a flappable officer. He was a professional soldier, son of a professional, a tall, red-haired man admired by his subordinates. This mission would prompt one historian to call him "a reincarnation of Frank Merriwell," riding to the rescue.

He summoned his battalion commanders back off the desert, where they were reconnoitering for their maneuvers, and issued his movement order half an hour after receiving his own instructions. He had to move his forces 789 miles at top speed through abominable weather. To lead the way, he chose Westmoreland and his 34th Field Artillery Battalion.

Westmoreland, as he packed his gear and supervised the battalion's preparation, told the men around him in the command post, "When you fellows came into the service, we took you from civilians and made soldiers out of you, then when we came overseas we separated the men from the boys, and now we're moving out, and we're going to make artillerymen out of you." He and his troops knew by the haste of their orders that this movement was going to end the waiting they had endured since Pearl Harbor, then since November, when the division landed in Africa without them. But when they pulled onto the road, their howitzers towed behind five-ton Diamond T trucks, at four o'clock that afternoon, they did not realize how urgently they were needed, or how rough their journey would be.

Patches of snow lay alongside the road. It drizzled. It was cold, and the Americans were unprepared for this. It was Africa, after all. In their quick departure, they had to leave behind foot lockers, extra clothing and shoes, to catch up with them much later. That first day, the column covered 210 miles, paralleling the Atlas range past the Foreign Legion headquarters at Sidi bel Abbes and on to Orleansville. There was only the briefest break for sleep. The trucks used blackout lights, snaking along roads dangerous in dry daytime. Westmoreland was everywhere, moving up and down the column, prodding, encouraging, asking individuals how they were doing.

As measured in miles, they were doing fine. They made 234 miles the next day, through Affreville to Mansoura des Bibions. The earth under them was fine clay powder when dry, but like white axle grease in the rain. When they halted, a 155 could sit stationary on the road and slowly slide sidewise into a ditch. Westmoreland would supervise the hitching of another truck onto the howitzer's prime mover, and the great slipping and shouting that accompanied its retrieval.

The column turned into the northeastern tip of the Atlas Mountains, and made only 135 miles though pressing forward without letup the third day of the march. Maintenance for the 155's and their trucks was tough; they carried their own repair and replacement equipment. One driver would stay at the wheel until exhausted, then another would shift into his seat, but the trucks themselves had to keep grinding away, in lower gears, up and down, clutching for traction on the primitive roads, day and night. Guns would slip off the road, be bypassed, and catch up at the next rest break. But they did catch up, and all twelve of them were ready for firing when the battalion reached its destination.

As the column came down out of the mountains, Westmoreland went ahead with officers from his operations, intelligence and survey staffs to check with units on the scene and find out where their guns would be positioned. They drove past a flood of Americans and Arabs fleeing to the rear. Rumors flew. Tebessa was likely to fall any moment. Air Corps personnel, supply and service units were pushing out of Tebessa, and their traffic at first flowed against and slowed Westmoreland's command group and the trailing artillery column. But then some, cheered by the arriving reinforcements, turned back toward the front.

Westmoreland reported to the division artillery's executive officer at Tebessa, and was told to go ahead and contact Irwin somewhere along the road toward Thala. He kept going into Thala, and after dusk located British headquarters. The British told him he was the first officer of the 9th Division to appear there—and that he was most welcome.

In the afternoon, before Westmoreland reached Thala, Rommel had become impatient and taken personal charge of the German attack there. His forces battered, then routed Dunphie's British, who withdrew under smoke cover after bravely delaying the advance. Dunphie's tanks pulled back into a break in the defensive line of the Leicesters, kept open for their arrival. This procedure, expected by the Germans, almost resulted in the loss of the entire final blocking position. The Germans placed a captured British tank at the head of their own column, and it tailed onto Dunphie's, leading German tanks into the British lines. When they were discovered, a fantastically confusing firefight took place, aimed at anything that moved in the dusk. After three hours, both sides pulled back, leaving the scene abandoned. Had the Germans pushed on through to Thala, they could have carried it and achieved their objective. As it was, tomorrow would tell. Rommel ordered an attack through Thala the next morning.

Westmoreland was in Thala during the fight on the ridge to the south. He was shown by British officers where his weapons would be emplaced. They gave him 1/50,000 maps of the area, but only one was big enough to include both his gun positions and the enemy target areas.

Kerner, in charge of the battalion on the road, brought it into Tebessa at the head of the division artillery column. He sent John Clemmey, a soldier from his message center, ahead to find Westmoreland. When Clemmey reported to him, Westmoreland demanded, "Where's the battalion?" Told it was several miles west, he sent word to Kerner to "get those guns up here." Clemmey returned to tell the executive officer that he thought he had better start the battalion moving "before we all get court-martialed."

Responding to this, the real thing, Westmoreland was snapping out orders to his staff. One lieutenant was dispatched in a jeep five miles west to select a rear echelon area. Another was sent forward to find observation post locations. With another, Westmoreland himself went to get a firsthand look at the batteries' gun positions. Then, his limited reconnaissance complete, he went back and met Kerner and the battalion, ordered the outfit to drop all nontactical equipment and load for action. He assembled his battery commanders and, there in the desert darkness west of Thala, issued the first combat order of his career.

The 34th was ending its fourth straight day of forced

marching. That day, it had added another 210 miles without halting. The whole column had made the punishing journey in one hundred hours, and arrived with 411 vehicles intact, 48 guns ready for combat, and 2,170 officers and men exhausted. As they rolled forward from Tebessa to Thala, many of the men straggling the other way aboard ambulances, trucks and half-tracks shouted to them to "git while the gittin's good," but they went on. When they reached Thala their appearance gave a noticeable lift to the British who were figuring how long they could delay Rommel before the inevitable withdrawal. Exhausted or not, the artillerymen were just beginning another working day.

Field Order number one of the 34th instructed the howitzer batteries to emplace along a trail running westward out of Thala, where they could use their relatively greater range to enfilade the main road from Kasserine Pass. Irwin, appointed commander of all artillery in the Thala area, passed the word that the newly arrived guns would be ready to fire at daybreak. Westmoreland ordered more specifically that his 155's would be prepared to register their fire at 6:45 A.M. The pieces were laid, trenches dug, six attached half-tracks carrying 75-mm. antitank protection were sited, while the Germans were distracted by a midnight sortie carried out by what was left of Dunphie's tanks.

Before dawn, individuals lay on the hard earth and tried to sleep. Kerner was among them, and he remembers that the fog and rain that had dogged the march were gone, and as he stared up at the stars above a silhouetted mountain crest they seemed to dance and swim in his exhaustion. There was an occasional rattle of machine gun fire off past the village, and now and then a searching German 88-mm. shell burst and broke his fitful nap.

The artillerymen had been positioned by map coordinates, because detailed night reconnaissance was impossible. Thus it was not until dawn on that George Washington's birthday that Westmoreland and those with him realized how desperate the situation was. The Germans were looking down on them from ideal artillery observation posts. Lieutenant Colonel Justin Stoll, commanding the 84th Field Artillery Battalion, a 105-mm. outfit placed farther forward, recalls that he was told one hill a thousand yards to his front was in friendly hands, and only found out that the Germans owned it when he sent a forward observer team out to try to use it. The newly arrived guns, the scraps and remnants of the British artillery and tanks, and the Leicesters, now down to three understrength platoons, sat there under the glare of the Germans. But they did not merely sit and wait.

At 7 A.M., General Fritz Freiherr von Broich, Rommel's subordinate, was about to move out on the advance he was sure would capture Thala. Suddenly, a rain of shells from the 9th Division guns fell among his forces. This jarred him. He telephoned Rommel. The two agreed that the fire came from guns that were not there the night before, and if such reinforcements had arrived, an Allied counterattack was likely. Rommel came forward to inspect the situation. As he did, the remnants of Dunphie's tank brigade played another bold role; they charged the German line, and though they lost five tanks, they bluffed the Germans into delaying their jumpoff and preparing for the expected counterattack.

The first 155-mm. shells from the 34th were fired at 8:54 A.M. by C Battery. Forward observers reported targets along the road south from Thala, and German 88's were pounding any Allied movement along the same route. Despite strikes by German Messerschmitt 109's, Junkers 87's (the screaming Stuka dive bombers) and twin-engine Junkers 88's, the guns kept up an impressive volume of fire all day, blasting a German gasoline dump and silencing an 88-mm. battery.

Stoll's 84th turned the muzzles of its 105's downward to use direct fire against a German tank probe about noon. It lost four guns, but knocked out three tanks and continued the bluff that convinced the Germans the Allied reinforcements were bigger and more potent than they were. The 34th encouraged this attitude, pouring out fire, enduring incoming counterbattery salvos, shuttling trucks back and forth toward Tebessa for ammunition resupply.

Rommel, uncharacteristically hesitant, talked with his superior Field Marshal Albert Kesselring that day. He decided that he could not risk pressing ahead. He was willing to call the campaign a draw, and turn his attention to the British Eighth Army, approaching back to the east. Martin Blumenson, the United States Army historian who has made the most complete study of the battle, concluded that "of all the units making their way to Tunisia, the 9th Division artillery reached the vital point at the decisive moment and exerted the conclusive influence on the Battle of Kasserine . . . the battle had ended that Monday morning of the 22nd with the opening volleys of Red Irwin's artillery pieces."

The vanguard of that rescue force, Westmoreland's 34th, was awarded the Presidential Unit Citation for its leading role. Its citation described the march from Tlemcen and emplacement by night, and recalled that, "Although enemy forces were entrenched only 2,500 yards distant and there were only three platoons of friendly infantry in front of the artillery, the unit maintained constant and steady fire with such deadly effect that enemy tank units were dispersed and driven back. The cold, determined manner in which the 34th . . . entered into battle after almost an incredible forced march contributed in great measure to the defeat of the enemy's attempt to break through the Thala defile. The gallant entry into the battle and the heroism with which the volume of fire was maintained despite terrific enemy fire are in keeping with the highest traditions of American military service."

But the war went on. Westmoreland sent out Lieutenant Donald A. Rencken, a forward observer, dressed as an Arab the following morning. Rencken, burnoose and robes above his Army boots, sifted within the German patrol lines. He reported the enemy withdrawing.

The rest of the 9th Division by now was catching up with the artillery and the 39th Regimental Combat Team, which had been torn up fighting farther north in the battle for the Dorsal ranges. After holding fast at Thala for several days more, Westmoreland's battalion joined the 47th RCT in a night move, shuttling forward into Kasserine Pass. The battalion spent most of March there before shifting south, en route to its second major battle at El Guettar.

The United States II Corps by now had the added strength that the Germans were convinced it had brought up at Thala. It also had a new commander, Major General George S. Patton, Jr., an officer devoted to forward movement. The corps's role was to push eastward toward the Tunisian coast as Montgomery shoved the Germans north. The first serious resistance to this pressure came at El Guettar Pass, through which runs the main road to the coast. Djebel (Mount) Berda rises abruptly south of the pass and dominates the flat, gully-sliced, treeless desert across which the Americans had to advance. The Germans were covered among the knobs of Djebel Berda. The 9th, operating as a division for the first time in combat, was to coordinate in opening the pass for a deep armored penetration toward the coast and the enemy's lines of communication. Heavy artillery preparations were scheduled against the strongly emplaced enemy as the infantry moved to the attack, using the protection of night as it crossed the open plain.

Westmoreland's 34th was to move at night, too. It arrived three miles below El Guettar village, north of the pass, at 11:10 P.M. March 27, and Westmoreland ordered preparation of a night command post. He had worked out a policy of using different CP's for day and night, to avoid artillery fire during darkness after being spotted during daylight. They were about 250 yards apart, the night position dug in deeply, covered with black canvas. Another Westmoreland experiment came when his howitzers kicked up so much desert dust that they were easily detectable targets as soon as they commenced firing. He directed that all available canvas, off trucks, trailers and elsewhere, be laid beneath and around the pieces to cut down this dusty visibility.

Up to El Guettar, he had followed the book closely in emplacing his batteries, and the result was that each battery's front was too narrow, making it too concentrated a target. Combining combat experience with what he had learned at Fort Sill and Schofield, Westmoreland devised a system of spreading each battery's weapons along a front of a thousand to fifteen hundred yards, and worked out with the communications sergeant a network of phones tying in at each gun, all running back to the executive officer. It involved so much wire it made the artillery unit look like a signal battalion, but it spread the guns out over ten times as much area as before.

115

Next morning, when the division was about to jump off in its assault, Westmoreland told Clemmey that he was about to hear one hundred guns "hub to hub" fire together —and he was right; it was as if one gigantic cannon had roared, and the battle of El Guettar was joined. But soon after the artillery opened, Westmoreland realized some of his enemy targets were pulling back beyond range of his outmoded 155's. He asked permission to push one battery forward to keep the Germans under fire. Patton's headquarters approved, and assigned Westmoreland's C Battery a position three miles ahead of its previous firing site, designating the exact map coordinates where it wanted the guns located.

Even on the nearly worthless 1/100,000 maps issued for that campaign, Kerner could see that the unit would be totally exposed to German fire, and he complained, but II Corps insisted on that spot. The battery moved forward at 3 A.M. Next day it took heavy shelling from German 150-mm. batteries, and its own guns could not be fired because the gunners could not even stick their heads above ground. The position was so conspicuous that it drew an attack from the first four-engine German bomber the 34th had ever seen, along with the same strafing and bombing suffered by the rest of the American corps.

The punishment taken by the battery grew so intense that Kerner suggested that it might be pulled back under cover of smoke. But Westmoreland went out to the position himself. "I don't know how in hell he made it; his driver was ready to walk the gangplank," Clemmey remembers. After conferring with the battery commander, Westmoreland returned to his CP and vowed, "I'll be damned if I'll pull that battery back." But at 2:10 P.M. that day, he ordered all spare camouflage nets sent out to C Battery to cover

dummy positions that would be left as the battery shifted—
not back, but to a position where it could use its own guns.

The Germans retained air superiority. Day and night,
they bombed, dropped flares, and rarely strafed. But American anti-aircraft protection was making them more cautious—especially improved .50-caliber machine gun defenses. In the jumpy first days, these weapons had knocked
down five U.S. P–38's in one day, although the unique twin-
boomed planes bore no remote resemblance to anything
flown by the enemy. The .50's gradually became more selective, and were successful in sharply reducing the terror
and destruction of the slow, obsolescent Stukas, which
dived within easy reach of the heavy machine guns. Later,
however, when American P–51 Mustangs replaced Spit-
fires in the increasingly frequent Allied umbrella overhead,
they too were victimized by the itchy-fingered machine gunners because they looked so much like the Messerschmitt
109. It was a gunner, Corporal Joseph E. Beebe, who became the first man of the 34th killed in action as he swung a
.50, tracking a strafing Junkers 88.

During the El Guettar fight, an aerial observer passed
word that a German outfit lined up regularly every evening
at mess trucks at a certain spot. Westmoreland obtained
enough white phosphorus shells to scatter the hungry Germans into their trenches with high explosives, then chase
them out with incendiary WP's, and back and forth. When
the fire mission began, General Irwin came speeding up and
ordered it halted, maintaining that using WP against personnel was a violation of the Hague Agreement. It took
several days for the staff to check and find out that it was
not, and after that the battalion never found such a tempting target for Westmoreland's combination of warheads.

Westmoreland called Stoll of the 84th one afternoon

and told him General Eddy wanted them to go to the position of the 39th Infantry to coordinate night defensive fires against an expected counterattack. They had to cross three miles of exposed, untraveled road to get there, and after conferring at the regimental CP hidden in a wadi they planned barrages to be called in by number, and headed back to the artillery positions.

The Germans were shelling targets on one side of the road, then shifting their fire across to tanks on the opposite side. The two colonels decided to wait until the enemy fire switched the other way and then "go like a bat out of hell." But when Westmoreland's speeding command car reached the point where the German guns traversed the road, it suddenly seemed to evaporate in a boom of dust. A shell, probably 170-mm., had exploded just off the left front fender, increasing the car's speed drastically. Infantrymen in holes alongside the road stuck up their heads and made the OK sign with their fingers as the officers' car raced across the desert away from the enemy salvos.

While the 34th was distinguishing itself and gaining sustained battle experience, the infantry regiments of the division were bruised by the enemy in his hilly fortress. But under steady pressure, the Germans gave up El Guettar on April 6, and the next day the Americans rolled to join Montgomery on the coast.

The enemy was being pressed hard from three sides, and as his lines shortened his resistance was more concentrated. The American II Corps now was to be pulled together and given a prize objective. But to accomplish it, the whole corps had to move back inland and two hundred miles north, defying the book by crossing the lines of communication of the busily engaged British First Army, and move into position on the northern sea flank of the Allied forces. The 9th Infantry Division moved farthest—from the southernmost flank to the northernmost. In place in the north and under another new corps commander, Major General Omar N. Bradley, the corps was assigned to drive toward the port of Bizerte. The 9th Division had two aims, one to capture the hill mass blocking the way to the coastal plain, the other to drive up the Sedjenane Valley, working with the French Corps d'Afrique. The operations were too far divided for the division's artillery to cover them both from a central firing area. Thus it was split, with the 34th supporting the 60th Infantry in the move down the Sedjenane.

Again, Westmoreland's unit pulled into an unfamiliar combat area in darkness. The battalion CP was set up a few yards from the graves of fourteen German soldiers, marked by blank wooden crosses, with steel helmets atop the mounds. A few yards from them was the unburied body of a British soldier. Westmoreland reminded his operations, intelligence and communications NCO's that they should keep a quart of gasoline and matches handy at all times to destroy documents in case of an enemy breakout. He himself probably would not be there to burn them; he was constantly out ahead of the guns, joining his forward observers, adjusting registration and fire missions. And when he was at the CP, he often had important visitors. Even Irwin and Eddy took the unusual step of coming down the chain of command to see him, to talk with a young battalion commander. Even in combat, one of his close colleagues noted, he was a "marked officer."

One of the most difficult targets assigned the 34th, in support of the infantrymen hacking their way through matted jungle, was a reinforced concrete gun emplacement near one of the lakes below Bizerte. It lay at the extreme range of Westmoreland's 155's—they could reach it only when the wind was right. The time fuses on the high explosive shells could not be set to wait that long, so Westmoreland used a technique he had employed against German armor farther south. He ordered use of charge six (for maximum range), with no fuses at all. The shells exploded when their cases cracked against the hardened target. It worked. The German guns harassed the infantry no longer; their emplacement was destroyed.

But this example of their ingenious use was no testimonial to the aged howitzers; as the battalion rolled forward along roads cut by the division's own engineers through the jungled hills, the 155's were giving Westmoreland serious trouble despite the self-service maintenance that had kept them going through country so hostile to any kind of machinery.

Setting up another long pace forward, the battalion CP was positioned in an Arab graveyard. It was cozy until the following morning at ten o'clock, when German 88 shells fell just beyond, then just short of, the tents. They had the CP bracketed, then laid ten more shells on a little mosque in the cemetery, which they had chosen as a registration point for their guns. No one was killed, but everyone was reminded of the theory of avoidance of conspicuous terrain features.

By early May, the main barriers to the division's advance had been reduced. One last string of djebels lay between the infantry and Bizerte. Flanking movements had put the infantry into position to make a final attack to attain the crest, and to do so it used a tactic the division called "leaning up against artillery." All available guns were registered just ahead of the assaulting companies, laying shells within one hundred yards of the riflemen, and their fire walked up the mountainside, enabling one battalion of infantry to take this key German strongpoint. The other djebels fell, and the way to Bizerte was clear. Grinding out ahead, half-tracks attached to the 9th Division won the race into the city. Snipers and artillery took potshots at them, so they withdrew until the next day, when the 47th Infantry and French troops were the first major forces to move into the evacuated port.

Artillery outfits sent their forward observers in with the infantry to seek targets among the retreating Germans. Kerner joined them, and radioed back to Westmoreland—transmitting his map coordinates in code—that he was there. Westmoreland skeptically queried his position. Kerner assured him where he was, and the battalion soon followed. It set up its headquarters under a real roof for the first time in months, but Westmoreland and Kerner prudently did not sleep in the first beds they had available in just as long a time. The rest of the staff did, and woke up speckled with bedbug bites.

The battle for Africa was won. Only mopping up remained. Thousands of prisoners had to be processed. But the 9th Division did not make its home in the cosmopolitan though crumbled metropolis of Bizerte. It was ordered back to Algeria, this time on a comparatively leisurely six-day, 910-mile march to Magenta, south of Sidi bel Abbes.

The division's official historian described Magenta: ". . . flies, intense heat, manure, choking dust and lack of things modern." It was the division's home for "seven long weeks" of training; resupply; repair of equipment; recreation in the form of sports, movies or swimming on the beach near Oran; malaria; liberty in Sidi bel Abbes, where soldiers

121

struck up friendships with Legionnaires; dysentery; and rest, less during the enforced afternoon siestas than through the cool desert nights. Westmoreland played on his battalion's softball team, pressed his troops on a schedule of drill, inspection and calisthenics, and concerned himself about the condition of his creaking 155's.

When General Irwin filed an annex to the division's operations report for northern Tunisia, he endorsed several of the innovations employed by Westmoreland: "Wide dispersal of pieces made artillery batteries unprofitable targets for bombing or counterbattery fire . . . Dummy positions draw enemy fire, and have been used to good effect . . . Massed artillery fire breaks up tank movement . . ." Irwin, however, had earned himself another star, and moved on to a higher command. His replacement as division artillery commander was an officer with whom Westmoreland would have extended close contact but very little rapport.

But the next step in Westmoreland's combat career was not to be with either his new artillery commander or his old division as such. At the end of June, the 34th was attached to the 39th Infantry and ordered back to Bizerte. In bivouac outside the city, the artillery underwent a heavy but haphazard air raid by German bombers who were frustrated by anti-aircraft fire on a mission against the harbor, and jettisoned their loads on the camp. There was much more bombing and shelling ahead.

7

Licata to Barton Stacey

1943–1944

There was widespread debate over where the Allies should move after eliminating the Axis from Africa. The Balkans? Southern France? Sardinia? The decision was Sicily, for it would not only help keep the Soviet Union in the war by opening another front closer to the enemy's homeland, but it would give the Allies control of the Mediterranean sea lanes, and it was close and accessible enough so that the offensive spirit generated in Africa would have an outlet, without a break in momentum.

The first assault unit ashore was to be the 82nd Airborne Division, commanded by Major General Matthew B. Ridgway. The 39th Infantry, with Westmoreland's artillery battalion in direct support, was among the forces scheduled to hit the beaches the next day, after the paratroopers' night drop. Four battalions of airborne soldiers were to jump onto the high ground behind the port of Gela, and protect the later landing there. But the air drop was jinxed from the start. A midsummer gale and inexperienced transport pilots combined to scatter the paratroopers sixty miles up and down the southwest corner of the island. Stray airborne soldiers still were wandering into their own lines a week later. General Bradley saw the bright side of the confusion, however, when he wrote later that the paratroopers' dispersion panicked the Germans and Italians into greatly exaggerating Allied strength.

Neither did the botched but effective air drop do anything to dissuade Westmoreland from his earlier enthusiasm for action with men of the airborne persuasion. He liked their direct approach to combat, and in fact contrasted it to the relatively stodgy action he expected with the 39th Infantry. His battalion had barely rolled ashore at the port of Licata on July 15 when he left Kerner in charge and went in search of the 82nd Airborne's headquarters.

When he arrived, Ridgway was briefing his staff and subordinate commanders on the outfit's next assignment. It involved moving fast up the shore of the island. Westmoreland stood in a corner of the tent and listened until Ridgway was through. Then he introduced himself to Ridgway. He said he had heard what the division was about to do, and he wanted to offer the general "the best artillery support you've ever had"—and added, almost as an afterthought, that four dozen trucks and other transport came with the deal. Ridgway may or may not have been impressed enough to accept the offer of artillery support from a brash young lieutenant colonel, but he did not hesitate to buy the idea of more wheels for his air-droppable, thus extremely lightly equipped division. He picked up a field telephone and told II Corps he wanted Westmoreland, and he got him.

Once the switched attachment was made formal, Ridgway sent his division artillery commander down to take a look at his newly acquired medium howitzer battalion. The artillery officer was glad to have it; he had asked for heavier supporting arms than the 75-mm. weapons organic to the airborne division. Being an artilleryman himself, he had commanded 155's of the same model, and he thought he knew all the tricks of handling them. But when he inspected the 34th, he found out somebody else knew them all, too. He was impressed, and made a point of telling Ridgway what a sharp unit they had come up with, then of inviting Westmoreland and Kerner to have dinner with him that evening. He was Brigadier General Maxwell D. Taylor. It was the first meeting in a friendship that was to have an important influence on Westmoreland's later career.

Westmoreland's 34th tied in with the 82nd Airborne at Agrigento, twenty-five miles up the coast from its landing at Licata. From there, it laid down supporting fires at Ribera, Santa Margherita, Sciacca and across the island's western-most bulge to Trapani for the fast-moving paratroopers.

Back at Fort Bragg, Westmoreland had worked out what he called a "blitz" formation for traveling light in a pursuit situation. He never had an opportunity to use it in Africa. The battalion had practiced it, so that every man knew what he was supposed to do when the commanding officer let out the single word "blitz," just as if he were calling a play in a football huddle. Advancing artillerymen had never traveled lighter than the 34th when most of its organic trucks had been turned over to the paratroopers, so "blitz" it was, and it worked, as the battalion displaced from one firing position to another five times, covering more than 120 miles in the eight days between debarkation and arrival outside the strategic port of Trapani.

125

Getting the promised trucks to where the 82nd wanted them was not as easy as it sounded. Kerner dispatched a convoy of "all available transportation" forward on Taylor's order, and a few hours later Taylor was on the telephone, demanding to know where it was. Kerner told him he had sent it, that he would scrape up whatever else he could find and bring them to him personally. As he hurried up the road at the head of the second convoy, Kerner was halted by the colonel of one of the 82nd's regiments, waving a pistol. The colonel told him matter-of-factly that he was taking the trucks. Kerner informed the colonel he had a pistol himself, that General Taylor wanted those trucks and was going to get them. Furthermore, he added, where were the others he sent through there a couple of hours ago? The colonel reluctantly produced them, and Taylor got his trucks.

Westmoreland's battalion was in direct support of his friend Colonel James M. Gavin, the airborne proselyter from Fort Bragg, as Gavin's regiment rolled the last mountainous miles toward Trapani. At every populated corner happy Sicilians were tossing fruit, bread and candy at the conquering Americans. For the artillerymen chasing just behind, the day turned into a "class reunion," for repeatedly paratroopers who stopped off to enjoy the welcoming hospitality for a while would hitchhike rides on the artillery trucks—and many of them turned out to be old members of the 9th Division, who had switched to airborne in the long-ago summer of 1942.

At about four o'clock that carefree, dusty afternoon, however, the atmosphere did a quick change. Just before the advancing column came into Trapani's eastern outskirts, its lead trucks hit minefields before a stoutly defended roadblock. The paratroopers bailed out of the trucks and deployed toward the sudden opposition, and as they did Italian guns on the hills across the city laid down a shaking barrage along the road.

It was heavy, but largely ineffective. It went on while the paratroopers maneuvered toward the roadblock and Westmoreland's guns, along with the 75's of the airborne artillery, unlimbered. The gunners began yanking lanyards furiously. Some of the targets were so far up the hillsides the 155's could not elevate sufficiently to reach them. But combined with clearing of the roadblock and occupation of the high ground on the flanks by the paratroopers, the heavy American cannon fire convinced the Italian naval district commander that his honor had been upheld. So Contrammiraglio Giuseppe Manfredi surrendered the battle, the city, his sword and his field glasses.

This period of rapid movement was ending, however, as Axis resistance became tougher toward the center of Sicily. The 82nd Airborne was pulled out and sent back to Africa to refit and prepare for its forthcoming action on the mainland of Italy. Westmoreland's guns then rejoined the 39th Infantry, in attachment to the 1st Infantry Division, attacking into the heart of Sicily.

Major General Terry Allen, the hell-for-leather commander of the 1st Infantry Division, had seen his men fight desperately to throw back a counterattack by the Hermann Goering Panzer Division on the hills behind the landing beaches at Gela, and they had been heavily engaged ever since. At the end of July, he picked the 39th Infantry to lead his attack against enemy forces in Cerami, which straddled the main road north of Mount Etna to the island's eastern coast. The 39th had a battalion in Cerami early the next day, but then it ground against stiffer defenses. The weight of 165 artillery pieces—including Westmoreland's

127

and the three remaining battalions of the 9th Division (which had landed through the reopened port of Palermo) —was called in upon the Germans in the hills. With this support, the infantry inched ahead, but the guns had a hard time following on the narrow, clogged road through the mountains. Luftwaffe fighters flashed over, and enemy guns laid accurate concentrations. A counterattack hit the point, but was broken up with heavy friendly artillery help. Yet the forward movement of the regiment, thus the corps, was held up before the next town along the vital road.

That was Troina, a natural fortress that looks down on any attacker from the west, totally dominating the road and the hill noses that push the road into repeated curves. The ground over which the Americans had to advance was steep, jumbled, and sown thickly with mines. As the 1st Division coiled to strike against Troina, the 9th Division was moved in on its left. The battle rocked back and forth, with the artillery laying tons of high explosives on German batteries in the hills, against a major enemy counterattack, and on the town itself. It was costly. The Germans finally began to withdraw on the night of August 5. When the Americans moved into Troina, they found 150 dead, most of them civilians, in streets and houses. The advance pressed on past the northern slopes of Mount Etna, with Westmoreland's battalion once more serving with its own 9th Infantry Division.

Westmoreland's reputation for always being out front was strengthened during this constant combat and artillery displacement. Not only that, but he was on his way to winning an Air Medal, something not accomplished by every artillery officer. In the late stages of the Tunisian campaign, his outfit had gotten its first spotter aircraft, little L–4 "grasshoppers," and Westmoreland, the frustrated aviator, spent as much time in them as his forward observers. When he found his 155's being completely overshot by a heavy German rifle, he went aloft with a pilot to try to find the source of the annoyance. They found nothing. As they were about to give up, Westmoreland told the pilot to pull up suddenly and look back. He did, and they spotted a giant railway gun easing out of a tunnel behind them. They noted its coordinates, and Westmoreland ordered the same no-fuse technique that had silenced the concrete gun emplacement at extreme range in Tunisia. It worked again.

Another German weapon that had begun to bother the Allies toward the end in Tunisia was the elusive Nebelwerfer, a six-barreled, 150-mm. rocket launcher whose projectiles came in with a high-pitched shriek more demoralizing than that of the now obsolete Stukas, and earned them the GI nickname of "screaming meemies." Westmoreland learned on Sicily that they could fire a salvo, unlimber and take off for a new position within three minutes. His forward observers found one way of hitting them with counterbattery fire. That was to adjust the American guns on a point several hundred yards removed from the Nebelwerfers, without alarming the Germans, then suddenly switch onto the enemy guns with a full "fire for effect" order, rather than warning the enemy by gradually creeping fire onto his position. Since the rocket weapons made a flash of flame some thirty feet high every time they loosed a salvo, they were easy to spot, but only when this system of calling return fire on them was devised were they easy to hit.

Late in the Sicilian campaign, Westmoreland mounted his command car and went scouting toward the front for new artillery positions. En route back, his driver tried to bypass a hole in the road, and as he drove along its shoulder, the car hit a German mine. There was a blast, and something from the car went flopping at least one hundred feet into the air. Stoll of the 84th Field Artillery Battalion saw it and was shocked, thinking it was Westmoreland himself. He ran to the car, and there sat Westmoreland in the rear seat, calm and unhurt. "What happened?" Westmoreland asked. He did not know whether he had been bombed, shelled or mined. The car's right front wheel had been blown off, and what Stoll thought was a body flying aloft was its tire. The mine was an eleven-pound German Teller. If it had been a heavier, antitank mine, the car and its occupants would have been destroyed.

The incident was cited in the official description of Westmoreland's leadership accompanying the Legion of Merit, awarded to him for action in Africa and Sicily. It mentioned Thala and El Guettar, and said that "in front of Troina, Sicily, because of the need of medium fire deep in enemy territory, he personally reconnoitered positions well in front of the light battalions, and closely supervised the occupation and firing from these positions. Although severe enemy firing was experienced in both positions, his mission was efficiently accomplished. He was constantly well forward, coordinating the work of his forward observers, and personally fired many missions from these observation points. While seeking forward observation near Ceasero, Sicily, his vehicle was demolished by mines but he calmly obtained another vehicle and continued his mission. His superior courage, devotion to duty and ability to work unceasingly was an inspiration . . ."

So Westmoreland survived and prospered in Sicily, but his 155's did not. They had been dragged in and out of firing positions fifteen times in little more than five weeks of fighting. Only five of the twelve 155's of the 34th were still serviceable at the end.

The fighting on the island over, the 9th Division was sent back to camp on the Tyrrhenian seacoast, and there it went into the same sort of rehabilitation-and-preparation routine it had scheduled on the desert at Magenta. Fresh meat and USO shows arrived. The officers had time to organize formal battalion messes, and Westmoreland could take stock of what he and his men had learned. He could not know it, but the action at Randazzo was the last time he would command the 34th in combat.

This lazy interlude lasted more than ten weeks. When the battalion was ordered to Palermo in early November, it went into a muddy staging area before sailing in the rain for England. Every soldier there knew what came after England.

In a convoy of twenty transports and eight destroyers, the division arrived in England the day before Thanksgiving. Westmoreland's 34th and the 39th Infantry with which it had worked in Sicily were detailed to make their home in Nissen huts and barracks at the tiny country town of Barton Stacey, about twelve miles up the road from Winchester, which in turn was about forty-five miles southwest of London. It was an ancient town, population 830, with only two pubs, the Swan and the Plow, where the enlisted men made friends. By Christmastime many were taken into the families of Barton Stacey.

The officers were taken in, too, mostly by well-to-do Englishmen who had come to the countryside to avoid the bombs falling on London. There were parties, and for Westmoreland the handsome bachelor, there was more attempted matchmaking. There were occasional trips to London for sightseeing and the theater.

But mostly there was business. The 34th was issued new 155's—modern, American-designed M–1 howitzers, easier to tow at high speed, with longer range, greater stability, wider traversing action and, above all, with plentiful spare parts. The 9th Division artillery was chosen to stage a demonstration shoot for the chief of the Royal Artillery at Lark Hill, Hampshire, and was commended for it. Westmoreland was picked as a member of a six-man team of officers from division artillery which toured other, less experienced United States units in England, giving lectures on various aspects of artillery in combat—communications, forward observers, choice of firing positions.

The artillery, the Air Corps, the ground-bound infantry all were pressing toward readiness, but none more eagerly than the units that would spearhead the great campaign ahead. Maxwell Taylor, promoted to major general and given command of the 101st Airborne Division, was seeking all the expertise he could find for the dramatic assignment his division would carry out. He remembered Westmoreland and the way his battalion had performed with the 82nd Airborne on Sicily, and when a colonel's billet opened up in the 101st, he thought he could tempt Westmoreland finally to go airborne. He offered him not only a full colonel's eagles, but a job as division artillery executive officer (divarty XO) of his division.

Westmoreland was standing by the road outside Barton Stacey before dawn one morning in early spring, supervising his battalion's movement to a firing range. Out of the darkness rolled the 9th Division artillery commander, Brigadier General Reese M. Howell, who told him that General Eddy had considered Taylor's proposal and replied that the

101st could not have Westmoreland. Instead, Eddy was transferring Westmoreland to become divarty XO of the 9th, with the promise that promotion to colonel would follow soon.

Westmoreland had mixed feelings about what almost happened to him, and what did. He admired Taylor, and he still had the itch to become a paratrooper officer. But he had formed strong ties with the 9th Division, and particularly with the battalion he had trained and led in battle.

He was never averse to advancement, but he did not take lightly the idea of leaving the 34th. Shared experience, especially shared danger, brings men close, regardless of age and rank. Westmoreland had lasting ties with radio operators, drivers, cannoneers, staff officers—friendships that he still kept up a quarter of a century later. One of them was with the Catholic chaplain of the division artillery, then First Lieutenant Edward T. Connors, a Boston Irishman who had many of his own kind in Westmoreland's battalion. The division's historian, Joseph B. Mittelman, called Father Connors "almost a legend, another 'soldier saint,' " and told how the chaplain hitchhiked his way into battle, holding services on flat rocks or jeep hoods, and how he won the Silver Star by rescuing men of a service battalion amid exploding ammunition trailers in Tunisia.

If Westmoreland, like Connors, left the 34th as "almost a legend," the priest himself was glad to help perpetuate that impression. It was he who described the young Captain Westmoreland back at Fort Bragg as having a visage "like a laser beam." He recalled the later time when Lieutenant Colonel Westmoreland was lecturing a soldier for failing to wear his helmet in the field, "when several enemy planes appeared overhead and began to strafe the area. In spite of the inherent danger to himself, his first concern was for the safety of the man. He took off his helmet and put it on the man's head, then pushed him into the foxhole and acted as a shield by falling over him." Father Connors said, "Many were the nights he would pace the command post, anxiously awaiting the return of special observation post or communications details, not turning in until the last man was safely in . . . He insisted that his men be briefed on all phases of impending moves and operations . . . This was carried out so diligently that an officer from one of the other artillery units complained, 'You men know more about what's going on than we officers do.'

"Throughout the almost four-year period when we had day-to-day contact with him, we never heard Westmoreland say even one slight 'damn.' He did not resort to gimmickry such as wearing fancy-strapped shoes, or pearl-handled pistols. Bluff and bluster were not in his nature . . . He used power but never abused it. His command was one of respect, not of fear."

Officers who were Westmoreland's contemporaries, competing with him, assessed him with harder eyes: "He was all Army. He had no time for anything else. He didn't equivocate, had a forceful way, but could take suggestions. He never blew up. He told his people what to do, and expected them to do it. He always wanted things done right, was really quite a perfectionist, but when things weren't perfect, he didn't lose his temper, he just made it clear he was disappointed. He was very concerned for the welfare of his troops. There was no question he was one of the most patriotic, dedicated men I ever knew. We said he would become chief of staff of the Army if he didn't stub his toe."

Those above Westmoreland, as well as around him, were watching him when he became division artillery executive officer on April 13, 1944.

8

Normandy to the Huertgen

June–October, 1944

For the first five months of the year, American troops in England trained in assault techniques from squad level up to Army Group. How to attack a fortified emplacement; how to control a company under fire on a hostile beach; how to move a battalion, a regiment, a division inland against carefully prepared defense in depth; how to mass the fires of four battalions of artillery quickly, accurately on a point target; staff exercises to coordinate mounting, marshaling, loading and unloading.

During this procedure Sir Bernard Montgomery, by then a field marshal, came to talk to the troops of the 9th Division, to reminisce about "the old days" in Tunisia and to look ahead. Winston Churchill, Eisenhower, Bradley (by then commander of the First Army) and Major General J. Lawton Collins, commander of the VII Corps to which the division was assigned, came and reviewed the 9th, which felt it was earning the name of a "show division."

By spring, the troops were ready for dress rehearsals for what was to come—though where and when it would come were closed secrets to the rehearsing soldiers. During one landing exercise at Slapton Sands, on the Devon coast below Dartmouth, Westmoreland was present as an observer. With some background in amphibious affairs gained during those drills off Virginia and North Carolina, he thought it would be appropriate for him to go up to the bridge of the command craft and chat with the brigadier general in charge of the landing division. It was a rare Westmoreland slip, a breach of naval etiquette, to do so without being invited, and the general ran the lieutenant colonel down off the bridge. Westmoreland, a stickler for precise propriety, was embarrassed. He never made the same mistake again.

Rehearsals over, the thousands of American troops were anxious and full of rumor. It would be Norway. No, France, Spain, Belgium, Germany itself. To stifle this talk, lest some of it be correct and leak to the enemy, troops were moved into marshaling areas, cut off from the surrounding countryside, guarded by counterintelligence operatives.

The 9th Division, going in as one of the "early buildup" units rather than in the initial assault waves, got six-hour alert orders May 21. On June 6, as infantrymen of the shock divisions were wading ashore in Normandy, the 9th Division artillery moved into the carefully camouflaged marshaling area outside Southampton. June 8, it began loading into a convoy of fourteen Liberty ships, with Westmoreland and artillery headquarters aboard the SS *James Caldwell*. The command group cleared its dock that night, anchored in the harbor, and sailed for France the night of

June 9. An air raid alarm woke all hands at 3:30 A.M., but the planes flew on overhead. The convoy arrived in the Bay of Seine that morning, anchored off Utah Beach at midday and put its forces ashore by landing craft at 3:30 P.M. The cannoneers trudged twelve miles to their rendezvous point south of Sainte-Mère-Église, and that night the air raid alarm was genuine.

Westmoreland's job as divarty XO was to coordinate a series of staff functions as well as to serve as deputy to the artillery commander. He had to tie together the G–3 (operations) effort with G–4 (logistics), trying to match the job assigned to the guns with the supplies of ammunition and gasoline to make it possible. He spotted firing locations, allocated daily rates of fire to the four battalions and their tank destroyer and anti-aircraft attachments, made sure medical services were available and replacements were requested before they were needed. In effect, his job was that of chief of staff to the artillery commander. And though it was primarily a staff job, the combination of Westmoreland's assertiveness and the qualities of the artillery commander himself were to give it more and more of a command role.

The 9th Division was committed to action on June 13. The first fire mission of its artillery came the following afternoon, against tank concentrations and troop movements, and the next day it broke up a tank movement and halted a counterattack before it got started.

But its most spectacular shoot of the Normandy campaign came early June 18, after the division's infantry regiments sliced across the peninsula, isolating the enemy in Cherbourg.

The Germans mounted a heavy counterattack before dawn, putting tanks, guns, trucks and other rolling equipment into a single column in the hope that its weight would punch through. Most of the guns of the division were called in against the counterattack.

As one artillery officer described it, "We laid the Germans out all over the landscape." The battalions coordinated by Westmoreland rained concentrations over a five-mile stretch of German hardware. The destruction was so complete that debris made the road impassable. The shoot obliterated much of the German 77th Division, fatally wounding its commander. Survivors regrouped with other stragglers in another attempt to break out of the peninsula, but it also was smashed by the division's guns.

Up the peninsula to Cherbourg, the artillery paced the infantry. As the port fell under siege, the 9th Division intercepted a radio message from the defenders, reporting that their resistance was "completely crushed by artillery fire." Then the division turned back for the slow, costly fight through the Normandy hedgerows. One of Westmoreland's spotter planes was shot down; fire directed from those bold "grasshoppers" broke up a series of counterattacks, but when it rained they were grounded, and forward observers tried to see over the hedgerows by climbing ladders into fruit trees, taking chances on getting shot by sniper-shy American soldiers.

Westmoreland got his promised promotion to full colonel in late July, almost simultaneously with the Allied high command's schedule for a mass breakout from the Normandy perimeter. He plotted the artillery concentrations that would help pave the way for attacking regiments of the 9th Division. Some twenty-five hundred aircraft were to lay a carpet of five thousand tons of bombs in a six-square-mile area ahead of the assault elements, then the artillery was to concentrate on specific known targets as they advanced.

This was the ill-fated Operation Cobra; the Air Corps became confused in the dust and smoke of the great raid, and splashed bombs onto the friendly infantry waiting to attack. In the 9th Division, one battalion was put out of action; some of Westmoreland's forward observer teams were among the lost. Telephone lines between artillery headquarters and the firing battalions were cut, so initial missions had to be controlled by radio. The offensive was held up and another mass preparatory raid planned. Almost incredibly, the same thing happened, though with less damaging results. But the Germans were hurt worse than the hapless United States troops, and Eisenhower's forces pushed through into the open, beginning a war of constant movement across France, weeks when the artillery was hard pressed to stay within firing range of the front lines.

The withdrawing enemy turned repeatedly and lashed out at his pursuers. In early August, he threw heavy forces against the thinly stretched 9th Division at Mortain. This counterattack was repulsed after heavy artillery concentrations fired immediately in front of the division's forward elements. Prisoners said the artillery cut their battalion to pieces, killing the battalion commander, and that heavy nightly harassing fires had caused serious damage.

This artillery damage was not all one-sided, though; the enemy was using rocket shells filled with flamethrower fluid, which exploded in huge blasts of flame. He dropped Nebelwerfer rounds and "butterfly" antipersonnel bombs on divarty. As August ended, the artillery reported difficulty coordinating fires because the speeding, crisscrossing advance laid other divisions' zones of action across the front of the 9th. Ripping north, the division crossed the Seine, led the American advance into Belgium and by early September approached the Meuse at Dinant.

The crossing of the Meuse was the first major battle to confront the new division commander. General Eddy had been rewarded with command of XII Corps. His replacement was Major General Louis A. Craig, described as "sincere, religious, a good listener, smaller than his predecessor but every inch a fighting leader." Craig was from an Army family, and his brother, Malin D. Craig, had been Army chief of staff before the war. He had two sons of his own under arms. He avoided personal publicity, trying to give credit to those who served under him, and they thought it significant that instead of wearing the handy little .38 pistol issued to generals, he preferred the hefty GI .45. Craig was fifty-three when he joined the 9th in August after Stateside duty training units bound abroad. But he was not unfamiliar with the Meuse River; in World War I, he had seen action in the Veste, Aisne-Marne, Meuse-Argonne and Toul sector campaigns.

Along the Meuse, the long race ended and grinding combat began again. Here, Hitler ordered a stand to give time to reinforce the Siegfried Line which guarded Germany's own borders. Craig knew his river crossing would be bitterly contested. He combined deception with head-on assault by ordering one of his regiments to feint at Dinant while actual moves were made north and south of the city. Crossing at night, his infantrymen were bled by pounding counterattacks. Heavy artillery concentrations and the timely arrival of a tank column, which had crossed farther north, helped the stubbornness of the riflemen pay off. The Meuse was breached, and the bruised 9th pushed patrols across the German frontier September 12. Two days later, units of the division's 47th Infantry stuck the first probe into the Siegfried Line.

Through the rest of the month, the division jabbed,

withdrew and jabbed again against the dragon's teeth and pillboxes of the Siegfried Line. Its artillery assigned guns to accompany riflemen to destroy fortifications with direct, point-blank fire. In one day, the artillery was credited with knocking out a dozen pillboxes. That was the same day troops at the northern end of the division's long front tapped a frantic enemy telephone conversation that testified to the efficiency of the guns.

At 10:30 P.M., a German officer called a comrade. "That artillery was a bull's-eye, it's banging hell out of us and the troops. We're moving the tanks back; it's unusual to concentrate artillery in one area so heavily. We've got to move them out fast. Hurry!" He reported a direct hit on the troops' billet. "We can't move them out, they're banging right on the line . . . Get ambulances as soon as possible, I don't care what the CO says; a hundred fifteen to a hundred twenty-five men are out of action . . ." The operator tried to find out what had happened to the commanding officer's line. "Maybe he was hit. Maybe the wires were hit . . . The artillery is right—" Someone screamed, there was a confused jumble of sound. "The men are running back, mixed up in another battalion . . ." The line went dead, and was on and off all night, each time giving the American eavesdroppers a picture of the enemy's hopeless efforts to escape the massed fires of the 9th Division's guns.

Westmoreland's role in this devastating application of supporting arms usually was played at a folding desk in the center of divarty's headquarters tent, amid maps, radios, telephones and the desks of staff officers. Sometimes he was out, scouting forward, checking targets in a "grasshopper," visiting the gun battalions. Also, the abrasive personality of the divarty commander, the fifty-five-year-old Howell, encouraged Westmoreland to take on himself the function of buffer between the general and the rest of the Army, with whom divarty had to get along if it were to do its job.

When officers from division or higher headquarters came to visit the divarty CP they were likely to be met at the jeep dismount point by Westmoreland, who made it seem purely coincidental that he was there at that particular time. As he escorted the visitor to the command tent, he would give him a concise, businesslike briefing that answered most of the questions he was likely to ask. He knew, and those visitors familiar with divarty understood, that Howell was likely to unburden himself of a collection of gripes, without covering the essentials about which the ranking outsider was curious.

In the opposite direction, downward, the young colonel often interposed himself to protect battalion commanders and others equal or junior in rank to himself from chastisement by the divarty commander. Once, Howell was tongue-lashing a gun battalion commander when the younger officer suddenly flared and told his senior that he would damn well do things his own way. Just as the divarty commander started to explode, Westmoreland stepped between them, tried to smooth over the argument, and probably thus saved the battalion commander from being relieved on the spot. Shortly afterward, medical officers discovered that the insubordinate battalion commander had a brain concussion and spinal leak, suffered when his jeep hit a mine.

It was inevitable that Howell became more and more annoyed at this confident young Westmoreland, who was always anticipating him, making him look slow by comparison, and in the older man's eyes, trying to take his command right out from under him.

One day in September, Westmoreland returned to the

command tent and found the general sitting in the chair the executive officer usually occupied, there in the center of activity. Westmoreland simply turned, opened the tent flap and quietly found something else to do for a while. When he returned again, the general was still there. Once again, Westmoreland busied himself elsewhere, but that night, he went to Howell's personal tent and asked him what was happening. The general declared that he was serving notice that he was running this outfit, and his executive officer was not.

In a scene reminiscent of a much greener Lieutenant Westmoreland sticking his chin out at his first battery commander over a poor efficiency report, the colonel told the general that if he was not to be allowed to do the job to which he was assigned, he preferred to be relieved. He added that he had been quite happy running the 34th Field Artillery Battalion before, and would be glad to go back to it. The matter was left hanging there as Westmoreland stalked out, and when a mutual working agreement was reached a day or two later, it merely papered over an increasingly uncomfortable situation.

It continued as the 9th Division prodded east, with the First Army offensive finally literally running out of gas, stalled in a swirl of German landscape known as the Huertgen Forest.

9

Via Remagen to the Elbe

October 1944–April 1945

★

General Craig, taking over the 9th Division in late summer, did not arrive from the States with his own staff in tow, as senior officers often are able to do when assuming a new command. His predecessor, Eddy, was an example: when he left to move to a corps command, he took with him many of the staff officers and senior NCO's who had learned in combat to function smoothly in running the 9th Division. Craig thus had to build a staff team of his own.

Several levels of experienced hands remained, but because they had operated under another general, Craig could not immediately impose on them his own techniques of staff procedure. And since July, even before his arrival, the division had been experimenting with several officers in search of a new chief of staff.

Craig was conscious of the age difference between himself and most of those under his command, and of the fact that so far he had not seen action in this war. Thus, for the chief of staff job, he wanted someone who was younger, who had combat experience, who was familiar with the men and units of the division, and whose duties had qualified him for that crucial position.

Ironically, but not surprisingly, the division artillery commander recommended Westmoreland for the job. Without stretching the truth an inch, Howell could tell Craig that Westmoreland was thoroughly capable of becoming chief of staff despite his youth—and at the same time ease the tension that existed within his own artillery command post. He did so.

Craig, less than two months with the division, had met Westmoreland and knew his reputation, but had not been able to form any firsthand impression of him. He checked out Howell's recommendation and heard repeated descriptions of Westmoreland's "very high integrity, completely unimpeachable character, extremely high personal standards, high intelligence, physical activity that made him able to stand long hours of administrative work in the CP." In addition, Westmoreland's experience with division artillery was as pertinent as any preparation, for it had a division-wide function, and with its heavy logistical and personnel involvement it often was a demanding job, especially when attachment of other gun, antitank and anti-aircraft battalions multiplied its jurisdiction. So Craig chose Westmoreland, and later said in restrospect, "Then my troubles were over."

The United States Army staff manual (FM 101–5) lays down the responsibilities of the chief of staff this way:

"He formulates and announces policies for the general operation of the staff; directs, supervises and integrates the work of the staff . . . ; keeps the commander and staff

145

informed of the situation, and represents the commander when authorized."

He also "receives decisions from the commander and makes or secures from the commander such additional decisions as may be required and gives necessary instructions to the staff . . . ; allots the detailed work of preparing plans, orders, reports, and other staff actions . . . approves or secures command approval; insures that subordinate commanders are alerted to the actions required of them; insures that all instructions published to the command are in accordance with the policies and plans of the commander; insures that orders and instructions of the commander are executed."

In addition, he "studies the situation with a view to being prepared for future contingencies; requires all staff officers . . . to inform him of any information or recommendations given directly to the commander and of any instructions they have received directly from the commander; secures from the commander information, recommendations, and instructions received from or given higher and subordinate commanders; insures establishment of liaison with adjacent, higher, subordinate and supported units, and supervises the operation of the war room, when established . . ."

But in every command, the job of chief of staff is no more nor less than what the commanding officer wants it to be. In many organizations, he becomes strictly an administrator, who remains at a desk in the CP, tying together the work of the general (personnel, intelligence, operations and logistics) and the many special (communications, medical, engineer, legal, signal, chaplain, etc.) staffs, and who never becomes known by face or seldom by name outside the staffs of subordinate units. Westmoreland was not to be excused from this administrative role, for Craig wanted them to develop such an understanding that he could make known his wishes in a general directive way, and have Westmoreland translate those directives into detailed, complicated staff procedures to be assigned to each section. But Craig emphasized the command aspects, trying to develop such a rapport with his chief of staff that when he, the commander, was away from headquarters, being seen by his line units or coordinating with other commands, Westmoreland was his representative—in effect, his deputy.

There was immediate potential for conflict in this system, because two generals in the CP outranked Westmoreland, and one of them carried the title of assistant division commander, standing in the chart depicting staff duties directly between the chief of staff and the commander himself. But Craig made it clear that they were not to obstruct Westmoreland's implementation of his instructions. Westmoreland was to absorb Craig's viewpoint so that he could express it in his absence, when the thirty-year-old colonel virtually was in command of the division.

Westmoreland moved into the chief of staff job October 13, 1944, a day after General George C. Marshall, chief of staff of the whole Army, had paid a secret visit to the 9th Division in the field. The division was a week into a renewed offensive to outflank enemy positions that had held up the division through September, to gain a crossroads as a funnel for further movement, and to eliminate the likelihood of a German counterattack through the dense woods of the Huertgen.

Charles B. MacDonald has described that forest as "a seemingly impenetrable mass, a vast, undulating, blackish-green ocean stretching as far as the eye can see. Upon entering the forest, you want to drop things behind to mark your path, as Hansel and Gretel did with their bread crumbs." To soldiers of the 9th, who already had lost hundreds of their comrades there, it had become "dark, forbidding, frightening and filled with an enemy who remained unseen much of the time. Here was a high, steep ground, a muddy lowland woods, a damp cemetery for hope . . ."

The division's line of attack lay directly through that cemetery. Resistance was fierce from the start. One battalion hit a fortified outpost soon after jumping off in the attack, and bloodied itself pounding it, trying to flank it for almost a week. A German counterattack cut into the left flank of the division. The Americans moved forward slowly, at great cost, in deep fatigue. By October 16, they had driven only three thousand yards farther into the forest, at a cost of more than a casualty per yard. But the enemy had suffered, too. Shifting priorities of attack allowed withdrawal of the battered 9th Division from the line, for rest at Camp d'Elsenborn, three miles inside the Belgian border. As the tired, depleted outfit pulled back, in its sector "the real winner appeared to be the vast, undulating, blackish-green sea that virtually negated American superiority in air, artillery and armor to reduce warfare to its lowest common denominator. The victor thus far was the Huertgen Forest."

Thus Westmoreland assumed his new job at a time when the division was physically in its most straitened condition since it first reached wartime strength back at Fort Bragg, and its spirits dragged lower than ever since El Guettar, or since the shock of massive bombardment by American aircraft in the Normandy breakout. The offensive into the forest already was losing its momentum when the order came to move back some twenty miles, for sleep, showers, hot food, treatment of trench foot and later of frostbite, repair of equipment and, before the division would face all-out combat again, assimilation of hundreds of green replacements. Under these conditions, Westmoreland began to exert his influence in the division command post.

That CP was at Buetgenbach, south of the main division cantonment at Camp d'Elsenborn. Both sites were on the main line of "Buzz Bomb Alley," the route across which the Germans fired V–1 missiles against Liége and Antwerp. Craig ordered all anti-aircraft weapons as far forward as possible, in an effort to stop the sputtering, self-propelled bombs before they came over friendly territory. The guns brought down some, but as one officer remembered it, "It seemed every one we winged would drop in the division CP." Westmoreland had set up a comfortable office in a former Belgian Army building, and one of the robot weapons, hit by anti-aircraft fire, dove into the ground just outside, blasting glass slivers in on him.

This jumpy low-pressure period was a good opportunity for a new chief of staff to accustom headquarters to his way of doing things. Westmoreland, stickler for detail and uniformity, held frequent conferences with individual staff officers. Noticing this, Craig asked him why—especially why he was spending so much time with one particular staff member. Westmoreland replied that he was trying to help him with procedures within his own section, and Craig, out of nearly thirty years experience in the Army, instructed his chief of staff never to allow a subordinate officer to come to him with a problem unless he also brought along one or more proposed solutions. Westmoreland accepted and remembered this advice.

Soldiers of the 9th Division luxuriated in their role of corps reserve until early November. That was when Generals Eisenhower and Bradley called on division headquarters, and Craig and Westmoreland found out what lay ahead for their combination of tested veterans and nervous replacements.

Eisenhower had to decide whether to hold through the winter along the line fought over all fall, building up men and supplies to drive into Germany and end the war in the spring, or to mount major offensive pressure during the cold season despite the worn condition of his forces. He decided in late October to push ahead, to continue attrition of German divisions, preventing massive last-ditch strengthening of positions within Germany, and hopefully to head off German mass production of jet fighters and proximity fuses. Either of those steps could endanger the air superiority that was an absolute requisite to prompt Allied victory.

The five-star general and Bradley outlined for Craig and his staff their plans to drive to the Rhine before deep winter. An intermediate objective was the Roer River, within a few miles of which the 9th had spent so much time and effort during the autumn. This overall offensive was to be preceded by an aerial bombardment on the scale of the one that broke the German lines around the Normandy beachhead. But this one was plotted much more carefully, with wider margins of safety to prevent another fiasco like that in July. After repeated weather delays, it came off and the offensive began. But not until early December did the entire 9th Division take a role in the continuing assault. Its mission was to attack eastward, aiming at the Roer city of Dueren.

Westmoreland shifted to a new CP at Bergrath, Germany, eight miles from Dueren, not quite four miles behind the jumpoff point for the infantry. The staff work involved in the new assignment was complicated, and once the offensive began on December 10, the employment of maneuver units on the ground was more so. Finally clear of the Huertgen Forest to its south, the division faced a series of carefully defended towns and villages en route to the Roer.

Earlier, the Allied high command had not realized how important a barrier that river could turn out to be. The reason: a series of dams impounding enough water to sweep down the valley, drowning troops and cutting off any units that might cross the river before the dams were in friendly hands. The generals knew of the dams, but under-assessed their defensive potential. Only in November did they begin to give the dams the weight they deserved in their planning. Desperately, the high command sought to knock out the dams by air attack before ground troops reached the river. The damage was negligible.

By mid-December, the 9th Division was on the banks of the Roer. It sent patrols over, scouting crossing sites. The Second British Army moved toward the river on a broad front to the north. In reaching for the dams, the 78th Infantry Division had come within two miles of one of the supplementary structures.

Then the Germans struck. They used stealth to open the gate to mass as they launched their desperate winter counterattack, the great gamble that created the Bulge. But they did not make their Bulge through the 9th Division.

The division was preparing to cross the Roer when scattered reports of enemy counterattacks started to trickle in. Westmoreland, with division headquarters and the main forces of the 9th, was given the cumbersome assignment of shifting south onto the line near Elsenborn. He headed in a jeep for the division's new CP site, and along the way passed Stoll, who had replaced him as division artillery executive officer, waving artillery traffic through a crossroads.

He slowed down, held out one hand and said, "Doc, you've just been promoted to colonel. I could only find one spare eagle, and here it is. Good luck." And then he drove off toward the Bulge.

Pulled out of line upriver and reinserted more than twenty-five miles south, the division helped form the northern shoulder of resistance, stubbornly refusing enlargement of the German salient that drove all the way back toward the Meuse, where the 9th had fought so bitterly more than three months before. The drive achieved almost total surprise, rolling the Americans back over fifty miles, along a frontage up to forty-five miles wide. Nor was it one single, all-or-nothing dash; where the 9th Division held, it had to fight off infiltrating enemy units, round up paratroopers who dropped behind its lines, stand firm against heavy tanks attacking under smoke cover, endure the heaviest artillery output from the enemy in months.

But it did hold, and the German offensive passed its peak by Christmas. The German generals' ambition of slicing the Allied armies in half, capturing immense stores of supplies in Belgium, was denied. Before New Year's Eve, the enemy salient turned into a trap, closing on the Wehrmacht soldiers whose offensive had been costly to both sides and may have bought Nazi Germany a little longer life.

In January, the worst enemy of the division was winter. It clamped down tightly, weakening individual soldiers, snarling transport. Patrols felt out enemy positions on skis. Casualties were evacuated from the forest on toboggans. The only consolation was that the enemy suffered too, and his misery was worse because it was that of the loser. It was time for the Allies to take up the offensive again.

By this time, the high command was totally converted to the necessity of capturing the Roer dams before pressing past that river. As part of a wide push east, the 9th Division was aimed upstream from the dams. Westmoreland issued Craig's order for night attacks by the division. Sifting through the woods, often leaving their mechanized support behind for the sake of silence, the infantrymen of the 9th moved through snow and blackness to surprise the Germans in predawn assaults, and crossed terrain the enemy believed impassable. Their line of attack zigged south, zagged north. They grabbed a village overlooking the Roer and repelled an armored counterattack before pushing on to the lake formed by dam number five, the Urft dam, second largest in the forbidding string of potential German defenses. They captured the Ordensburg Vogelsang, a "thousand-year-Reich" training school for young Nazi leaders. And from it, one company made a sudden two-mile lunge and snatched the Urft dam before the German detail assigned to blow it up could act. The division, though meeting unrelenting defensive pressures, was jabbing ahead with a speed it had not been able to achieve since the surge across France.

Recitation of these twists and turns in geography and strategy, swings in initiative from Allies to enemy and back, cannot compare in excitement to descriptions of the infantryman's war at the foxhole and platoon level. Division orders are written on paper, or disappear into telephone lines strung through the snow. An army on the move involves so many human beings that it loses its human quality and becomes more like a natural force, a glacier. But an idea of the weight Westmoreland was bearing, of how little sleep he was getting in that winter of 1944–1945, is gained best by referring back to the staff manual's description of his job, and imagining an officer formulating, announcing, directing, supervising, integrating, informing, representing, deciding, allotting, insuring, studying, recommending at

153

each of the complex staff steps required by all those twists and turns. Craig felt that he and his chief of staff had developed quickly the rapport he deemed invaluable. It and the confident, take-charge tendency with which Westmoreland complemented it were never demonstrated more to Craig's satisfaction than in the operation that began with a gobbledygook phone call the morning of February 8.

The Urft dam, second largest, had been taken. But the largest, Schwemmanauel dam, remained in enemy hands. Behind it were twenty-two billion gallons of water, which had not been loosed by thousands of tons of aerial bombs but could easily be sent flooding down the valley across Allied lines by one enemy soldier twisting an electric detonating device. Since they decided in October that the dams were necessary to operations beyond the Roer, American generals had sent four divisions toward Schwemmanauel, and all had ground to a stop against German defenses in depth, short of their objective. The 78th Infantry Division was last in this series of determined, not yet successful units. It had taken the town of Schmidt, more than three miles from the dam, and there its offensive thrust had drained away.

This was the situation when Craig drove back to corps headquarters, an hour-and-a-half jeep ride across frost-broken roads that were "just waves," on the morning of February 8. There, Major General Clarence R. Huebner, corps commander, told him that the Allies had an enormous movement toward the Rhine ready to roll as soon as the Roer was safely breached. Huebner had been given "either-or" orders by Lieutenant General Courtney H. Hodges, First Army commander, to secure the ominous dams and unlock the way east. Huebner had spent the previous day overseeing the 78th Division's stymied drive. He could see that it alone did not have strength left to take the ridgeline across its front.

Huebner also knew the 9th Division; he had fought alongside it as commander of the 1st Infantry Division. He turned to Craig with the same urgency with which Hodges had spoken to him. How soon could the 9th Division put a force into the attack in the sector now covered by the 78th? Craig's troops were momentarily disengaged after capturing the Urft dam; he replied that it could be done almost immediately. Ordered to make good this estimate, he cranked a field phone and asked for his chief of staff. Security regulations forbade discussion of operations by telephone, so, reminding himself of a vaudeville double-talker, he spoke with Westmoreland in slang, nicknames, and hidden meanings. His messages clicked with Westmoreland immediately. Craig hung up and headed back for the division CP as fast as the jeep would carry him.

When he arrived at his own CP, it already was in motion. Westmoreland had two regiments on the road, following Craig's instructions to leave one in the division's current position. It was a march that reminded artillerymen of their race across Algeria and Tunisia to Thala. The infantry regiments led the way, and division artillery joined the column. For the operation, a total of thirty battalions of guns had been placed under control of the 9th's divarty commander, and ammunition restrictions were lifted. This column, with all its supporting units, had to move under a dull drizzle, over nearly impassable roads, and be in position to attack before dawn the next day.

As another division officer said, "Westmoreland ramrodded it." What is more, he added, "I don't think it occurred to him that there was anything unusual about it." Pressing on through the clammy night, lighting its way with anti-aircraft searchlights bouncing their beams off low-hanging clouds, it moved into attack on time. Against heavy opposition, the leading 60th Infantry fought into the town flanking the dam. By nightfall, the north end of the dam was in friendly hands. The 60th fought all night, springing units of the 78th Division free the next morning to push on to the dam itself. A deep gap had been blasted in the roadway across the dam, a pillbox at the other end kept firing, and the water gates were blown, letting go enough water to raise the river level three feet downstream to the north. It caused a reshuffling of Allied plans, but had none of the impact in hopes of which the Germans had clung so resolutely to the dam and its approaches.

General Huebner wrote General Craig a letter of commendation:

"You will recall that at 11 o'clock this morning I made the decision to have you attack through the 78th Division and capture Schwemmanauel dam, and thereby accomplish the corps mission. The importance of the . . . mission was such that it affected future action on the entire Western front. In order to execute my decision it was necessary that you turn over a large part of your sector, move your division some 20 kilometers over most difficult roads, and launch an attack through another division which at the moment was engaged heavily with the enemy. I further required that this be done with all possible speed.

"Your attack was launched at 0530 hours, 9 February, 18 hours and 30 minutes after receipt of orders. The displacement was admirably coordinated and successful. The division accomplished its mission. All this is indicative of 'know-how.' The operation was a combination of smooth, efficient and experienced staff work, as well as sound, decisive and rapid command . . ."

There followed a few words of compliment to the "Old Reliables" of the 9th Division, and the troops picked the phrase for their nickname.

Huebner's letter was addressed to Craig, but Craig is quick to point out that it was Westmoreland who took the assignment in that jabberwocky telephone conversation and "carried it out perfectly."

Orders from corps switched the 9th Division back south, near the point from which it had begun its overnight march to Schwemmanauel, before being shifted again, this time to positions near the Huertgen Forest. Its next move, part of the massive Allied offensive, was to cross the Roer. In preparation, engineers spent dangerous nights sneaking across the swollen river in flat-bottomed boats, sinking cables that would be used to secure the assault boats on jumpoff day. The division and its supporting arms were ready to go when, suddenly, that plan was scrapped and alternate orders were issued to exploit successes farther north. One regiment was to sideslip, cross the river on bridges thrown across there, then turn back upriver to outflank the division objective area while the assault crossing took place. It worked. From there, it was all downhill to the Rhine.

Nideggen . . . Mueddersheim . . . Roevenich . . . Juntersdorf . . . Geich . . . Oberelvenich . . . Gross Vernich . . . Neukirchen . . . Heimerzheim . . . Pech . . . Bad Godesberg on the Rhine. Working with a combat command from the 3rd Armored Division, the 9th inexorably pressed back the German 3rd Parachute Division, which fought a skillful delaying action before its commander surrendered in Bad Godesberg.

The 9th Infantry was not the only division moving fast

toward the Rhine. The 9th Armored, thrusting ahead tanks and infantrymen on half-tracks in a combat command under Brigadier General William M. Hoge, surged forward ten miles in one day to enter the river town of Remagen on March 7.

The Allied high command had a master plan for ending the war in Western Europe which called first for the juncture of the First and Third American Armies along the west bank of the Rhine, in order to trap the enemy forces still on that side of the river. Then the principal drive eastward would be made by the Armies under Montgomery at the north end of the front. The 9th Armored was instructed to reach the river, then pivot right to meet forces from the Third Army paralleling the stream north.

But an unexpected thing happened to the mechanized combat command on its way to meet Patton's men. In Remagen, the tankers expected to be able to rest while other Allied troops mopped up west of the river. Then, as they topped the town's hilly approaches, one of them spotted a railroad bridge across the Rhine—intact, with soldiers and civilians straggling across to the opposite bank. Everyone on the Allied side, from squad to supreme headquarters, assumed that the Germans would destroy every bridge across this last great natural barrier before the invading Allies came close. In October, the Ludendorff bridge at Remagen had been reported downed by Allied air, but it was promptly restored. It was hit again, and left hanging by only its upper bracing, but again strengthened, and carried a heavy share of traffic toward the advancing front lines. So the men of Hoge's command were surprised to see it still standing, and when they did, they expected it to go up in a great explosion at any moment.

The stream of Germans across the bridge was a tempting target, but not until midafternoon did it sink into any of the attackers that they might capture the bridge whole. The Germans blew a huge antitank hole in its western approaches, and as the first United States riflemen gathered to sprint across, the enemy set off another charge toward the eastern end. But the span held, and Company A of the 27th Armored Infantry Battalion daringly crossed the bridge under fire. In late afternoon, when it had dug in, flushed German soldiers and civilians out of the railroad tunnel near the bridge's eastern ramp, and climbed onto the abrupt heights above the scene, it notified Hoge that the bridge was in American hands. Then he had to make a risky decision: take the initiative of reinforcing the bridgehead with everything under his control, or follow his orders to slide farther south down the river's western shore. He sent over all the infantry he could muster, then reported to his division commander, who turned to corps headquarters, who turned to General Bradley at First Army. Bradley wanted to forget the earlier plan and exploit the bridgehead, but Eisenhower's G–3 complained that adherence to the original directive was best. So Bradley called Eisenhower himself, who quickly endorsed the buildup of the bridgehead. One of the first steps taken to carry out this chain of decisions was to bring the 9th Infantry Division into the action.

Craig had indirect word that "a bridge" had been taken, and though that seemed unlikely, he told Westmoreland to draw up contingency plans in case the 9th had to respond. Shortly after, Hoge sped into the 9th Division CP and announced, "We got a bridge at Remagen; I need a regiment!" Craig gave Westmoreland a few words of guidance and headed for the 9th Armored's headquarters for a complete briefing on what was to come.

He and his command group were to take charge of the

entire bridgehead operation. This word was passed to West-moreland, who trimmed down the division headquarters to absolutely essential personnel, leaving behind logistical and clerical specialists, and put it on the road trailing the 47th Infantry toward the bridge. The 60th Infantry followed up.

Again, it was an all-night forced march, through rain, over unfamiliar roads, through chaotic, blacked-out traffic. In the morning darkness of March 8, after moving twenty-five miles under these conditions—the last eight slogging on foot through the mud—the 2nd Battalion, 47th Infantry crossed the river and immediately went into battle. Its sister battalions followed it during that day. Craig was assigned a guide by the 9th Armored, and crossed during the night in a jeep with an aide and two military policemen with machine guns. Westmoreland, groping his way ahead of his jeep, showed up with the reduced CP group at 2 A.M. and they took over the bridgehead. They set up their command post some four hundred yards north of the bridge, alongside the river.

By that time, the Germans had recovered from the shock of the bridge's loss and were throwing everything they could command into an effort to crush the bridgehead. They lay heavy concentrations of artillery on the bridge itself, reaping serious casualties among the American MP's stationed there to guide the flood of oncoming traffic. Engineers working under this fire hustled to brace the bridge to support tanks. A handful of armor crossed, and was deeply involved in fighting off determined enemy counterattacks. The defenders held, and the next day a broad assortment of units started pouring into the new salient.

Craig describes a bridgehead thus: "You start with very little space and just jam people into it—it's a hell of a mess." Colonel Stoll, of division artillery, said, "Battalions

and other outfits came barging across without announcement." Westmoreland supervised the assignment of these
arriving units in the perimeter. His main directives from
Craig were to restrict bridge traffic to one-way east, and to
keep artillery on the far shore because of the ammunition
supply problems they would have if they crossed the river.
It was all a military juggling act. Westmoreland was putting
stray battalions together into regiments, seeing that supplies
trucked over the bridge went to the neediest destinations,
prodding the engineers in constructing parallel spans,
scrounging German river boats to start a ferry service to
carry supplies and ammunition east and hundreds of American casualties back west. All of it went on under mounting,
increasingly better organized enemy pressure.

The German High Command recovered from its shock
quickly and appointed General Fritz Bayerlein, commander
of the Panzer Lehr Division, to assume charge of the struggle to erase the bridgehead—much the same way Craig was
ordered to handle varied units on the offensive side. Bayerlein had three panzer divisions of varying strength, plus a
panzer brigade. In addition, his effort became a magnet,
drawing to the antibridgehead drive nearly all the reinforcements being transferred to the west from the Russian
front. Bayerlein, one of Hitler's most talented and forceful
generals, decided to concentrate against the center of the
bridgehead, with the aim of cutting it in two and then rolling up Allied troops along the river in both directions.
Lacking success in this, he hoped to push close enough to
the bridge to destroy it.

The Luftwaffe joined this all-out effort. Though deeply
depleted, it flung all it could fly against the bridge. Stukas
of 1939 vintage, a few jets just off underground production
lines flashed across, their bombs making the shaky span

161

tremble but not downing it. Many bombers were lost, because the Americans had concentrated around Remagen the biggest collection of anti-aircraft artillery of the war— half again as many guns as protected the Normandy beachheads. Spent rounds and falling fragments from friendly weapons were just as much a hazard to troops in the bridgehead as the growing crush of German artillery trained on the bridge. Still the bridge stood. Hitler ordered German "frogmen" to try to blow it up. A team of six made a brave try, but they were spotted and their attempt broken up. Finally, the enemy risked use of the gigantic, supersecret V–2 rockets. But while the V–2's had their effect on a widespread, crowded target like London, they were not intended for employment against a point target like the Ludendorff Bridge. Eleven were fired. None hit the bridge, but some further destroyed Remagen.

Thus neither repeated pounding by Bayerlein's tanks and infantry nor frantic shelling and bombing could crush the bridgehead or drop the bridge. But the combination of the abortive demolition charges, enemy rockets, shells and bombs, the concussion from heavy American artillery emplaced nearby, heavy vehicle traffic and the constant hammering and cutting of engineer repair crews finally did in the bridge at Remagen. On St. Patrick's Day its single intact truss quivered and snapped, and the bridge crumpled into the Rhine. Twenty-eight engineers were killed or missing.

By then, however, the engineers had pontoon spans across the river, and men and supplies continued to pour in without letup. Westmoreland was acting as chief of staff of a corps-size force, supervising insertion of the 78th and 99th Infantry Divisions into the expanding bridgehead line, integrating the operations of scattered armored units which scurried from probe to probe around the perimeter.

The bridgehead forces were not fighting a strictly defensive war, however. The German commander explained to his superiors that the reason his major counterattack plans had not been carried out was that every time he designated a point for jumpoff in the assault, that point was taken by the Americans before the appointed hour. By the time the bridge collapsed, infantrymen of the 9th Division were slogging toward Stroedt, a town more than five miles from the CP beside the river. Three days later, troops of the division moved ahead to the Wied River, more than six miles beyond the Rhine. That was the day Westmoreland and the division CP shifted forward from Erpel, near the bridge, to Kalenborn station. With that move, the success of the bridgehead operation was stamped official. From Kalenborn, the command post directed operations to and beyond the Wied, and it was only six days before it displaced eastward again.

Despite the chaos in the bridgehead, Westmoreland viewed the operation with a sense of order. He considered it "one of the division's most outstanding achievements," comparable with its cutting of the Cherbourg peninsula.

"It was one of the toughest, if not the toughest, fights the division ever experienced, because the enemy appreciated its importance," he told a combat interviewer. "The enemy put his best and most troops at the points where we were driving to expand the bridgehead."

He was talking about the center of the perimeter, particularly the sector of the 47th Infantry. "There is an engineering parallel between the bridgehead and the construction of an arch. An arch is the strongest type of bridge; pressure can be applied at any point, and the arch will withstand the pressure as long as the keystone is intact. If the keystone is pulled out, the arch will crumble. In the

Remagen bridgehead, the 47th was the keystone. They provided depth and strength to the bridgehead. When the bridgehead was established, there were some who advocated an elongation of the bridgehead along the banks of the Rhine, as this was the path of least resistance. The enemy actually allowed expansion of the bridgehead along the riverbanks because he was interested in concentrating his thrust and building his defenses against the strengthening of the arch," Westmoreland said. He did not add that it was the good judgment of Craig, the division operations officer and himself that kept the bridgehead in the shape of that consistently rounded arch, with a many-times-tested regiment as its keystone, rather than allowing it to stretch along the river in a thin string that might have been bisected by the enemy.

Craig recognized Westmoreland's contribution by awarding him the Bronze Star. His citation said that "despite the swift advance of the assault elements . . . and the difficult operations by which the Remagen bridgehead was expanded from a foothold to a secure salient, Colonel Westmoreland preserved the maximum integration of staff effort possible and supplied the commanding general with sound recommendations on matters ordinarily within the immediate field of staff members whose advice was unobtainable due to difficulties of communications or transportation. His expert judgment, executive ability and thorough knowledge and grasp of the tactical situation contributed materially to the success . . ."

The next barrier, the Wied, was not a strong one, for the enemy behind it had recoiled, waiting for the next major punch by the Allies. That was to be a huge double envelopment, taking advantage of the unplanned bridgehead, with Montgomery's forces driving across the Rhine to the north and the American First Army pushing out of the Remagen crossing east and north to join it. Their objective was to encircle the Ruhr, industrial heart of Germany, and trap a third of the enemy's remaining western forces. The 9th Division was to work closely with armor in extending the southern edge of this great noose.

The division moved in a much larger-scale version of the "blitz" formation Westmoreland had used when his battalion chased the enemy up the Sicilian coast. In this pursuit situation, Westmoreland was making notes and devising improvements much as he did in training his battalion at Fort Bragg. Should more infantry be made organic to the armored division? Yes, because "during a pursuit operation it is essential to clean the woods and isolated pockets, or you will have your service troops fighting in the rear . . ." Limited roadways call for attachment of an infantry combat team to the armored division. When possible, "it is better for the fighting morale of the men to fight as a division . . . Furthermore, if an entire regimental combat team is attached to an armored division, the armored division has no use for the regimental headquarters, cannon and anti-tank companies and service elements. These elements of the RCT go to waste." For Westmoreland, school was always in, whether at Bragg or on the road to Ober Steinebach, the next CP of the fast-moving 9th Division.

As chief of staff, he also was continuing the habit of personal observation that he had developed while working with artillery. Although he had his pilot's license, he never flew "grasshoppers" by himself, because he was not authorized to take charge of airborne government property. But he was frequently aloft, and his reconnaissance missions were often a harbinger of action to come. Some soldiers of the division were aware of this; when they saw him take off, they said, "Oh God, start packing, there goes that crazy colonel again!"

By March 27, the 9th Division had such impetus that it was able to make twenty-seven miles forward in a day. Soon afterward it held up while armored elements turned north and linked up with troops from Montgomery's command. Thus the loop around the vital Ruhr was formed, but it was thin and the Germans were determined to break out of it. The 9th Division was sent into the mountainous Sauerland, following up the armor even before the noose was completed, with the assignment of blocking enemy escape routes.

It was not routine mopping up. The Germans had a more urgent appreciation of that corridor than did the Americans. Panzer and infantry units slowed down battalions of the 9th in counterattacks. Against desperate resistance, the corps drove ahead until it was held up by a last-ditch enemy effort to keep open a highway bottleneck. First Army struck at this opening with a composite command from the 9th Division and the 7th Armored Division.

As Westmoreland described it, they "fought the terrain as well as the Boche, and had considerable difficulty getting road net for supplies. Lack of sufficient communications also plagued us." As the task force sped north, then west, the other regiments of the 9th ground out yards, helping reduce the pocket until April 10. It and the other involved units had trapped 317,000 German soldiers who became prisoners. And it was the 9th that had held tight the jaws of the trap.

While the 9th and adjacent commands had been busy closing the Ruhr pocket, other divisions had pressed eastward to reach toward a rendezvous with advancing Soviet forces. The 9th's mission was now switched to clearance of the Harz Mountains, a natural fortress that could provide a haven for an extended holdout by the enemy.

The road took the division into the town of Nord-hausen. There, the infantrymen found an aspect of the war around which chance had guided them till April 1945. It was the Nordhausen concentration camp. The sight of dead and dying prisoners, some still barely living but already placed in communal ditch graves to await death before being covered, struck the men of the 9th as they paused. When they moved on to the attack, they had a new concept of the enemy they were eliminating.

Craig and Westmoreland sent combat teams curving up into the four-thousand-foot mountains. The advance was steady but not cheap; the S.S. troops knew they could up-hold their honor and vindicate their fatherland now or never. But less expectable was the courage with which indi-vidual American soldiers took chances at this late stage of the war, assaulting and not letting up against nearly certain prospects of death, as if they were defending their own homes rather than wiping out an enemy who could not stand much longer. So the rifleman, as always, bore the brunt of the step-by-step fighting. After mid-April, however, the corps again combined infantry with armor, in another spear-head that thrust around the remaining Germans in the moun-tains, and convinced more than fourteen thousand enemy soldiers that they were encircled and might as well quit.

This feeling spread. On April 19 and 20, the 9th Divi-sion captured more than 8,600 prisoners. In the last of the night attacks in which it specialized, the division sent its troops against a holdout company of Germans in the town of Drohndorf. At 1:15 A.M. April 21, the town fell, and the last important combat of the 9th Division in World War II was over.

10

Victory and Occupation

1945–1946

★

No striped pants or swallowtail coats were issued; the uniform was still olive drab. But beginning in late April of 1945, Westmoreland's duties and those of most other staff officers among the Allied forces in Germany had more to do with diplomacy than with tactics and logistics.

After reducing the Harz Mountains redoubt, the 9th Division moved to the line of the Mulde and Elbe rivers, beyond which Western Allied units were ordered not to advance. The Russians approached the same line from the east. Thousands of Germans, soldiers and civilians, fled ahead of the oncoming Soviet Army, preferring to surrender to the Americans on the western side of the river dividing line. After chasing Germans two thousand miles across Africa and Europe, the 9th Division found itself cast as reluctant sanctuary for former enemies to whom enmity was a relative affair.

But the order to Western Allied forces was that only liberated friendly soldiers and German troops wishing to surrender could cross the river westward. Civilians were not allowed. Line companies of the 9th Division were strung along one riverbank to enforce this rule. Thick along the opposite shore were Germans wanting to cross. Enemy military units were herded across bridges, their hands clasped atop their heads. Not all of them quit without a last hurrah; a patrol sent across the river was badly shot up. But that was an exception to the rule of prisoners flowing steadily westward.

Civilians tried to cross under cover of night. They tried to masquerade as surrendering soldiers. A handsome woman beseeched a company commander of the 60th Infantry at midbridge, offering to come share his quarters with him, showing him jewels she would give him, if only he would let her cross. He did not, but there was a tiny area of discrimination left to those guarding the river. He exercised it when he allowed a chemist with I.G. Farben documents, one of the inventors of detergents, to bring his talents west.

Patrols across the river were like hands reaching out to greet the Russians. Finally, at 6:30 P.M. April 27, a unit of the 60th Infantry met a Soviet patrol, and the next day its regimental commander made the juncture official and arranged for a formal meeting between division commanders and staffs.

Thus Westmoreland and his colleagues salvaged from the bottom of much-abused clothing rolls and foot lockers the Ike jackets, blouses and ribbons cached there back in England against the possibility of such a ceremony—or of a furlough in Paris. They invited the Russians across to exchange greetings and coordinate occupation plans. Craig stood at attention, trousers somehow sharply creased, right

169

olive drab glove removed to shake hands with Major General Sokhonov of the Soviet 121st Infantry Division. His staff arrayed behind him looked as if it were on parade at Fort Bragg, despite the battle wear of its uniforms. The tall, square-jawed Russian general wore jackboots, epauletted tunic and medals. His own staff stared at the first Americans most of them had met.

Things were not so rigid the next time the officers of the 9th confronted the Russians. Much had happened in between. Berlin was surrounded and fell. Hitler was reported dead. Troops of the 60th Infantry had the division's last quick firefight with a German company that refused to surrender because it wanted to defend its village against the Russians. Westmoreland scouted eastward, and northeast toward Berlin, in a "grasshopper." A Soviet division occupied positions along the opposite side of the river. Then, as the operations report recorded it, "This division received a message on 7 May signed by General Eisenhower stating that a member of the German High Command had signed the unconditional surrender of all German land, sea and air forces in Europe to the Allied Expeditionary Forces and simultaneously to the Soviet High Command at 0141 hours Central European time, 7 May, and that effective immediately all offensive operations by Allied Expeditionary Forces would cease and troops were to remain in present positions."

There was no massive celebration among the staff and units of the 9th. All of them had lost many friends between Casablanca and the Elbe. They had finished one war, but none knew yet whether they would have to ship halfway around the world to finish another one. Every outfit was addressed by its commanding officer, and every commanding officer's main message was one of congratulations to men who had been the hard, grinding core of the American forces in battle after battle. The next morning, Craig faced more than a thousand liberated French prisoners and spoke to them in that language to mark the occasion.

For the Russians, May 8 was more conclusive. For them, the German was the only enemy who mattered; the war was over. They celebrated, and invited the 9th Division staff across the river to join in. The Americans' performance was one duplicated by striped-pants diplomats many times since.

When Craig, Westmoreland and their comrades arrived at the Soviet headquarters, a group of smiling officers greeted them, along with a soldier laboriously squeezing an accordion. Only after much conversation and handshaking did it dawn on the Americans that the accordionist was honoring them by trying to play "The Star-Spangled Banner." Their embarrassment was momentary, however, as they were led to a long table with bottles, sausages, cheese —the division's creditable effort to duplicate banquets going on that very day behind the towers of the Kremlin.

The Russian technique, diagnosed quickly by American officers used to feeling out enemy tactics, was for a single Soviet officer to walk up to a group of three or four Americans and propose a toast—to victory, to the USA, to the USSR, to Stalin, to the late President Roosevelt. Russian toasts are bottoms up, or else their proposer theoretically is offended. This system would have had the Americans drinking three or four times as much as their hosts had not Westmoreland and friends managed often to slip their vodka into various flowerpots, into bottles of white wine or anywhere else convenient, just as cabaret girls are wont to dump expensive champagne into ice buckets. A Russian corps commander became miffed because Craig was not drinking. Through an interpreter, Craig told him drinking made him sick. The Russian general said this was an unacceptable excuse, and stomped out. But Craig stayed, and when he and his staff departed at 4 A.M.—twelve hours after arrival—all of them were still on their feet. Some of the Russians were not.

A few days later, the 9th Division sent Colonel Stoll across the river to invite the Soviet officers for a return engagement. He could not find them. He asked other Russian units, and they maintained they knew nothing about the division. Partying between the erstwhile Allies was over. Churchill had not yet coined the phrase, but the Iron Curtain already was dropping.

It did not merely end social contact between Eastern and Western soldiers. Promptly, on the basis of agreements made at great-power summit conferences, the victors shifted into zones of occupation that were to harden into two Germanys for decades to come. The 9th Division was ordered south, from its position inside the Soviet zone, some fifty miles southwest of Berlin, to a sector of responsibility along the Danube in northern Bavaria. For a change, it was a move without the likelihood of hostile fire. Division headquarters was assigned to the town of Ingolstadt, on the Danube north of Munich and little more than ten miles from the line between the American and Soviet zones of occupation.

Almost simultaneously with this transfer, General Craig was ordered to leave the 9th and assume command of XX Corps. When Westmoreland learned of this, he had a farewell conversation with the fatherly commander who had placed so much trust in him. With the war over, career soldiers had time and reason to start thinking again of their own professional advancement. Craig knew his own career had only a few more years to run. But he realized also that in a sense Westmoreland's was just beginning. Westmoreland's early success had been in an expanding Army, where competent officers inevitably moved into more and more responsible billets. But soon, the Army was to shrink drastically. Those who rose and prospered in its ranks would be carefully selected. Craig recognized Westmoreland's "tremendous potential" in this situation, and reached into his own and his family's long background of successful military service to offer Westmoreland some advice.

It is commonly accepted that the best upward route for an officer lies through a variety of command and staff assignments. Those who decide which specific jobs he will fill take this into account, and try to alternate him between such billets when what is most contributory to his career does not conflict with the needs of the service. The objective, of course, is to mold an officer who has experience handling troops and weapons at successively higher echelons, and acquires familiarity with all the operational and administrative details on which command decisions must be based. Ideally, an officer headed for the higher ranks will get staff duty at one level before having a command assignment at the next lower echelon. Westmoreland had been able to approximate this sequence, beginning as a battery (company-level) officer at Fort Sill, working on battalion staff before becoming a battery commander, moving back to staff work before taking command of the 34th Field Artillery Battalion, following that with what was essentially a dual command/staff billet as division artillery executive officer, then being promoted to division chief of staff. He clearly was ready for another command assignment.

Craig's career guidance for his chief of staff took all this into account, but its gist was simpler: switch to the infantry. Despite his successful service as senior staff officer of an infantry division, Westmoreland still was identified as an artillery officer. All of his command experience was in that branch. Specializing in artillery does not rule out higher advancement, but there is no question that the infantry is considered the single line of work in which most other lines converge. Dedicated infantry officers indoctrinating their troops are not above saying that all other soldiers exist for the eventual purpose of supporting the rifle company. The infantry remains not only "The Queen of Battle"; it is the one branch within the ground forces which is not a specialty, but a combination of specialties. While years spent in artillery, engineers or communication should not be a disadvantage to an ambitious soldier, the same experience in the infantry will be rated by some promotion boards as a positive advantage.

Westmoreland did not change his primary MOS (military occupational specialty), the official designator of his main training and experience. But neither did he disregard Craig's advice. He insists that not switching was a matter of principle, that an officer should not hop around just because opportunity may look brighter in another line. He believes any good officer, specifically including an artilleryman, can become qualified to command combined arms. Within a month of his conversation with Craig, he moved to solidify his own qualifications by accepting a transfer to command of the 60th Infantry Regiment.

Commands were shifting rapidly as experienced officers and units were tapped for duty in the continuing war against Japan. Thousands of men of the 9th Division were eligible for transfer home because they had amassed the magic total of eighty-five rotation points, figured by a formula combining credit for months overseas, decorations, wounds and other evidence that an individual soldier had done his share. Almost simultaneously with Westmoreland's taking command of the 60th Infantry, the whole division learned that it had been chosen for permanent occupation duty rather than reassignment to the Far East. And as veteran soldiers of the regiment were rotated to homeward-bound units, they were replaced in wholesale numbers by low-point troops from the 65th Infantry Division and other outfits headed for the United States.

From his regimental CP at Geisenfeld, south of the division headquarters at Ingolstadt, Westmoreland was charged not only with running the 60th Infantry but also with overseeing almost every phase of life among the Germans in that corner of occupied Bavaria. Detecting and capturing enemy units trying to sift unnoticed into civilian life; distributing food, assigning housing; sorting thousands of displaced persons brought into Germany as laborers; uncovering stores of German munitions and archives. Military government authorities worked through a separate chain of command, but they answered to the Army commander in each sector. Westmoreland busied himself, moving throughout the regiment's area.

In the regiment, Westmoreland's most persistent concern was morale. Everybody wanted to go home. Those who had spent many months with the outfit felt they had earned the trip. Those who had joined recently from other commands did not arrive with any pride in their new unit that might have motivated better deportment. Westmoreland met these problems with a stringent training program, partly to maintain combat capacity, importantly to keep his troops busy. He organized athletic programs, including a softball league. He held down right field on the officers' team.

The spit-and-polish life of troops in barracks gradually replaced the more permissive approach of men in combat. A platoon of the 60th Infantry was selected to do the honors at ceremonies marking July 4 at division headquarters. On August 1, fifth anniversary of the reorganization of the division back at Fort Bragg, General Patton flew in to review the whole command, lined up along the strip at Manching airfield.

But there was relaxation, too, for the war in Europe was weeks, then months in the past. Westmoreland would have his staff in for dinner with him. There was great camaraderie, with the chaplain saying a blessing, the surgeon telling funny stories. An officers' club had been created in an old bierstube, and drinks were dispensed thinly on a monthly ration. The colonel and the group around him usually would drop in after dinner, and often there was singing. Westmoreland himself had then and still retains a liking for the original Kipling version of "Gentlemen-Rankers," to the tune better known as "The Whiffenpoof Song." But its lines about "to dance with blowzy housemaids at the regimental hops . . . the home we never write to, and the oaths we never keep . . . We have done with Hope and Honor, we are lost to Love and Truth, we are dropping down the ladder rung by rung . . ." and its whole air of resignation to decline and debauchery were and are so totally inapplicable to Westmoreland that their attraction to him had to lie in their irony. However slightly, they were more pertinent to others. The regiment had captured a supply of a local alcohol that was mixed into a liqueur called "green death." Westmoreland and his retinue would have one of these, and one only. Others might have more.

As for the "to dance with blowzy housemaids" part, the colonel was sitting in the club one July evening when the radio announced that the ban on fraternization with Germans had been lifted. There was no perceptible reaction for a few minutes, except for discussion. But gradually, the club emptied of young officers. Westmoreland realized it, and was seriously perturbed, but officially he could not halt it. Promptly, word was circulated in the regiment that he did not think it very ethical to socialize with such a recent enemy. Most of the more experienced officers, who shared memories with Westmoreland, felt the same way.

The regimental commander scouted the area and the unit rounded up a stable of good horses. Westmoreland picked for himself a black stallion, a jumper that could clear two meters, but he had to ride alone because the stallion was untrustworthy around either mares or geldings. He rode almost every afternoon, from four to six o'clock, and tried to organize a regimental polo team, but there was not enough riding talent available. On one occasion, he took part in a horse show in Munich.

If there ever was a nagging awareness on the part of a conscientious soldier thus enjoying himself while a war went on elsewhere, it was lightened by the news that came in the morning darkness of August 15—V–J Day. A burst of celebration was followed by formal division ceremonies the following day. And that, inevitably, was followed by even more urgent desires on the soldiers' part to get home, and on their relatives' part to have them there. The further reduction of occupation forces in late September caused the 9th Division's zone of responsibility to be widened. Westmoreland's 60th Infantry shifted its headquarters to Ingolstadt, where the division had made its CP.

He began military competition between units, with

scores being kept in mortar and machine gun drill and other skills. He found an old German training area near Hohenfeld, and although another regiment was using it, he ordered platoon, company and battalion exercises to be run there through the fall. This training for subordinate units was not entirely to keep restless troops busy and bring newly assigned ones to standard proficiency, either: the regiment got orders to prepare a contingency plan for reinforcing the 88th Infantry Division at Trieste, on the Italian-Yugoslav border. Into one of the earliest cockpits of cold war tension, Westmoreland sent a reconnaissance team to gather information on which the regimental staff based its movement and operational plans. The contingency plans were never used, but Westmoreland's concentration on them typified his insistence on careful advance staff work.

Looking back, rather than forward, he also was examining his recent past for lessons that might be useful in the future. The result was a study, based on his own experience and that of veterans in the 60th Infantry, of what changes might be made in the unit's organization to make it more effective. Its primary recommendation was that tanks should be made an organic part of the infantry regiment.

The regimental CP's new location at Ingolstadt put it within easy driving distance of a Red Cross club at a nearby tank training center. A pretty Red Cross girl named Jenny got into the habit of coming to Ingolstadt for the stated purpose of mooching supplies for her club. It was clear she took to Westmoreland. In the building he shared with several other officers was a guest room, and Jenny invited herself to stay over there. Westmoreland, not totally confident about how to cope with this, told his S–4 to find promptly whatever supplies she wanted so she would go away, but this did not always work. In fact, there was an afternoon when the colonel and the Red Cross girl went for a ride with two of his colleagues in a two-horse barouche he had uncovered someplace. One of the officers got out during their spin around the Bavarian countryside, and snapped a photograph of the others that later caused his own wife a brief twinge of unfounded jealousy. But for Westmoreland, Jenny, like others in the past, was a pretty passing acquaintance.

Neither were the regimental officers successful in organizing mass substitutes for the fraternization on which their colonel frowned. On one occasion, the adjutant went to the hospitals at Nuremberg, Munich, Augsburg and other cities, and got promises by perhaps half a dozen nurses each for a party planned at a lake beside the Danube at Ingolstadt. Then he struck a previously undiscovered lode of sixty-two civilian displaced women, working as translators of Eastern European languages at a censorship office. He invited them, sight unseen, and brought back word to the regiment. A spiffy array of regimental officers drooped quickly when its guests arrived—all beyond forty-five years old, and none apparently having suffered from malnutrition during the war.

Special issues of captured liquor, brandy and wine helped cheer the troops at Christmas and New Year's. Then their unit exercises were held across terrain which has been the wintertime goal of thousands of skiing holidayers in the years since Germany's rebound. The basketball team of the 60th Infantry was leading the division league when Westmoreland was ordered on January 30 to become acting chief of staff of the 71st Infantry Division.

It was not, as it may sound, a demotion. The 9th Division was taking over the zone of occupation of the 71st, and the 71st was preparing to sail for the United States. Many men of the 9th made the switch along with the colonel described by the division history as "the ever-smiling Colonel William C. Westmoreland, one of the last old-timers left with the division . . ." Two weeks after joining the 71st as acting chief of staff, Westmoreland became its division commander. Neither, in this case, was it a big promotion for a young colonel. But it was a sizable administrative responsibility, for his task was to see the 71st Division home.

11

Airborne at Last

1946–1950

Home, for the 71st Infantry Division, meant reversion to inactive status. For Westmoreland, it meant South Carolina.

His new orders were to the Operations and Planning Division (OPD), a "super operational staff" in Washington, ranking even above the general staff of the Army, a division with a hypersecret communications center related to the often publicized, seldom seen "war room" used by the Department of Defense and the President in later years. His selection was a tribute to the reputation he had earned as chief of staff of the 9th Division, and clear notice that he still was being watched by those at higher echelons. It appeared that his brief, mainly nontactical period as commanding officer of the 60th Infantry and of the 71st Division would have to suffice as a full layer of command

181

experience in the command-and-staff alternation considered so desirable.

With his orders to OPD, Westmoreland, for the first time in well over three years, went back to take leave with his family, which had moved recently to Columbia, South Carolina. They were proud of him. His father had followed his only son's progress, not only his advancement in rank and billet, but moving vicariously with him across the maps of Africa and Europe when censorship let the name of the division slip into the regular theater communiqués. His mother and Margaret, who was married by then, admired his eagles, and made sure their friends saw him in uniform complete with ribbons. It was while Westmoreland was enjoying this adulation, and the unscheduled days and home cooking that came with it, that he received a phone call from then Major General James M. Gavin, the same Gavin whose paratroopers Westmoreland's gun and trucks had supported up the coast of Sicily. Gavin had advanced fast since then, leading the 82nd Airborne Division's jump into Normandy, becoming its commander during the fighting across the Elbe and during the occupation of Berlin. Gavin was famous, and he wanted Westmoreland.

"How would you like to take over the 504?" he asked. That was one of the three parachute regiments of the 82nd Division.

When Taylor had tried to recruit him into the 101st as the European campaign began, Westmoreland had a sense of loyalty to the 9th Division developed over more than three years with that unit. It matched Taylor's offer, and he stayed. But in 1946, Westmoreland had acquired no loyalty to OPD, an outfit to which he had never yet reported. Gavin was offering him a choice regimental command, and

182

the crack at the airborne life into which he had tried to switch when he was at Fort Bragg in 1942.

Westmoreland was eager but cautious. He reminded Gavin he had never been to jump school. The general replied that that could be arranged, it was no problem.

"Well, I've accepted the job with OPD and I don't want to be wishy-washy about it. I don't feel I should go for a better assignment when I've already made a commitment," Westmoreland replied.

The conversation was left there. But when Westmoreland reported in to OPD shortly afterward, he found his orders had been changed—at Gavin's request. He may have felt it slightly improper, but he was delighted.

The 82nd Airborne meant Fort Bragg again. Briefly, he filled the division's assistant chief of staff billet, but this was just a temporary orientation period before his assignment to jump school at Fort Benning, Georgia.

In the spring of 1946 Westmoreland was a thirty-two-year-old full colonel, still young for his rank and experience, but approximately ten pay grades senior and more than ten years older than the average student at the airborne school. He also was more dignified than most Army officers, of whatever age and rank. But he, like all students, went through jump school following the same training schedule, submitting to the same discipline as the most recent nineteen-year-old graduate of basic training.

Officer trainees at Benning lived in their own quarters, and retained the off-duty perquisites of their rank. But once they joined their classmates for each day's jump training, they were required to react as if by reflex in the reverse role of being taught by tough-lunged NCO's. They double-timed when everybody else double-timed, shouted back their part of such catechisms as "Airborne—all the way!" They did the same calisthenics at the same hours, took the same scratches and lumps when they made mistakes in prejump drills, and on the great day when they graduated with their first genuine jump from the sky, they leaped out the door of the slow-moving transport at the slap of a cocky sergeant's hand on the fatigues across their fanny.

Westmoreland, with his lifelong physical fitness consciousness and his thoroughly schooled self-reliance, took both aspects of the Fort Benning discipline without faltering. Nights, he made notes on each day's experience. And despite his self-sufficiency, jump school and the assignments to which it led created a rah-rah attitude about the airborne forces which was to be the closest thing to boyishness discernible about him through his entire career.

The course lasted just six weeks, and then he was back at Bragg—this time as commanding officer of the 504th Parachute Infantry Regiment, 82nd Airborne Division.

But his moving behind the desk of the regiment's commanding officer did not mean he had arrived yet with the veteran paratroopers of the 504th. A high percentage of the senior NCO's and officers had made combat jumps in Normandy or at Nijmegen. For most of their months at war, they had been led by Colonel Reuben H. Tucker, "a legend among the airborne." They were not eager to admit a substitute, his paratrooper wings still bright from the PX, into full membership until he had proved himself—be he commanding officer or not.

Paratroopers are taught to be contemptuous of "straight legs," that is, soldiers who go out in polite society without wearing highly polished jump boots around the tops of which their trousers are bloused. Now here was a young colonel applying to replace Tucker, and he had not even been an infantryman in the war, much less a paratrooper. One of the regiment's officers has compared Westmoreland's assumption of command to a fresh second lieutenant's taking over seasoned troops.

That situation did not last long. Westmoreland was aware of it, and came determined not to push too fast, to stick to the book of leadership, but to go all out when challenged in the daring specialties by which paratroopers judge men. This was most true in jumping—he was leading men who had dozens, even hundreds of jumps behind them. Thus when the regiment's first jump from the then-new C–82 transport was scheduled, he led the way. The following day, he jumped from the new craft last, and with nobody to send him off leaped out and down with such force that the steel connecting link of his parachute whipped up and cracked into the back of his helmet, knocking a deep dent into it and sending Westmoreland to the ground with his chute open, striking and recovering without further mishap. But for twenty-four hours he did not remember a thing about reaching the ground or anything else. He regained his awareness in the post hospital, suffering from a concussion. The blow did him no lasting damage, but had it knocked him out instead of just silly, he probably would not have survived.

A technique used with great effect by Westmoreland in those days of testing with his new regiment was his seeking of advice from the officers and sergeants who had more jumping experience than he. If he could start them talking, he would listen seriously, picking their brains—not merely to learn about the paratrooper business, which he had to do, but also to establish himself with them as a leader who did not play God. He would call together his NCO's for pep talks about the regiment's plans and about leadership methods. Still a bachelor, he was affable with his regimental officers, often going with them to the club after hours. There was the weekend night when the officers of the 504th had a party at the club, and somehow a big, expensive mirror became broken during the goodwill. The club was placed off limits to the regiment, which was not conducive to better morale. Westmoreland went to the post commander, who happened to be the former 9th Division artillery commander, Irwin, and told him he would personally guarantee the behavior of his officers henceforth. The club ban was lifted.

Not immediately, but promptly, Westmoreland arrived in the regiment in all senses of the word. And when he did, one of his battalion commanders relates, there was no doubt at all which regiment was going to be the pride of the division. Gavin seemed to concur. He had a paternal interest in the 505th, which had been his own in combat, but it was the 504th that he chose for a series of compliments.

Westmoreland was ordered to develop for his regiment a plan for emergency defense of the atomic installations at Oak Ridge, Tennessee, more than two hundred miles away across the Smokies. The first West Point cadets sent into the field for training with line units after the war were sent to the 504th. It was the regiment picked for escort duty when Mexico's president called on President Harry S Truman in Washington. The 504th was alerted when a national railroad strike threatened, and officers and NCO's who lived off post were kept at their stations, on call. When this alert stretched on, Westmoreland softened its effect on his outfit's home life by arranging a series of functions at the officers' and NCO clubs on the post, and inviting the wives of the alerted leaders aboard for face-to-face conversation, if nothing more.

Soon after Westmoreland had climbed atop the new job, his telephone jangled with another of those calls bringing fresh challenge into his life. This time, it was not the voice of a general talking gobbledygook which he was to translate into orders to capture a dam, or offering him a command he had wished for but hesitated to grab. This time, the voice was feminine, and what it said was:

"Remember me?"

It was Kitsy Van Deusen, no longer the pig-tailed horsewoman of nine, now a nineteen-year-old college student. After meeting her at Fort Sill and making friends again at Schofield Barracks, Westmoreland had seen her briefly visiting at Fort Bragg in 1941. Since then, Colonel Van Deusen had been heading the ROTC program at Cornell, and she had started college there. Kitsy, a smart girl, was aware that the years between thirteen and nineteen are dramatic ones in any girl's life, and she was prepared when young Colonel Westmoreland asked her whether she had grown up yet.

"Why don't you come on over and see?" she replied.

He did, and she had. He took her to dinner at Gavin's that night, and was forced to make a drastic but effortless revision of his impression of the cute little girl who had told him not to grieve over the loss of one youthful sweetheart, because later on he could marry her instead. He began a concentrated courtship.

With her father back at Fort Bragg, Kitsy transferred to the Women's College of the University of North Carolina, at Greensboro. It was purely coincidental that to date her Westmoreland had to drive back and forth over the same route he had taken with his hurriedly discharged date that Pearl Harbor weekend six years earlier. Wearing colonel's eagles, commander of an outstanding regiment of some three thousand outstanding soldiers, there he was on week-end nights, on the doorstep of a college dormitory, saying good night to an undergraduate with big dark eyes and dozens of friends who hung out of the dorm windows sighing over Kitsy's good fortune. One of the housemothers had been a Wave, and perhaps appreciated such things better than her charges. She told Kitsy that the colonel was much too old for her, that she should introduce him to someone more his age. Kitsy declined.

Some of Westmoreland's colleagues say that during those postwar months at Fort Bragg he seemed to relax more than ever since they had known him—certainly more than at any time since he came to Bragg that first time, from Hawaii. The war was over. A vague great deal lay ahead, but the wartime urgency was gone. Other friends maintain that while the broad tendency in the postwar Army was to let down, to assume that the job was done and nothing else would ever be so important, Westmoreland kept his eye fixed on his duty and career. The two recollections do not deny each other. Westmoreland held his regiment at an exemplary level, amassed parachute jumps to bring his record into the same league frequented by his subordinates, and studied the leadership example of those senior to him, such as Gavin. But he had to acknowledge that the war was indeed over, and that he had done as much as most soldiers to win it.

Besides, it was about time he abandoned the guarded game he had played with the girls in high school, at West Point, as a young officer and overseas. He was an established Army officer, with solid past and promising future. He was approaching thirty-three years old. He let himself go, brushed aside the opportunities that came from introductions to sisters of wives of many of his colleagues, and proposed marriage to Kitsy Van Deusen.

Kitsy said yes.

The date was set for May 3, 1947, the place St. John's Episcopal Church in Fayetteville. The wedding party drew from Westmoreland's South Carolina boyhood friends, his West Point classmates, wartime companions and especially the officers of the 82nd Airborne, and on Kitsy's side from her classmates at college and her close friends among fellow "Army brats" she had known at Sill, Schofield and Bragg.

Conrad Cleveland, Westmoreland's pal from Boy Scout days in Spartanburg and from The Citadel, drove over to act as best man. It was his duty to get the ultrapunctual groom to the church on time. Cleveland, after The Citadel, had advanced during the war in service with anti-aircraft units in the Pacific. He told Westmoreland that to avoid well-wishers who might decorate the newlyweds' car or pull some other unwelcome practical joke, they had better approach the church via the back roads of Fort Bragg. Repeatedly, military policemen halted the automobile at roadblocks, explained that secret exercises were under way, and demanded to see the two officers' credentials. Repeatedly, Cleveland's were inspected and approved, but Westmoreland's were checked and rechecked, questioned doubtfully while the anxious colonel eyed his watch. It all was preplanned by Cleveland, who after adequate alarm had been stirred did get the groom to St. John's on time, and in a ceremony resplendent with brass and lace, Westy and Kitsy became Colonel and Mrs., and exited laughing beneath an arch of crossed swords.

The bride and groom, then and now, are strikingly different persons. Kitsy's spontaneity, her immediate relaxa-

189

tion with newcomers, her readiness to laugh and party contrast remarkably with her husband's formality, his friendliness which though genuine seems carefully considered, the caution with which he approaches a second cocktail. Apparently it was the unanimous opinion of their well-wishers that she would be a good influence on him and an asset in the peacetime Army, in which officers' wives can help or hurt their careers a great deal. She was not only smart and vivacious, but versed through a whole young lifetime in what was right and wrong in Army society. So, in the late spring of 1947, Colonel and Mrs. Westmoreland set up housekeeping in a duplex in officers' country at Fort Bragg.

Even in a career as patterned to success as Westmoreland's had been, there were occasional bumps. It was in 1947 that a board of officers was convened at Bragg to decide whether an officer who had served with the 9th Infantry Division in Europe should be allowed to remain in the regular Army.

The question arose during the bitter fighting into the Huertgen Forest in the fall of 1944. The officer involved was serving as executive officer of a battalion of the 60th Infantry. The battalion was ordered to take a German pillbox holding up the regimental advance. En route forward, the battalion commander was wounded, and after retiring to his CP in another captured pillbox, decided to call off the offensive effort for the day. But the regimental commander ordered the battalion to go ahead and take the objective by sundown. The key to success was getting two tanks across a firebreak in the forest to provide direct fire support for assaulting the pillbox. One made it across, but another hit a mine. A company of the battalion pressed on and got onto the pillbox, but could not hold it and had to pull back for

Brigadier General Westmoreland lands first among troops of his 187th Airborne Regimental Combat Team in a training operation on the Han River sandbars near Seoul, 1953. U.S. ARMY PHOTOGRAPH

Westmoreland is congratulated on winning his second star by General Maxwell D. Taylor, then chief of staff of the Army, as Kitsy looks on at the Pentagon, 1956. U.S. ARMY PHOTOGRAPH

Westmoreland's parents greet him after a speech at Columbia, South Carolina.

General Westmoreland, COMUSMACV, talks with Vietnamese popular force trainees, south of Saigon, 1966. PHOTOGRAPH BY AUTHOR

Inspecting a Special Forces base under construction in enemy territory, southwest of Saigon, 1967. PHOTOGRAPH BY AUTHOR

Talking with refugees being resettled by the 25th Infantry Division from Viet Cong areas into a camp in Hau Nghia province, 1966.
U.S. ARMY PHOTOGRAPH

the night. The battalion executive, in charge since the commander was wounded, was relieved from his post by the regimental commander.

Now, almost three years later, the former battalion executive had to appear before a board to show cause why he should be retained on the rolls of the regular Army. One witness on his behalf was the commander of the company that attacked the pillbox, who made his case with detailed maps and overlays. The next witness was Westmoreland, who had been chief of staff of the division at the time of the Huertgen Forest incident, and had assigned the 60th Infantry the objectives beyond the stubborn pillbox.

Westmoreland had a choice of speaking up for an officer junior to himself, already in trouble, or for an opposing officer who was his senior, who remained active and could someday have an influence on his own career. But to him there seemed no choice at all; his mind was made up, and he told the board that while he had not been on the spot during the action, he felt the regimental commander had acted arbitrarily in relieving the battalion executive, that in fact he seemed to have used the junior officer as a scapegoat for the regiment's lack of progress that day. The case against the battalion executive officer was dismissed.

Westmoreland's testimony before the board had nothing to do with it, but within a few months he was wearing silver leaves again instead of eagles. As of June 30, 1947, there was a wholesale cutback in the ranks of those whose progress had been accelerated during wartime service. Westmoreland was a lieutenant colonel again—a standing he had achieved first back in 1942, when he was the brand-new commander of the 34th Field Artillery Battalion there at Bragg. But both he and his regiment knew that the reversion was servicewide, not aimed at him, and his subordinate

191

officers say he led then with as much élan as ever before—
perhaps with a little more.

This was not to go on much longer, however. He was
wanted at division headquarters. In the continued ebb since
V–J Day, every division remaining on the active rolls had
been cut far below the nominal strength shown on the
tables of organization. But in late 1947, the Army decided
to reorganize the 82nd Airborne, bringing it up to a full
strength of some sixteen thousand men. Its purpose was to
test new equipment, tactics, and training methods. Proper
tactical training should be carried out with standard, not
skeleton, units. Because every outfit in the Army was under
strength, field testing of aircraft designed specifically for
transport of airborne forces, and of such weapons as the
75-mm. recoilless rifle, had been delayed. So, at further
sacrifice among other existing divisions, the Army was bol-
stering the 82nd. One veteran war correspondent noted
prematurely that "the choice of an airborne division is significant, for there is a strong theory among military men
that this, rather than the oldtime infantry division, will
hereafter be the principal unit in ground combat."

To help him run the 82nd Airborne at this time of
growth and innovation, Gavin wanted Westmoreland as
chief of staff. Among Westmoreland's reactions was the
realization that this was a billet like the one he already had
filled during nine active months of combat in Europe. Without attending, he had received constructive credit for graduation from the Armed Forces Staff College, on the basis of
his wartime staff experience. But, after all, he was a lieutenant colonel again, he was due for another stint of staff duty,
and in the proffered job he could place his own imprint on
the development of doctrine for an outfit considered to be
the coming thing in Army warfare. Besides, Gavin wanted

him, and to be requested by name by an admired senior carries great weight with a young officer—a fact Westmoreland was to remember in assembling his own staffs in more responsible assignments ahead.

The staff officers who reported to him at 82nd Division headquarters maintain that neither marriage nor the birth of his first daughter, Katherine Stevens, in December, 1948; neither reversion in rank nor return to a position he knew so well, subtracted anything from Westmoreland's enthusiasm and seriousness. Every morning his section heads would come in to present their written proposals or responses to questions that had arisen on previous mornings. Westmoreland would approve most on the spot, but would ask that others be left behind so he could read them. Once he surprised a personnel officer by asking why he had not recommended any change in the division's policy for officers' leave. It had not occurred to the G–1. But Westmoreland thought the policy should be liberalized, and implied strongly that the G–1 should have anticipated his desire.

Anticipation was his primary characteristic as chief of staff. It lay partly in his own nature and training, nurtured by his service with Craig, who wanted a chief of staff who could start from an understanding of his individual approach and solve most problems to his satisfaction before they ever crossed the commander's desk. All commanders do not encourage this kind of thinking ahead by a subordinate; it takes an officer with firm confidence in himself to allow a younger, often ambitious man to take action in his name, without fearing that the result will be the impression of weakness or lack of leadership on his own part. Such men were Gavin's successors, Major Generals Clovis E. Byers and Williston B. Palmer. Westmoreland had known Palmer as artillery commander of VII Corps in France.

When Palmer got his orders in Washington, he was concerned that he could not take over immediately on the departure of his predecessor. But General J. Lawton Collins, then Army chief of staff, told him not to worry, that Westmoreland could run that division without any help. It was a significant compliment for a chief to make about a lieutenant colonel, and interesting also for the fact that Collins talked about the division's being run by its chief of staff—who is not, in the command chart, the second ranking officer in the division.

Directly between the division commander and his chief of staff comes the assistant division commander (ADC). It is an ill-defined position, whose function depends largely on the whim of the commander and the assertiveness of the ADC. More often than not, the commander uses his assistant to represent him in the field while he is tied to headquarters, to remain with the rear echelon headquarters during a displacement, or to handle special assignments, such as command of a separate task force of subordinate division or attached elements. Rarely is an ADC as involved with the daily detail of the division's performance as the chief of staff. Thus, in any organization where the personalities of ADC and chief of staff fail to dovetail, the potential for friction exists. At the 82nd, Westmoreland did not find himself in a situation comparable to his frustrating time as assistant artillery commander of the 9th Division, but there was at least one occasion when the ADC, a pleasant officer with few specific duties, spent so many hours in Westmoreland's office chatting that Westmoreland went to Palmer to complain that he was unable to get his work done.

Again, Westmoreland complained that he had to spend his time at headquarters, and had too little chance to move around seeing the division at work. Palmer told him bluntly that he had no intention of doing Westmoreland's work for him while the chief of staff went out and did the commander's work for him—that if he wanted to move about, he should develop someone on his own staff to whom he could entrust things. He never heard the same conversation from Westmoreland again.

This did not connote that Palmer was unhappy with his chief of staff. He was constantly impressed by the fact that Westmoreland walked in with a plan, suggesting that "I think we should do this," and if he approved, he usually found that Westmoreland had the staff work done, ready for action. Often, in turn, Palmer would make a suggestion and find that Westmoreland already had the plans in hand.

The chief of staff was given charge of a conscientious public relations campaign, intended to create more mutual understanding between the division and the civilian community around Bragg. Fayetteville was mainly indifferent to the post by then, and less forgiving of soldierly misconduct than when there was a war on. Those who were not indifferent showed it by continuing price gouging at the soldiers' hangouts, in the tradition begun in 1941. Westmoreland arranged for the Chamber of Commerce to come to the division area to watch demonstrations, to have lunch with companies which had decorated their mess halls out of their own contributions. It was a community relations program on which Westmoreland expanded greatly at later steps in his career, and one that Palmer copied without apology when he later commanded Fort Hood.

But Westmoreland did get out of division headquarters now and then. In 1949, for example, he was ordered to take a battalion of the 82nd to Washington to march in the annual Army Day parade. General Omar N. Bradley, Army chief of staff, had passed the word that he wanted the parade to be made up of working soldiers in their everyday uniforms, with none of the fancy white shoestrings and other gimmicks of the parade ground. The battalion commander was leery when Westmoreland passed this word, noting that his troops might look mighty drab. Westmoreland replied that that's what Bradley wanted, and the 82nd would go by the letter of his order.

So the battalion went in everyday khaki, and had the misfortune of following the Old Guard (the 3rd Infantry, the ceremonial unit from Fort Myer, in Arlington) in the order of march. The Old Guard wore what were for it everyday uniforms, all show business, and the paratroopers did look mighty drab by comparison. Westmoreland still insisted that he had done right by following orders exactly.

When a new parachute was being considered for airborne use, Chief of Staff Westmoreland tried it, making a free fall. He said he did it simply because he felt he should be familiar with the new equipment. Whether impressing his fellow paratroopers was part of his motivation or not, they do remember it still.

He had put in nearly four years with the 82nd when a letter arrived from a personnel officer at the Pentagon, suggesting that his next assignment should be as a student at Command and General Staff College, at Fort Leavenworth. Westmoreland was indignant. The prospect would have been welcomed by most captains, majors and lieutenant colonels, but he had, after all, served almost three years as a full colonel, and his experience covered the curriculum at Leavenworth and more. He went to Palmer for advice, and the general calmed him.

"Don't worry," Palmer said, "your career is being guided on a different level, one that officer knows nothing about."

At this stage, Westmoreland was considered by some contemporaries as an outstanding officer but one whose path it was best to avoid—"you couldn't stick your neck out, or he'd step on it." Some who served with him have argued more recently over which adjective, ruthless or merciless, fit him best in the late 1940's. His seniors of that period recall that on occasion he did speak out in the face of those above him, but explain that this is not unheard of, even in the Army, for an officer who had built a reputation like his. Everyone who watched him in that period does not think he was either ruthless or merciless; all do agree that both his interests and his personality seemed to "flange out" eventually, making him easier to talk or to serve with. At any rate, Palmer was correct when he said Westmoreland's career was being guided "on a different level." Westmoreland simply did not answer the letter about Leavenworth. Later, another message came. He was being assigned to Leavenworth after all, but as an instructor, not as a student, and with the expectation that better things were promptly forthcoming.

About half of the lieutenants commissioned in a given year can expect to study eventually at the Command and General Staff College (C&GSC). When they have reached approximately battalion officer level and shown enough promise to indicate that they will rise higher, they are assigned to Leavenworth for studies that lay the groundwork for command at regimental or higher level, or staff billets at division and above. In many ways, it is a refresher course in staff procedures, a means of familiarizing officers with tech-

197

niques that have been revised since their West Point or specialty school days. It deals in specifics, the how-to of tactics and logistics, more than in theory. Hundreds of officers from nations allied with the United States have attended C&GSC since World War II.

Westmoreland was detailed to the school's Department Four, which included his specialty, airborne warfare. He and Kitsy moved onto the post and particularly enjoyed meeting the broad variety of foreign officers and their wives, whom they entertained with a verve originating on her side of the partnership.

Yet for Westmoreland, it was frustration, for that same June, a new war had started in Korea, and he was not there. His teaching career at C&GSC was intended as an orientation period before he shifted to a similar but more prestigious assignment. This time, he became an instructor at the newly reorganized Army War College, "the senior institution in the Army educational system." He made the transfer in October 1950, with part of his attention nevertheless directed toward the Far East.

The Army War College was founded after the Spanish-American War at the urging of Elihu Root, then Secretary of War. Captain John J. Pershing was in its first class, when its exclusive instruction was offered on Lafayette Square, across Pennsylvania Avenue from the White House. It is a long step above C&GSC, being the institution where "selected officers are given instruction to prepare them for duties as commanders and staff officers in the highest positions in the Army and in joint commands." Whereas half of each year's crop of new Army officers can look forward to C&GSC, only about one in ten can expect assignment to the Army War College. Between 1905 and 1940, the college graduated some two thousand officers, and of those, six hundred became generals. With the coming of World War II, it was suspended. After the war and the brief height of the trend toward unified services that culminated in the National Security Act of 1947, its reorganization was recommended.

In peacetime, instructors at the college would be drawn from the lists of its graduates, but in the postwar period, there were few war college alumni of the proper rank, so officers whose experience approximated the course were selected. Civilians who have been connected with the college for decades consider that first postwar faculty the best the college ever assembled.

The faculty flexed considerable influence. It proposed courses in outline, and those accepted were drawn up in detail by the submitting officer. Its members guided students in studies and decisions, yet never suggested what solutions were acceptable or not. They monitored seminars as well as visiting lecturers, and were expected to state in writing whether and why they thought those visitors should be invited back.

The college's subject matter was not just an updating of tactics and techniques learned at an earlier level. It was as near as any military education is likely to get to the cosmic approach—foreign policy, national economics, political trends, not only in their application to purely Army problems.

No sooner had the reborn college begun operation than it was moved from Leavenworth, where it had temporarily squatted in the quarters of C&GSC, to Carlisle Barracks, Pennsylvania, and the site of the old Carlisle Indian School. There, Westmoreland and Kitsy occupied a brick three-bedroom duplex, not quite as roomy as quarters at some other posts, but looking out on a parklike back area, and just across an elm-shaded street from the swimming pool and the Carlisle stadium where Jim Thorpe had performed four decades before.

Westmoreland regained the colonel's eagles he had worn during the war, and began the most academic interlude in his career, more exclusively so than duty as either cadet or superintendent at West Point might be. He spent part of every day in the library, where one of the researchers remembers him as gentlemanly, tenacious and never asking for reading that did not pertain to his work.

Concentrating thus on his specialty, he recommended a course on "Airborne Forces and Logistical Use of Air Transportation," with subheadings on independent operations, large mobile forces, theater concepts, strategic reserves, replacements and mobilization plans. His other proposals included "The Impact of the Atomic Age on the Economic Structure of the United States," and "The Influence of Public Opinion on the United States Military Posture." In addition, he found himself involved in courses on joint war planning and theater planning. His faculty group bore responsibility for studies of "United States Policy Toward Establishment by the Soviets of a Separate German State in East Germany" and "Allied Campaigns in Western Europe"—the latter a consideration of how the recent European war, from invasion planning to Rhine crossing, might be fought in the atomic age.

This was heady, broadening stuff, but Carlisle was not where the action was. It was in places like Taegu and Inchon, Sukchon and Chorwon. There is no evidence that Westmoreland's impatience at being pinned down in Carlisle as the Korean War went on a year, then into its second year, had anything to do with his attitude toward speakers who came to the campus. But while most instructors were finding nothing but glowingly favorable things to say about the lecturers, Westmoreland wrote that one admiral should not be invited again because he talked too long and had a monotonous voice, and that a major general made no important contribution because he apparently had not been properly briefed on the purpose of his lecture.

Palmer, by that time commanding X Corps in Korea, was almost as eager for Westmoreland to come there as Westmoreland himself was. He asked that he be sent out as his chief of staff, but Lieutenant General Anthony J. McAuliffe, then making personnel decisions at the Pentagon, refused to approve the transfer because Westmoreland did not have the rank to fill the brigadier general's slot of a corps chief of staff. Palmer argued, reminding him that Westmoreland already had been chief of staff of two divisions and had commanded two regiments. McAuliffe remained firm, but time changed that.

Westmoreland himself gave a lecture on April 30, 1952; his talk was in several ways prescient. In introducing a Bell Aircraft Corporation film on the use of the helicopter in Korea, he explained to the war college just how the Army and Air Force were interpreting the 1948 agreement that defined which military aircraft would be operated by each of those branches. Quoting the agreement, Westmoreland said, "The Army takes all this to mean they can use the helicopter instead of the truck, and the Air Force says it means helicopter support is their function, since they provide airlift." Citing the Air Force's arguments, he summarized: "To put it bluntly, the Air Force is most unenthusiastic about the Army's building up large quantities of helicopter aircraft," and "although the Army has gone ahead and assigned operational and procurement authorities, procurement has to be done through the Air Force with the contractors . . . The helicopter troop program for the Army is very meager at the present time," because "the General Staff has taken the stand that the helicopter should be like any other equipment—before integrating large numbers, we should give the vehicle complete field tests and work out doctrines and techniques for its combat employment." Westmoreland was pro-helicopter.

Within a dozen years, he was to be running the first "helicopter war" in history, within four years he was to be unwillingly in the midst of the continuing debate between the Army and the Air Force over roles and missions, and within little more than three months he was finally to be watching helicopters in Korea with his own eyes, not via a movie projector.

He had been no good at concealing his growing impatience from Kitsy. She knew he wanted to go to Korea, and no doubt knew he eventually would. So when he got his orders to report to the Eighth Army that summer, she stood like a good Army wife at the foot of the plane's ladder, and pretended to smile as her husband waved back, ending the between-war years that had stretched on too long to suit him.

12

Combat and Detigerization

1952–1953

The troops of the 187th Airborne Regimental Combat Team were bivouacked in a crabapple orchard outside Taegu. F–84 Thunderjets whooshed off a fighter strip alongside, shuttling forward to harass Chinese efforts to bulwark their bleeding forces in a war of static attrition. The paratroopers were awaiting action. Not that they had been idle; they had filled a variety of assignments in Korea in the previous ten months. But it was the straight-legged infantryman and Marine who were fighting most of the war. Somebody up there still had not learned what the experts had been predicting five years before—that in future wars, the airborne "will be the principal unit in ground combat."

The 187th was formed in 1942 as a glider regiment, and assigned to the 11th Airborne Division. Redesignated an airborne infantry regiment in 1949, it had arrived in the Far East in time to fight around Kimpo airfield outside

Seoul in the days after the bold Marine landing at Inchon had turned the tide back northward. Then it was pulled out of the attack and its particular talents were used in the first combat parachute operation of the Korean War. Jumping into the Sukchon area above the North Korean capital of Pyongyang, it was assigned to block the enemy's lines of retreat. That the enemy was fleeing faster than expected, and the drop date of October 20, 1950, was too late, was no fault of the 187th. The combat team (regiment plus attachments of artillery, tanks and other support units) then operated around Pyongyang and north until the tide of Chinese intervention swept the American forces to the toe of the peninsula again in December. When the shifting front rolled back north, the regiment jumped again in an effort to cut off retreating enemy units south of Munsan-ni. That was in March 1951. For much of the following fourteen months, the 187th reverted to its role of theater reserve, standing by at Beppu, Japan, for any emergency or opportunity into which the RCT's carefully designed mobility could propel it on short notice.

That emergency arose when Communist prisoners on Koje Island, off Pusan, revolted. Starting with demands on their captors, they became more and more aggressive, arming themselves with homemade weapons, getting beyond control of the prison guards, asserting themselves so strongly that an American officer who went into prison compound 76 to bargain with them was grabbed and held as hostage. The situation was about to slip out of hand when Brigadier General Haydon L. Boatner, assistant commander of the 2nd Infantry Division, was assigned to break it up, and was given the 187th Airborne RCT as a tool. The unit flew from Beppu to Pusan, and rode landing craft ashore on Koje. Authorized to use any force necessary, Boatner sent the paratroopers into compound 76 against entrenched enemy prisoners wielding spears, knives, Molotov cocktails, clubs, hatchets, barbed-wire flails and other threatening weapons. The airborne soldiers, using concussion grenades, tear gas and fists, advanced through the trenches until they hit a hard core of three hundred still resisting, and when six Patton tanks rolled in, the resistance fell apart. Thirty-one prisoners were killed, some by their comrades, and one soldier was speared to death. After this display of determination by the captors, the two other troublesome compounds quickly complied with Boatner's orders. The revolt was over.

Thus the 187th RCT was between jobs, training intensively for whatever its next assignment might be, when its new commander flew into Taegu on July 29, 1952. It was Westmoreland, keyed up to the first chance he had ever had to handle a maneuver force, rather than supporting arms, in combat. His new command had arrived in Korea nearly two years earlier, heavily loaded with combat experience and airborne skill. Almost every officer of battalion or higher level had commanded units of similar size in World War II. But, largely by chance, the RCT had not added greatly in those two years to its own or the airborne forces' reputation. Extended time ashore at the resort of Beppu had encouraged the good life, including extensive shacking up with the girls of Kyushu, and this permissiveness was related directly by some regimental officers to a parallel relaxation of interest in the troops' military reason for being there. Westmoreland's predecessor in command, Brigadier General Thomas J. H. Trapnell, had started tightening up the RCT. Westmoreland, well briefed on the unit, arrived with the stated assumption that the command was being downgraded when it was turned over to him, still wearing a colonel's eagles. He hit the ground running.

At the airstrip, the deputy commander in charge of the RCT was waiting. He happened to be a colonel who had been a class ahead of Westmoreland at West Point. After a formal exchange of salutes and handshakes, the two went to the van that would be Westmoreland's quarters. Without further civilities, Westmoreland looked the deputy in the eye and said flatly that he was going to run things, adding that if this would make the situation awkward he would arrange for the deputy's prompt transfer. Without hesitation, the deputy said no, he preferred to stay as Westmoreland's assistant.

Taking it from there, the deputy asked whether Westmoreland wanted to get up at 4 A.M. the next day to go up to an observation post and watch a practice shoot by the RCT's 4.2-inch mortar unit. "Of course," the new commander replied, and in the breaking dawn he was hustling up a hillside at a pace with the officers around him, though he was fresh from the sedentary life at Carlisle and they had been tramping in the field for weeks. The mortar shoot had hardly begun when one of the guns had a sandbag slip under its baseplate, throwing it askew so that a round crashed directly onto the observation post where Westmoreland was watching. Seven men were wounded. The commander hastened to each, seeing that he was properly cared for, and then down to the firing position to find out what had gone wrong. The mortarmen, and in turn the whole RCT, were shaken when they imagined what kind of outfit the new commander would think he had inherited.

Within another few hours, Westmoreland had made a training jump with his new troops, who were directed during periods in reserve to be ready for a combat jump on order. He made a point of brushing aside a personal chute, packed especially for him, and took one off the same line the troops used. He made jumping as soon as possible after arrival a personal tradition, carried out every time he assumed command of an airborne unit.

Replacements were being woven into the 187th as it prepared for movement, and by August 4 they were assimilated and the RCT boarded train and trucks to roll to Chipo-ri, a marshaling area for further movement north. There, Westmoreland ordered stepped-up physical conditioning, sending the paratroopers up and down nearby mountains much like those in their forthcoming area of operations.

Westmoreland and key officers of the 187th gained map familiarity with that area in a briefing on August 8 from the 17th Infantry, of the 7th Infantry Division. The 187th was to relieve the 17th Infantry secretly in its positions above Changnim-ni, in the Iron Triangle, the bottleneck which through history had let invaders down into Seoul. A company of the 7th Division screened the transfer area, keeping out all strangers, while Westmoreland went forward to reconnoiter and select positions before the RCT moved up. So slickly was the movement carried out that soldiers in adjacent units knew nothing about the switch until word was passed down to them that it had taken place.

The war of maneuver in Korea was over, and had been since United Nations and Communist negotiators had sat down at Kaesong the previous year. Neither the 187th nor any other UN command was allowed to conduct more than limited offensives, local thrusts and parries to take control of dominating terrain, to deny the enemy an observation post, to capture prisoners, to keep the other side guessing.

This did not mean a unit had to carry on a passive war, however, and the lines across that section of the triangle became active on arrival of the 187th. Many of the positions it inherited were poorly sited, considered by Westmoreland indefensible. He promptly started adjustment of his lines, straightening bulges, covering avenues of approach, pushing out five hundred yards here, a thousand there. He also ordered quickened patrolling and raiding, sending out platoon-size combat patrols to strike enemy positions across the valley.

To his paratroopers, the most impressive thing about their new commander was his care for detail. When a patrol was dispatched, he did not routinely glance at the map overlays and approve it on the assumption that the staff and smaller unit leaders knew what they were doing. He wanted to check every turn in a patrol route, often suggesting alterations. He insisted that whenever possible, patrols rehearse over ground like that forward of the lines before setting out. All day, Westmoreland would troop through their positions, squinting along fields of fire where machine guns were laid, asking sergeants and lieutenants what they would do if this or that happened, inspecting outposts ahead of his main line of resistance. One of his battalion commanders characterized Westmoreland's command: "He makes you feel like he's looking over your shoulder all the time."

This habit of omnipresence combined with what a general has called his "battlefield magnetism—he always happened to be where something happened" to produce some exciting moments for Westmoreland. There was the day he went forward with a battalion commander along a cleared lane through minefields to take a look at a pair of outposts on pimples of land in the Kumwha valley. They were under clear enemy observation from Papa-san Hill (Hill 1062), and suddenly two or three recoilless rifle rounds exploded within a few feet of them. The battalion commander flattened alongside the trail, but Westmoreland was at that moment negotiating a wavering bridge across a small stream, and he spread-eagled into the water. He managed to laugh. More than once, he returned from a day touring units with his jeep riddled by shell fragments. He would go about his business in the CP, and his curious staff would have to quiz his driver to find out about that day's narrow escape.

The temperature was bubbling at 102 degrees on an August afternoon when a returning platoon-size patrol from the 187th's A Company was pinned down forward of the lines by heavy Chinese artillery fire. A second platoon was sent out to reach the trapped men and guide them in, but when it came close to the patrol, it too was sent ducking for cover by enemy artillery. The Chinese, seeing a potential victory at little risk to themselves, ordered out skirmishers who advanced on the isolated paratroopers. Corporal Lester Hammond, a radio operator hiding near the trapped unit, spotted the Chinese troops and called down friendly artillery fire around his own position as the enemy moved past him toward the platoon. Hit repeatedly by fragments, he kept adjusting fire until the enemy surge was broken up—and he was killed by his own artillery.

When the two platoons were able to move back under cover of friendly fire, Hammond's body was left behind. A sergeant from C Company took a tank out to bring it back. The tank mired in the rain-filled paddy. Another was sent, stuck, then three or four, then eight or ten tanks, all trying to tug one another out of the deep mud. Suddenly from the 187th observation post, those watching through field glasses saw Westmoreland himself there directing operations, under the nose of the Chinese on Papa-san. The 674th

Field Artillery, part of the RCT, was ordered to fire a protective box about the paratroopers as they sweated to extricate the tanks. The late afternoon fog rolled in, night fell, and Westmoreland and the tankers worked on. Deep in darkness, the party finally brought out the tanks and the body of Corporal Hammond, who was posthumously awarded the Medal of Honor. As for Westmoreland, he had to answer to Eighth Army because the 674th Field Artillery Battalion exceeded its ammunition allotment that day.

During insistent pressure from higher headquarters for capture of prisoners who might tip off enemy intentions, Westmoreland devised an elaborate plan to comply. Under cover of night, he put a platoon in an ambush position, up a draw ahead of the lines. Next day, he sent an observation plane skimming low over Chinese positions. When the inevitable enemy small-arms fire crackled, smoke began to pour from the aircraft and a body fell out, trailing a parachute, coming to earth close to the draw and the waiting platoon. The plane banked, seemingly out of control, and wobbled behind a hill where there was a loud explosion. Shortly, a Chinese patrol probed carefully toward the fallen body and parachute. Before it reached them, the paratroopers sprang their ambush, killed four of the enemy and captured two. The Chinese could not have known that the smoke from the plane was created by a smoke grenade, that the falling body was a dummy and that the explosion heard behind the hill was not a crashing aircraft but a satchel charge set off by the 187th. It was a practiced, perfectly executed ruse—except that one of the prisoners died of wounds and the other was killed trying to escape.

In the chill of late September in the Korean hills, the RCT worked hard at constructing bunkers and outposts along the new defensive line Missouri, across the Hanton-Chon and Namdae river valleys. Still trying to bring in prisoners, Westmoreland sent out patrols and beamed daily loudspeaker broadcasts against enemy positions on Sugar Loaf Hill. Visiting generals appeared frequently, and Westmoreland escorted them through his portion of the 7th Infantry Division's zone of responsibility.

One of the innovations he could describe to them was an application of his artillery background to the supporting weapons of the 187th. He took a mathematical approach to employment of the outfit's 4.2-inch mortars and antitank cannon. Considering the 4.2's essentially artillery pieces, he gave them an artillery-trained commander, and tied them in with the artillery battalion's fire direction center. He increased training on the countermortar radar sets that could track the path of incoming mortar shells quickly and accurately enough to allow plotting of prompt answering fire, and planned to leapfrog such equipment in any offensive situation, to keep one echelon in operation at all times. He liked the quadruple-mounted .50-caliber machine guns, intended for anti-aircraft use, and put them into play for overhead fire in support of advancing units, as well as sighting them in for sporadic harassing and interdictory fire against enemy trails and fortifications during the night.

Some of those touring VIP's were treated to a rare Westmoreland gesture toward humor, when their host asked them repeatedly during their visit whether they would like to relieve themselves at one of the mortar shell packing tubes that are always scattered about, stuck in the ground for that purpose, when any American unit is in the field. Given any response at all, the RCT commander felt justified on the guest's departure in presenting him with a gaudy medal—the Korean Order of the Piss Tube, with the rank of Marksman, Second Class. But all visitors did not depart in a spirit of levity. A bestarred kibitzer was present one day as Westmoreland's men ran a raid on enemy positions to the north. The paratroopers got onto the Chinese-held hill and into the trenches there, but brought back no prisoners and reported no enemy killed. The visiting general gibed, "Well, you got no blood up the risers today," which is, of course, airborne talk, with reference to a song about the risers that lead up from the parachute harness to the canopy above. Westmoreland was annoyed, and did not pretend otherwise. He told the general that his troops had run the operation as planned, and it was chance rather than ineptitude that dictated the result. The VIP left promptly afterward.

The 187th was pulled off the line in early fall. In an effort to lure enemy forces into the open, thus exposing their positions and making them vulnerable to American air and naval firepower, higher headquarters was planning an elaborate feint off the east coast of Korea. Westmoreland was to prepare for an airdorp, and Eighth Army was to go through the motions of readying itself for a major offensive to link up with an amphibious operation that would move toward the beach at Kojo. General Mark W. Clark, theater commander, told General James A. Van Fleet, Eighth Army commander, that his forces, including Westmoreland's RCT, were merely to attack designated land objectives, rather than assaulting enemy emplacements or attempting then to drive north. The planning and rehearsing were realistic; in fact, most of the men involved thought the offensive was to be genuine. But when the amphibious forces made their landing pass October 15, enemy response was disappointing. The follow-up moves by land and air were called off. And the net of the operation was a sag in morale of the American units which had thought they were about to move to break the stalemate of outpost warfare.

Thus out of action, the 187th received orders to revert to theater reserve in Japan. Back at Beppu, Westmoreland's assignment was to keep the RCT ready for quick deployment to any spot in Korea. That called for a constant high state of training, combined with prompt availability of the soldiers who would move out within hours of a command from higher headquarters.

This mission neatly complemented Westmoreland's diagnosis of what the RCT needed. That was more work and less cohabitation with the friendly population. Westmoreland began a training schedule intended not only to keep the RCT sharp in individual and unit combat skills, but also to wear the paratroopers down so that by evening they had little energy left to fuel a search for off-post diversion. He also ordered a halt to overnight passes, a regulation that caused a temporary wave of grumbling—including at least one protest by an officer directly to Westmoreland. Many commanders have enforced such restrictions in problem situations. This was a case in which the commander's course of action happened to fit exactly his own tight personal standards of conduct. Whether another RCT commander would have met the problem at Beppu the same way has to remain a hypothetical question. But morale in the 187th reflected Westmoreland's concern for his troops, and their realization that his regulations did not mean he was an antagonist toward them. He encouraged their organization of an enlisted men's beer club, called the Rakkasan Club (after the RCT's nickname, the Japanese word for "falling-down umbrella"). He stood up for them against the Beppu post commander, an older officer who had his MP's harassing the paratroopers for piddling offenses, and who seemed to resent the youthful success of the 187th commander.

That youthful success had its most solid confirmation when Westmoreland was notified he had taken over the RCT with a false assumption—the assumption that the 187th was being downgraded by the assignment of a colonel, rather than a brigadier general, to its command. The commander was upgraded to the level of the RCT on November 7, 1952, when Westmoreland was awarded his first star. He was thirty-eight years old, an age when most officers still are majors or lieutenant colonels.

Kitsy flew out for the promotion ceremony, and then moved in with him at Beppu. It was "practically Stateside living" for the officers who could bring their dependents to the resort city. Westmoreland and Kitsy lived in a big requisitioned house that had two hot baths, one fed by the famous mineral springs of Beppu. After work, Westmoreland and his staff would keep in shape by workouts with medicine balls or other exercise, then follow Japanese custom with a hot bath and a subsequent bull session. For hours of relaxation, Westmoreland bought himself a highly visible houndstooth jacket from Kolzinoff, the local White Russian tailor, and he taught his colleagues how to make what he considered the finest martini, a touch he had learned in turn from General Eddy. That was to mix according to the individual customer's preference for dryness or wetness, then to add a couple of drops of sweet vermouth. Those of his staff who did not endorse the recipe attributed Westmoreland's enthusiasm for it to his own limited experience in that specialized field. The Westmorelands remained in the requisitioned Japanese home until after the peace treaty was signed in 1953, when they had to move back onto the post.

But in both places they were able to entertain, and the post wives were able to organize for bridge and other activities, as if they were back at Fort Bragg.

A war was still going on only two hours away, however, and the first order of Westmoreland's business was to be sure that the 187th was ready for combat. As ideal as Beppu was for family living and off-post social life, it was like most military stations in Japan in its lack of adequate training space. Crowded Japan, where land is more efficiently used than anywhere else in the world, has few areas open enough for realistic maneuvers by battalions or regiments, for live firing of tank guns or artillery, for dropping strings of paratroopers from aircraft flying in formation. The RCT's 674th Field Artillery Battalion and one infantry battalion had to be stationed ninety miles from Beppu, across a mountain range. The Air Force wing with which the RCT worked was stationed at Ashiya. And the drop zone used by the 187th was at Oita, a tricky peninsula with habitually shifting winds and salt water on three sides.

Continuing his practice of seeing and being seen by his troops, Westmoreland made frequent trips over the mountains to inspect the artillerymen, or to accept social invitations from them. Normally he flew in a light plane, but occasionally he had to take the train when the weather closed in across the range. His dignity was dented on one such trip when he flew one way but was obliged to take the train back, wearing his starched fatigues, packed in among Japanese women with their babies and luggage slung on their backs. The commander also made a point of visiting the airmen at Ashiya, attending parties there, often inviting the officers to watch his troops jump. The result was that the 187th had fewer problems obtaining aircraft for training than would have been likely if the relationship had been confined to official paperwork channels.

At a firing zone near Beppu, where occasional duds occurred in the RCT's mortar ammunition, the local Japanese made a business of scavenging through the forbidden impact area for scrap. One of them was killed when he picked up a dud round. The incident fed resentment of the Americans' presence, and was used by leftists in Oita to stimulate the press and anti-United States demonstrations. To offset this, Westmoreland had meetings with the mayor and other officials, invited them to dinner and joined them at parties where he sipped sake and danced the *tankobushi* (the coal miners' song, a pantomiming exercise done in a circle, highly popular at Japanese parties in the late of the evening). The result was that what began as a liability turned into a military-civilian relationship evaluated as the best in the Army's Southwestern Command.

The drop zone at Oita inevitably was the scene of the paratroopers' best-remembered training adventures. Westmoreland, however, would prefer to forget the shiftiness of the winds there, for on one occasion he jumped and drifted earthward, guiding himself onto the drop zone, and at the last instant before he struck the breeze let up and plopped him directly into a "honey well"—one of those pits scattered thickly throughout agricultural Japan into which farmers dump human fertilizer from "honey buckets" slung on poles across their shoulders. Westmoreland crawled reeking out of the fermenting fertilizer, and stayed in the field for the remainder of the training problem. Then he headed back to Beppu to lead his staff and commanders in a critique of the day's operations. But the session was only a few minutes old before the odor became too much, and Westmoreland excused himself, headed for his quarters, stripped out of his clothes at the door, bathed and returned in fresh uniform. Unlike the time he flopped off the bridge under shell fire in Korea, he was unable to muster a chuckle.

The unpredictable winds at Oita could be dangerous. In the late winter of 1953, a flight of C–119 Flying Boxcars roared over the zone, spewing blossoming parachutes as they cut across the peninsula and headed out to sea. Aboard the last transport were some thirty soldiers who leaped just in time to come down near the beach—all but seven of them. Those seven splashed into the water off-shore. They had training in water landings, which included slipping out of their harnesses by popping quick release levers well above the water's surface, thus avoiding being dragged under by the soaked parachute. These men apparently thought they could tug their risers hard enough to swing themselves onto dry land, but they failed. Rescue boats were on station, as during every drop at Oita. But they were too late. All seven paratroopers were drowned before they could be recovered. The accident came during a severe Army crackdown on training accidents. Starting promptly, higher headquarters began insisting on a formal report on the deaths, with the implication that blame had better be fixed, and fast. Although he had not been directly involved, Westmoreland in effect took the blame by refusing to point to anyone else. He told the impatient officers above that they would just have to wait for the findings of the board appointed to investigate the accident. When it did report, it found that a series of seemingly minor hitches, which would have caused little or no trouble if scattered as usual over a year of jumping, had taken place within seconds on the C–119. The pilot had delayed turning on the green "go" light, the senior jumper had slightly delayed his jump, one of the later troops had hesitated—and by the time the last seven men tumbled out the door, they were commited to landing in the water.

Westmoreland's handling of the Oita tragedy typified his careful relationship with the officers junior to him, on whom he had to depend so heavily. Throughout his time with the RCT, he never relieved an officer—though one was relieved just before he arrived, and he confided that in that case he wished he had been there to order it himself. He came close to relieving another because of his apparent lack of aggressiveness in combat, but decided against it, and his judgment was corroborated. As his adjutant put it, "he kept no sword of Damocles hanging over his staff and battalion commanders." They could be confident that if they took an initiative Westmoreland would back them up publicly, although they might hear a later, private discourse on their mistakes.

A young lieutenant in the RCT's pathfinder platoon had an idea for his unit which Westmoreland avidly adopted for the entire 187th. It was the concept "Every man a tiger," and to carry it out he ordered a "tigerization" program of accelerated physical conditioning, training in hand-to-hand combat and small unit problems. Its aim was to have the paratroopers roaring for action when they were needed again in Korea. Westmoreland also made extensive use of training and leadership techniques that always have appealed to him for their simplicity. He prepared step-by-step outlines of the sequence for combat orders, the main points in relations with the civilian population and other items on which the memory might need hasty jogging under pressure. He liked to have these printed on pocket-size cards so his subordinates could carry them around and thus have no probable excuse for forgetting their contents.

He also composed letters on leadership, and addressed them to officers at the battalion and company level. To avoid offense, he began such a message to one of them, "I know you don't need this, but I wanted you to see what I'm telling the others . . ."

As the summer of 1953 began, the lengthy talks at Panmunjom had finally crossed the major obstacle of prisoner exchange terms. A cease-fire, no longer remote, became a genuine possibility. Looking in that direction, the Chinese began a June offensive against a bulge in the Eighth Army line, running from northeast of Kumwha across the territory of the South Korean II Corps to Mundung-ni. Heavy artillery fire preceded ground attacks concentrated against Korean-held Allied positions. After gaining some ground and causing heavy casualties, the Chinese held up again. But the attack had impressed Clark and General Maxwell D. Taylor, then commander of the Eighth Army. They rushed the 187th RCT (and the 1st Cavalry Division) back to Korea. The paratroopers were alerted June 20, and two days later their artillery was in action. When the enemy began another intensive drive July 13, Taylor attached the 187th to the 2nd Infantry Division.

The paratroopers were operating around Kumwha, astride Route 3, the "bowling alley" down toward Seoul. It was the same neighborhood in which they had occupied lines almost a year before, but when they were assigned to the 2nd Division's flank alongside a Korean outfit they moved into positions unfamiliar to them. Westmoreland placed one battalion on Hill 624, which covered the entire corps front, looking down on routes east and west along which the corps artillery was employed, dominating the potential invasion corridor through the valley.

Knowledge that the enemy was coming in great strength seemed to inspire Westmoreland. He went forward to his 3rd Battalion, where he called in the officers and senior NCO's of the line companies and told them what was expected. "You are here," he said, drawing a line in the soggy dirt with his foot. "If the enemy comes, you may go here." He took a side step, and with his other foot drew another line about thirty inches behind the first. "No farther." Looking up at them, he declared, "Here you will stand and here you will die, if need be."

Back at his own CP, Westmoreland reviewed the situation, including the fact that two Chinese divisions were in position to attack through the 187th if they chose that route. Almost rubbing his hands together in anticipation, he turned to his artillery battalion commander and said, "Okay, Fly, let's fight this war together now." He was confident that he, his troops and their positions were as ready as they could be, and he was still eager, for he still had missed the opportunity to command a line unit in the vortex of a full-scale battle. But both the Chinese and his immediate superior had plans slightly different from his own.

The commander of the 2nd Division was Major General William L. Barriger, a surname which Westmoreland, to the general's annoyance, insisted on mispronouncing "Barringer." Relations between the two were not ideal, and the 187th had not been dug in on Hill 624 and the adjacent ground for long when Barriger reacted to the Chinese push against neighboring units by ordering Westmoreland to pull his battalion back off 624. It was a night of torrential rain, "darker than the inside of a cow" according to one of the RCT's officers. Westmoreland was being told to make a move he considered tactically wrong, under abominable conditions, into totally unknown new positions so far back that they would be in the rear of his RCT command post. He telephoned Barriger to express his "earnest recommendation" that the shift not be carried out.

The division commander was adamant. He considered the move necessary. Westmoreland, outranked by one star, nevertheless engaged the general in a heated argument. When Barriger would not withdraw his order and threatened a court-martial, Westmoreland insisted that he put the command in writing. The conversation clicked off with Westmoreland's proceeding as ordered, notifying the commanding general that he was acting under protest and had requested a written order to show that the move—the mistake, in his opinion—was not being made at his own initiative. Even as he complied, he tried to change it before it was irrevocable, by going over Barriger's head, sending his own deputy to corps headquarters in an effort to get a rescission. It did not work. The move was executed, under such unlikely conditions that a captain thought the order was for a hasty retreat, rather than an orderly shift of positions. He thus burned a quantity of communications gear he could not stack aboard his vehicles. Westmoreland made him pay for it. But there is no evidence that Westmoreland himself ever paid for sticking out his neck again, directly defying a senior officer under combat conditions. It is the consensus of his colleagues who were there that he was right in his stand. Barriger retired in 1957 as a major general.

That Chinese offensive, which was aimed again at the South Korean forces, was the last major action of the Korean War. The 187th was not hit hard, although its flank units had to throw back heavy local attacks, and its responsibility for standing fast was great. There were casualties and paratrooper heroes in the fighting around X-Ray Hill, Finger Ridge and other juts of otherwise undistinguished terrain. Small patrols of Chinese raided the RCT's lines, seeking prisoners, just as the Americans raided them. There were skirmishes and fire fights, infiltration through the barbed wire at night, and on July 20 the Chinese led with artillery and made a limited advance alongside the 187th's positions, taking a hill occupied by the South Koreans.

And then, on July 27, Westmoreland received official notice that the armistice would begin at 10 P.M. He ordered his troops to clear their weapons beginning at 6 P.M., to avoid incidents that could upset the agreement. At seven, a jeep driver was killed by a burst of machine gun fire from the enemy side. As one paratrooper said, "I remember a full moon, as we sweated out the hours until 2200. We could hear fire above Sniper Ridge until about 0300 in the morning. Artillery and 90-mm. fire continued throughout the night. The Korean soldiers were singing in their bunkers."

It was over. Westmoreland sent his troops forward of the lines the next day, policing up empty cartridge shells, cigarette butts, C-ration wrappers. They dumped the garbage in the stream that ran between their lines and those of the Chinese. The enemy soldiers were "like ants, crawling all over Sniper Ridge." Two men of the paratrooper machine gun squad armed themselves with C rations and went toward the Chinese on a souvenir-swapping mission. When two Chinese waved submachine guns at them, they changed their minds and came back, disappointed. Westmoreland's orders were to destroy the bunkers and strong points along his main line of resistance, and to pull back to the former Nebraska line. There, he set his men to construction of a new, potentially permanent position that tied in more strongly with the truce line approximating the thirty-eighth parallel. They called it their "Blackjack Bastion." It straddled the "bowling alley" leading to Seoul, and into its timbers and sandbags the troops poured the leanness and meanness that the "tigerization" program had whet in them in anticipation of more extensive combat. Though sticking to his ban on mustaches and insistence on short haircuts, Westmoreland let them shed their shirts and get deep suntans while digging. This was halted by a break during which the RCT made a training jump onto the Han River sandbars near Seoul. Then it was back to "Blackjack Bastion" until early October.

Westmoreland had badgered his superiors in Japan and then in Korea for assignments for the 187th to make combat jumps, often presenting them with operation plans all worked out just in case. By autumn he felt the RCT was wasting its time in a static position along an armistice line. Then he started petitioning Taylor and his staff for transfer back to Japan, where more regular airborne training was possible—and, incidentally, where the dependents of himself and many of his troops were waiting. Eventually, the move was ordered. On October 3, the RCT moved out of the Kumwha area to Inchon, boarded the transport USS *General Pope* and headed for its Japanese home port.

En route to the port of Moji, Westmoreland and his subordinate commanders laid emphasis on a need keenly felt—the "detigerization" of a regimental combat team of paratroopers who had been away from bars, women and other aspects of civilization long enough to be hungry. Not only was there the obvious potential for rambunctiousness among the civilian population, but to make matters worse, the United States Navy had moved into Beppu in the absence of the 187th. As the RCT history euphemizes it, "A reorientation program to review conduct with civilians and Japanese-American relations was initiated that was to affect all the paratroopers."

The RCT troops arrived at Beppu by train on October 6, and Westmoreland had them rig combat gear and uniforms for an arrival parade up the local "Broadway" to their post, which they had named Camp Chickamauga. The local merchants and politicians laid on a generous welcome, and the townspeople turned out to watch. But in the crowd there also were enough jeering American sailors, most of them with their arms about the waists of local belles, to put the paratroopers in the mood for some of the hand-to-hand combat they had anticipated in their "Every man a tiger" phase. Westmoreland foresaw this, dropped an early curfew on his men that night, and went to call on the captain of the Navy ship. With the captain, he arranged a boxing competition between the champions of the paratroopers and the ships in port. Meanwhile, he ordered inspections of barracks, equipment, vehicles and anything else inspectable. He restricted passes each night to about 10 per cent of his command. Then, when the boxing series ended with a paratrooper victory, the 187th felt vindicated, and there had been only a minimum of blood shed in unscheduled Army-Navy bouts outside the ring.

By mid-October, Westmoreland had the Rakkasans back on a training schedule that made the one he had approved the previous year seem sissy. His tour with the 187th was nearing its end, and he would be able to leave it on the upbeat. At about this same time, Kitsy had to undergo surgery, and went to the hospital at Kobe, at the other end of the Inland Sea from Beppu. So Westmoreland managed a temporary liaison assignment with the Marine headquarters at Gifu, in order to be nearby while she was recovering. From there, they headed back across the Pacific. For the first time in his career, Westmoreland was Washington-bound.

13

At the Neck of the Funnel

1953–1958

Most Army officers throw up their hands at the suggestion that they are destined for a tour of duty at the Pentagon. They say they prefer working with troops, trucks, maps and cannon to shuffling papers in the presence of thousands of other officers, one as anonymous as another, with such distinctive addresses as 2D757. But it is possible for their dismay to be phony. For a man whose ambitions run toward the very top of the military hierarchy, it is essential that he learn by experience the circuitry and internal politics that are at their most intense and complex in the Pentagon itself. He can be truthful in saying that he would rather have the satisfaction of commanding several thousand men, and at the same time be conscious that at a certain stage of his career, advancement will be served best by an assignment in anonymity.

Westmoreland had risen to general officer status, put in

more than seventeen years of commissioned service, without a day of duty at the Pentagon. Through Gavin's intervention, he had barely missed a tour with the Operations and Planning Division on his return from Germany in 1946. On his return from Korea in 1953, the inevitable could be postponed no longer. He was assigned as Deputy Assistant Chief of Staff, G–1 (personnel), for Manpower Control.

The job sounded like the ultimate in Pentagon obscurity. In Korea or at Fort Bragg, a one-star general is a respected, perhaps feared, man. But whoever heard of the Deputy Assistant Chief of Staff, G–1, for Manpower Control? The G–1 field is one in which Westmoreland had no previous direct experience, other than briefly in his artillery batallion at Fort Sill, although as a division chief of staff and regimental commander he had to concern himself with personnel problems every day. Personnel is not a specialty which draws many talented volunteers, as are the other general staff lines of operations, intelligence and even logistics. Sharp nonspecialist officers may find themselves doing a tour as a battalion S–1 or a division G–1 along the way, but often those billets at the lower echelons are filled by less impressive, less ambitious men who have settled down to become career adjutants.

Yet Westmoreland's assignment to G–1 came at an interesting time. In the post-Korea letdown, the Army's strength was allowed to sag again, and when the business-dominated Eisenhower administration and the first Republican Congress since immediately after World War II combined interests with the new chairman of the Joint Chiefs of Staff, Admiral Arthur W. Radford, the Army suffered more than any other branch of service. Radford and General Nathan F. Twining, chief of staff of the Air Force, encouraged Charles E. Wilson, Secretary of Defense, in his efforts to obtain "a bigger bang for a buck." This meant assigning the major slice of the defense dollar to nuclear and thermonuclear weapons and means of delivering them. The obvious beneficiaries were the Air Force's Strategic Air Command and the Navy's carrier forces. The concept fit in smoothly with the missionary effort of John Foster Dulles, Secretary of State, to enlist all the nations of the world as allies or condemn them as enemies. In such a black-and-white world, the theory continued, there would be peace or else—and or else meant all-out, thermonuclear war. There was no place in this approach for fuzzy thinking that dwelt on the likelihood of an in-between situation, a limited war for which a large, ready, well-equipped Army would be essential and weapons of mass destruction would be useless.

Westmoreland, despite the obscure sound of his title, thus was closely involved with the headlines of the day. He dealt with both military and civilian manpower, Selective Service requirements, personnel procurement and distribution, determination of the special skills required, and the almighty budget that governed the rest.

Wilson called for a study to ascertain just how far the Army could be cut below its post-Korea level of 1,540,000 while still maintaining the same number of divisions, which was then nineteen. The report from Westmoreland's office came back contending that the divisions could not be continued properly with any troop total far below the current figure. Almost as if in direct response, Wilson ordered a reduction of 100,000. The G–1 section appealed this decision, and Westmoreland argued against it up the chain of command, through the vice chief of staff, the chief, the Secretary of the Army and Wilson's aides, who were not markedly sympathetic. Rather than holding the Army's strength

227

where it was, Wilson sliced it another 100,000, then another, then down to 1,175,000.

To back up his decisions, Wilson send down a memorandum asserting that, given proper leadership and training, the Army could maintain its nineteen divisions with the number of men it had been allowed. General Matthew B. Ridgway, then chief of staff, felt personally insulted. Eventually, Westmoreland sold the chief on a scheme which admittedly was "phony as hell," but which was intended to satisfy Wilson. It reorganized the commands in Alaska and Panama under division designations, and kept the remaining seventeen divisions at a level approaching their tables of organization. Wilson, who was most interested in having the nineteen divisions on paper as evidence that he could cut manpower without hurting capability, accepted it.

A sensitive part of Westmoreland's job was selling Congress on the Army's manpower needs. He presented most of the testimony at the Capitol for the G–1 section, and once ordered preparation of a pamphlet to answer persistent congressional questioning about exactly how all that manpower was being used. The first draft did not please him; he sent it back nearly twenty times more before deeming it suitable to back up his case before the legislators. But he won the reputation with his subordinates of supporting their papers to the limit once he had approved them.

Another Westmoreland innovation was accepted only after he bypassed a senior staff officer and took it directly to the chief of staff. It was designed to save dollars by closing the Puerto Rican base where new soldiers were being given basic training, ineffective because of their language handicap. He wanted to concentrate on teaching the Puerto Ricans English for six solid weeks, then send them to regular basic training courses on the mainland. The G–3 opposed the idea, but when Westmoreland presented it to the chief, it was approved.

While her husband was in the G–1 assignment, in July 1954, Kitsy gave birth to their son, James Ripley II, named for his grandfather. Thus she stayed behind in Washington that fall when Westmoreland accepted an opportunity that never would have arisen in the old, prewar Army.

Sending Army officers back to school is a common policy now, proven as a means of keeping them up to date on civilian research or management techniques, or broadening their background for development of a military speciality. Most often, this extra education comes at the junior or field-grade level. Westmoreland not only had never attended any formal Army institute such as the Command and General Staff College, but also had missed connections with these temporary assignments to civilian education—until, as a brigadier general, he was sent to the Harvard Graduate School of Business to take its advanced management course.

One hundred sixty-six executives registered for the course that fall in Cambridge. Only eleven of them were military men. The others were presidents, vice presidents, treasurers, purchasing officers or other officials from business and industry, all in the thirty-five to fifty age bracket. They wore suits or sport shirts to classes, and dressed this way, Westmoreland seemed to his classmates very much one of them. Not only his appearance and personality, but somehow his experience too fit in with those of the men around him. "He wasn't different," one of them recalled. "He might have been the vice president of a corporation."

The courses included Administrative Practices, which was a seminar discussion of case histories of business problems; Business and the American Society, an examination of the social and economic forces influencing business administration; Marketing Management; Cost and Financial Administration; Problems in Labor Relations, a series to which union representatives were invited to discuss their side of the issue; and Business Policy, which dealt with policymaking and administration at top management levels, occasionally using case histories of failed enterprises.

No written work was required, and the course did not conclude with grades. It was based on discussions, exchanges of experience brought to bear on one problem at a time—much like "brainstorming," in the current jargon. A student could contribute as much as he wished, remaining silent and listening, or talking too much. Westmoreland seemed to want to contribute more than his share, but took an exploratory, rather than dogmatic, approach to the problems. He was interested in the Administrative Practices series, which concerned itself with things as simple as how to handle a bothersome telephone operator or as complicated as reorganization of a whole office or business procedure, and in the Business Policy course, in which he had some spirited disagreements with the professor.

But the one that brought forth most enthusiasm from Westmoreland was Business and the American Society, which studied how executives could get along with people, as individuals and groups. This should not surprise anyone aware of his conscious, methodical development of his own techniques of leadership. Some of the discussions found the class breaking down along partisan political lines, and though they do not remember his declaring himself, the Democrats considered him one of them. Whether he, as an Army man, was obviously unhappy with a Republican administration then favoring the other services, or whether they simply assumed he was a Southern Democrat because of his South Carolina roots is less clear in their memory.

Westmoreland took part in evening conversations with the other seven men in his "can group" (the residents who had to use the same dormitory toilet), and often went to the daily cocktail session sponsored by the university for participants in the course. He played squash and golf when he could, and otherwise joined in whatever was proposed, in class and out. He had been able to see Kitsy only occasionally during the three-month course, but insisted that she come up to meet his colleagues during a three-day round of parties and ceremonies when it ended in December. She objected because she still was nursing Rip, as the boy was inevitably called, but he arranged baby-sitters and she came, recalling that she simply nursed Rip between cocktail parties and he never was a happier baby.

Westmoreland's classmates saw him in uniform only twice, once at graduation and once when he accepted an invitation to spend an hour telling the class about the compensations of military life. In gist, he said that anybody who made the Army his career had to be dedicated, because he had no prospects of getting rich that way. The general made a deep impression on those at Harvard with him. He was forty-one, prime executive age, and one of his contemporaries said, "I'll bet at least twenty companies would have hired him at the snap of a finger." Some did make him proposals, in fact, and he still has standing offers from the firms represented by several classmates. Even if he had never been promoted beyond brigadier general and become well known, one of them said, he would have been easily the best remembered military man in the class.

The Army had sent Westmoreland to Harvard to improve his efficiency and perhaps give him some ideas for the improvement of procedure in an office like that of the Deputy Assistant Chief of Staff, G–1, for Manpower Control. But when he returned from Cambridge, he stayed in his manpower billet only a few more months. Once again, he found that those above had plans for him.

General Palmer, Westmoreland's former commanding general with the 82nd Airborne, had risen to become vice chief of staff of the Army. Maxwell Taylor, whose path Westmoreland's career had crossed several times, was selected to become chief of staff. Their combined decision brought Westmoreland into one of the most influential, yet still largely faceless, jobs he ever held. It was the billet of secretary of the General Staff, an assignment which Palmer knew would be open. He also knew that Westmoreland was in G–1, just back from his temporary duty at Harvard. He staved off several other candidates for the job until Taylor arrived, when he suggested Westmoreland, backing up his recommendation with an account of Westmoreland's service as his division chief of staff at Fort Bragg. Taylor did not need convincing; he accepted Westmoreland immediately.

Taylor himself had served in the office of the secretary of the General Staff (SGS) during General George C. Marshall's term as chief of staff. Bedell Smith, Eichelberger, Bull, others with famous names had been assigned to that key post or the chairs around it, and this fact is testimony to the job's importance as a stepping-stone to higher assignments. There have been thirty-seven officers in the SGS billet since the job was created in 1903. Westmoreland was the thirty-first.

Those who have filled it consistently describe the job the same way: the SGS is chief of staff to the chief of staff.

Major General Elias Townsend, the 1967 incumbent, said the prime personality requirement is that "you have to be selfless . . . You yourself are not anybody. Your anonymity is the measure of your service to your boss. Instead of setting your own pace, you adjust to others' pace." When Taylor later expressed his appreciation for the work of the Army staff, coordinated by Westmoreland, he said that "insofar as I have allowed them, they have fulfilled the role of the perfect staff officer who sees to it that the Old Man's mistakes are neither too big nor too numerous."

The SGS job can be likened to a funnel with a sieve in it. Every official piece of paper that arrives in the Army staff office crosses his desk, and he determines which questions must be brought directly to the chief of staff's attention, which should be sent to the vice chief, and which can be handled without the personal attention of either of those four-star generals. The chief accepts no document which has not been initialed by the SGS.

This traffic flows in both directions. The General Staff itself is a circle of three-star generals, each with a subordinate staff, each dealing with such a broad field as administration, research, operations, logistics and comptroller matters. They originate plans and programs for submission to the chief, and they carry out studies and policies at the initiative of the chief. Going and coming, these affairs flow through the SGS. In addition, the SGS is responsible for putting the flesh of detail on the bare bones of general directives from the chief. To help with this load, he has his own stable of colonels and lieutenant colonels, men he is allowed to select from anywhere in the Army.

Methodically, Westmoreland organized his staff procedure so he could handle a heavier work volume than his predecessors. He made it more formal, requiring his colonels to come in with a stack of work and take only about ninety seconds to summarize each paper. To each presentation, Westmoreland would say simply "approved," or "disapproved," or less often, ask that the paper be left for closer study and possible reference to Palmer, the vice chief.

Clearly, more than sifting paper was involved for the SGS. Westmoreland handled downward relations, with his own group of colonels, confidently because he knew and had chosen these officers. His relations with Taylor, the chief, were of much the same nature as those he had established with General Craig in the 9th Infantry Division. He had to understand Taylor without hearing long explanations or often without being addressed directly by him, as when he would sit in on the chief's staff meetings or conversations with individual generals, and in eavesdropping pick out the "action items," note them and get them done. So close was his tie with the chief that he always had to watch his own language, because others were likely to assume that whatever he said represented Taylor's thoughts and wishes.

Working with Taylor and Palmer was smooth, because they knew Westmoreland well and did not hesitate to rely on him. Often, he was more closely informed on a given subject than either of them because they took turns swinging out to Army posts around the country and the world, while he had the continuity gained by his constant presence at the neck of the funnel. These conditions encouraged his seniors to give him more authority for making and recommending decisions than the SGS traditionally carried, and Westmoreland characteristically exercised it. Still, there was occasional awkwardness when he transmitted to the three-star generals of the staff the desires of Taylor or Palmer, since their desires, however indirectly communicated, carried the weight of orders.

Taylor took some of the delicacy out of this relationship by promoting Westmoreland to major general on December 1, 1956. The SGS position had begun as a two-star billet fifty-three years before, then been downgraded to one-star and later, during George Marshall's tenure as chief, to colonel. Marshall apparently believed all available officers of higher rank should be overseas, rather than in Washington desk jobs. But after World War II, the job was at one-star status until Taylor decided, in Westmoreland's case, to bring it back to two-star level. Westmoreland was forty-two, the youngest major general in the Army.

Kitsy, by then mother of another daughter, Margaret Childs, eleven and a half months old, was there to help as Taylor pinned on her husband's second star. The ceremony came just after the SGS had stirred a minor flap by signing a memorandum expressing the chief's disapproval of the exchange of Christmas cards among Army families bumping elbows with each other in the capital. Taylor grinned, and said, "Westy, I don't know why I should give you another star after all this Christmas card business." Then, "Well, I'll give you the star, but I'll be damned if I'll send you a Christmas card."

With all his application to efficiency to save time for Taylor, Westmoreland still was not concerned solely with procedure as SGS. He was at the crossing point on all the issues that deeply shook the entire Army or merely quivered its subordinate branches during the Eisenhower administration. With his background in G–1, he figured economies in the Army staff, for example cutting back the personnel assigned to the Quartermaster General. That department insisted it could not operate so understaffed, but Palmer backed up Westmoreland and told it to go ahead and try, and of course it did. On a broader scale, Westmoreland worked with Palmer on reorganization of the whole Army staff, initiated by the vice chief. The staff had its five three-star deputy chiefs plus a wide scattering of special branch officers, and responsibility upward and downward for their activities was hard to establish. The reorganization put the special branches under the closest related deputy chief, and this streamlining made much clearer who had to answer to whom about what. Westmoreland read every paper, listened to conversations, studied the leadership and decision processes of his superiors on every question faced by the Army.

The single most pressing question was the same one that had squeezed the Army since the change of administrations and the end of the Korean War, both in 1953. Wilson and Radford, with important congressional support, continued to prefer more and bigger bombs and bombers, within a smaller overall budget, which meant that the non-bomber forces—the Army and Marine Corps—had to suffer. The trend continued when Twining replaced Radford. And competition for the defense dollar sharpened when the Army and the Air Force found themselves working on different species of the next generation of weapons—missiles.

Ridgway, as Army chief of staff since 1953, had fought hard against the Wilson-Radford trend. He was often an isolated individual in debate within the Joint Chiefs of Staff, and retired under pressure in 1955. Taylor was his replacement. He was determined to fight just as hard, and in the months after he had been selected but not yet sworn in, he thought he detected some encouragement in the attitude shown in a National Security Council review of the administration's "new look" in defense. Hoping to solidify this hopeful inkling, he drew up a statement of his own beliefs, and on arrival in Washington turned it over to Westmoreland and the rest of the Army staff for "criticism and refinement." The result was a document entitled, "A National Military Program." Its primary contention was that the purpose of armed forces is to deter war and aggression; its most controversial section, as read by the Joint Chiefs to whom it was submitted, said: "The National Military Program must be suitable for flexible application to unforeseen situations. It cannot be geared to any single weapons system, strategic concept, or combination of allies . . . [It] should include all reasonable measures to prevent general and local war and at the same time contain the potentiality of waging any war, large or small, in such a manner as to achieve our national objectives and to bring about a better world upon the successful conclusion of hostilities." In short, a world unrazed by thermonuclear blast and fallout.

This was the basic Army position, and it was to stand through Taylor's time as chief and Westmoreland's parallel period as SGS, despite shifts in the emphasis of the civilian administration and the inordinately influential chairman of the Joint Chiefs. The Army document was intended as a position paper for consideration within the Joint Chiefs and wherever else the debate led within the government. It was basic, and a series of other papers supported its generalities in terms of individual weapons and specialities. Soon after the document was read and politely put aside by the Joint Chiefs, a much less diplomatically worded summary of it, plus comparable presentations by the other services, broke into print. The interservice controversy became more public than the Pentagon thought was proper.

"Staff studies" were leaked to newspapers by Army partisans, and countered by similar propaganda from the Air

Force and Navy. The issues of nuclear reliance, reduction of ground forces, aircraft carriers' potential and missile development—the whole debate over roles and missions of the services—were spread on the public record, in the words of subordinate staff officers who could sharpen points because they themselves were unidentified. Because it originated among the officers of individual staff sections, the Army side of the controversy was referred to inaccurately as "the revolt of the colonels."

Eisenhower was furious. So was Wilson. So was Taylor, though he was less embarrassed by the substance of the publicity than by its emanation from his headquarters. So was Westmoreland, for as Townsend has said, a main duty of the SGS is "to be sure the chief of staff is never embarrassed." Wilson admitted that he and top Defense officials had not read the documents, and insisted that they represented in many cases the views of individual officers, not of the services involved. Taylor said simply, "I disavow them."

Westmoreland went to Palmer and said, "General, we can't have this. These people are causing trouble for the chief of staff, endangering him. We can't have this here so close to him." If Wilson had not read the offending papers, it was understandable. For Westmoreland, it was a more personal situation, although he had not read them, either. Mark S. Watson, writing in the Baltimore *Sun* May 19, 1956, was speaking with more authority than he made obvious when he noted that the leaked papers were "not top-level . . . it does not yet appear that the respective services' secretaries of chiefs of staff even saw them." Palmer agreed with Westmoreland that "we can't have this," and the SGS busied himself trying to tamp down the fuss, to see that it did not flare up again. But though it did not recur in exactly the same terms, another leak did occur that summer, and this time it was to the short-term benefit of the Army.

Radford not only gave short shrift to the Army's basic position, he laid down a proposal that went far beyond anything he had urged previously. It would have made drastic cuts in Army strength in the next four years, allowing only token American units in major theaters abroad. Taylor arrived at the Joint Chiefs meeting called to consider the Radford proposal armed with a detailed rebuttal, whose contributions from his staff sections had been coordinated by Westmoreland. It was strongly worded, concluding that the Radford proposal "represents an unacceptable military program for the United States." Predictably, his statement landed on ears tuned out. A decision was withheld, but approval of the chairman's proposal seemed certain. Then Anthony Leviero of the *New York Times,* whose reporting had been at the center of the furor in the spring, did it again. He laid down in print the approximate outlines of the Radford plan, and another controversy blew up, with investigations and recriminations. Radford's proposal was shelved, but only for a while. In 1957, Wilson announced a series of military personnel cuts, each hitting the Army hardest, bringing its combat strength down from eighteen to fifteen divisions, thinning them dangerously. Watson commented, "There is not much fat left. Muscle must now be cut."

The official theory that future wars would be atomic encouraged at least one change for which the Army could show genuine enthusiasm. That was the reorganization of the combat division to give it smaller, less cumbersome maneuver units, intended to operate independent of the traditional front lines of earlier wars. Westmoreland was closely involved with Taylor and his operations staff in devising the new commands and giving them a name—the "pentomic" division, made up of five battle groups instead of three regiments. That the change would mean sizable reductions in the manpower of each combat division made unaccustomed harmony with the concepts of the Defense Department and the administration; that it meant the same number of men might be stretched to fill more divisions helped the Army think it was a way of adjusting to the persistently dominant advocates of the bigger bomb. The "pentomic" structure would cut the standard infantry division by 3,700 men from a total of 17,455; an airborne division by 5,600 from 17,100; and only a "minor" number out of the 14,684 assigned to an armored division.

To put the new concept into effect, Taylor decided to reactivate his old division, the 101st Airborne. He pulled cadres from the 82nd Division and Westmoreland's former command, the 187th RCT, to form the new 101st at Fort Campbell, Kentucky. Gradually acquiring its nominal "pentomic" strength of 11,500 men, taking time out to send elements to Little Rock in the school desegregation crisis of 1957, the 101st taught its subordinate units the tactics envisioned by Taylor and his staff. It eventually was ready for a shakedown operation called Jumplight. From the division's trials and errors, standard operating procedures for the new Army organization were found and disseminated to other divisions shifting to the "pentomic" structure at home and overseas.

As 1958 began, Westmoreland had spent more than four years on Pentagon duty, more than making up for the absence of experience there on his earlier record. He was ready for another change, and if precedent were served he was ready to shift again from staff to command. Taylor was impressed by Westmoreland's performance as SGS, and gratified by his loyalty. He showed it by offering him command of the 101st Airborne Division.

It was a choice command. Considering Taylor's attachment to the division he had led into Normandy and across Europe, it came as a high compliment. This was not the only time Taylor had demonstrated his regard for Westmoreland. He had recognized the class of his artillery battalion on Sicily, tried to bring him into his 101st for the Normandy operation, quickly accepted him as the secretary of his General Staff. He was to be instrumental in later, loftier steps in Westmoreland's career—so much so, over a period of two decades, that some were to refer to the younger officer as Taylor's protégé.

Taylor no doubt saw something of himself in Westmoreland, especially after the rapport they had developed as chief of staff and SGS. But he also recognized that successful officers of Westmoreland's generation had led a different, much less leisurely career than those of his own level, who won their commissions in the 1920's. He felt that Westmoreland's impression of being all business, with little time for spontaneity or frivolity, was closely related to the circumstances of his life in the Army. Westmoreland's group was commissioned just before the war, and when wartime expansion began it moved ahead at a rate that sometimes turned its elders green. Taylor, for example, was graduated from West Point in the Class of 1922, and thirteen years later made captain. The same procedure for Westmoreland took four years; in thirteen he was a senior lieutenant colonel, and had served as a full colonel for three wartime and postwar years.

The end of Taylor's own term as chief of staff and his first retirement were approaching when he selected Westmoreland for command of the 101st. He seemed to speak for both Palmer and himself when he acknowledged that "those of us about one generation ahead" were always planning the career of Westmoreland and promising officers like him. In fact, he considered it "one of life's pleasures" to be able to do so. But he insisted that he had always done it for the good of the Army, not merely to advance Westmoreland or any other younger officer. Men do not advance in easy jobs, Taylor believes. You bring out their best by challenging them.

14

Challenge at Campbell

1958–1960

Westmoreland leaned forward between the pilot and copilot of a C–130 as the Hercules circled above Drop Zone Suk-chon, a clearing in the forest of southern Kentucky named for the objective where his old 187th Airborne RCT had made its first jump into action in the Korean War. The parachutes blossoming below him this time were not lower-ing soldiers into combat, but into a realistic training exer-cise called Operation Eagle Wing. His 101st Airborne Divi-sion had been scattered to air bases across the near Middle West, in Tennessee, Kentucky, Indiana, Ohio and Missouri. From those starting points the first companies of the 101st were converging on a precise schedule at Fort Campbell, tumbling from transports onto DZ's below, assaulting ter-rain objectives, preparing then to act as aggressors against the battle groups that would follow them down the next day. Westmoreland had been division commander for three weeks; this was the first large-scale maneuver over which he exercised direct control—at Fort Campbell or anywhere else.

The day's weather forecast had been marginal, with wind speeds expected to approach the danger mark. But the veteran Brigadier General Reuben Tucker, former commander of the 504th Parachute Infantry Regiment, was on the DZ as control officer, carefully monitoring an Air Force anemometer. The wind velocity registered below the prescribed maximum, he radioed the word to Operation Eagle Wing headquarters at Seward Air Force Base, Tennessee, and set off green smoke markers to invite the paratroopers in. The first strings of jumpers from the assault companies drifted in, collapsed their parachutes and sprinted off into mock battle.

Then, suddenly, Westmoreland saw field ambulances scurrying onto the DZ. The sight of their red crosses there among the parachutes chilled him. He was thousands of feet above his men, and they were in trouble. He radioed Seward, strapped tight his parachute, and bailed out into the same tricky wind that had created the emergency. His aide jumped behind him. Landing without incident, the commanding general started supervising first aid efforts among the injured paratroopers.

After that first element of safe jumps, the wind had increased and shifted. A shear and turbulence had developed above the DZ, and the anemometer on the ground was unable to detect it. The later jumpers were blown off target, hitting near the edge of the broad DZ, then being dragged up to three hundred yards into piles of rocks and debris bulldozed off the zone. There were scrapes, fractures, cuts and concussions among the paratroopers who were being loaded into the ambulances. Westmoreland had been on the ground for minutes before medics realized that some of the injured were in fact dead. Two were banged and impaled in the debris, which was as thick and deadly as a Civil War abatis. One had strangled on his denture in fighting his chute as he was dragged. Two had been choked by suspension lines in the same struggle. Dozens of living were sent to the base hospital.

This was the kind of unforeseeable challenge Taylor had picked Westmoreland to meet. Operation Eagle Wing had hardly begun. It could be called off, in a spirit of mourning and with certain resultant damage to the morale of the highly trained and motivated division. It could be continued, at the risk of further accidents and of having the officer who made that decision appear callous, even reckless.

Westmoreland continued it. The following day, he was the first man to dive out of a transport onto the same DZ. It is tradition among airborne troops that the senior officer jumps first, and Westmoreland had followed that tradition when he had the 504th Regiment at Fort Bragg. In this operation, Colonel Talton W. Long, commander of the leading battle group, had preceded his men out the door and tradition had been served. But Westmoreland, ever sensitive to relations with his troops—and with the public— made it policy in his 101st after that for the commanding general, not merely the senior officer of the individual unit involved, to lead the way. Operation Eagle Wing was carried through, and about two thousand soldiers leaped without major mishap after the first day's disaster.

After the operation's completion, Westmoreland was determined not to let the accidental deaths pass by without their somehow serving a useful purpose. What could be learned from them, how could the odds on recurrence be lengthened? He ordered his staff to prepare a study, not to fix blame but to try to give the incident a positive ending, however outweighed by the fact of the deaths. The study determined that aside from the caprices of the wind, always a potentially disastrous factor for airborne operations, the difficulty had been with the parachutes used that day. They were the recently introduced T–10 model, with canopies longer and more bag-shaped than the familiar broad, mushroom-shaped chutes. They were of more porous material and their design effectively made them more stable, reducing swinging back and forth on the way down. But once on the ground, they were much more difficult for troops to collapse. With the flatter models, a man can chase the chute, run onto one edge and tip the top edge under. But this was hard to do with the T–10. Westmoreland concluded that a reliable quick-release device was more necessary than ever with the new parachutes. The study recommended it, and he pushed it until testing began. The T–10 now in use has that quick-release handle, which can free a jumper from his harness either before he strikes the ground or immediately after landing.

In the remainder of Westmoreland's time at Fort Campbell there were many jumps, few injuries, no fatalities, no discernible loss of morale, and very few of the "quit slips" by which a paratrooper can formalize his feeling that his luck has run far enough, and he wants to jump no more.

The mission of the 101st Airborne was readiness. Its standing plans for an emergency called for movement of leading elements within six hours after receiving an order. Westmoreland always kept one of his five battle groups on two-week day and night duty as a division alert force, following a training schedule that kept it close to the base. Within that battle group, one company was designated as "immediate ready," with its men kept either in barracks or very nearby. Their individual equipment was packed, combat vehicles loaded, post property inventoried, and their assignment was to be ready for departure to any destination on two hours notice. Another company had orders for movement only an hour after the first, and the whole reinforced battle group was trained to be at planeside in three more.

When they grabbed their gear to respond to such hurry-up orders, the soldiers could not know where they were going or for how long. They were prepared for permanent change of station. The entire division kept up its wills, powers of attorney and immunizations, prepared to head for the tropics or the North. At division headquarters, there was an effort at heightened administrative readiness, emphasizing, for example, the use of business machines instead of old-fashioned typewriters to prepare rosters and records. The time needed to turn out a single aircraft manifest was cut from two hours to less than four minutes.

Westmoreland maintained that keeping a division in an edgy state of readiness was a harder job than preparing it for imminent combat. It was, he said, like "preparing the Army football team for the Navy game and postponing the contest to a day in the indefinite future to be selected without warning by the Navy."

Practice alerts and inspections helped keep the division on its toes. One afternoon when Westmoreland had been commanding general for six weeks, one of these inspections was under way. Brigadier General Charles Rich, assistant division commander, was looking over the 506th Battle Group, which was assembled with its "go" equipment. At the same time, the telephone rang at division headquarters. It was the Continental Army Command, calling Westmoreland. "You are about to get a real mission for your division," CONARC told him.

It ordered Westmoreland to assemble immediately six hundred men, commanded by a full colonel, for flight to Ramey Air Force Base, Puerto Rico. Further orders would be issued there. The unit's mission: to parachute into Caracas, Venezuela, if necessary to rescue Vice President Richard M. Nixon from the United States embassy, where he was besieged after his car had been damaged by spitting, jeering leftist demonstrators during a procession through the capital.

Westmoreland immediately gave the job to the 506th Battle Group, summoned its commanders and staff and briefed them while the troops were moving from inspection field to airfield. The division's G-3 called in Air Force C-130's which had a training drop under way. They landed, refueled, took aboard a helicopter, ammunition, enough rations for a five-day operation, and the troops of the 506th. Two hours and forty minutes after the first telephone call, the first Hercules took off. It was followed by others at approximate fifteen-minute intervals, in a long string headed for the Caribbean.

Officers of Westmoreland's command chortled when they heard that a concerned reporter in Washington had asked the White House where the Marines were who were supposed to protect Nixon in such an emergency. "I don't know where the Marines are, but the 101st Airborne Division is on the way to Ramey Air Force Base, Puerto Rico," is the way they relate the presidential spokesman's reply. Eight hours, twenty-five minutes after the alert order, the first planeload of paratroopers landed at Ramey, sixteen hundred miles from home.

Westmoreland realized his G–2 formerly had served as a military attaché at Caracas, and assigned him as deputy commander of the mission. He took part in preparing an assault plan as the troops winged south. The operation would drop two companies onto a golf course across the street from the embassy, to secure the embassy itself and a landing pad for the helicopter to evacuate the Vice President.

The battle group stood by in Puerto Rico for a day, until it was notified that Venezuelan police and soldiers had moved Nixon safely on his way. When the paratroopers were ordered home, Westmoreland squeezed the most possible in training value out of the expedition, and had them make assault jumps onto the Fort Campbell reservation on their return.

Because the performance of the 101st had been good in this emergency, Westmoreland decided it should be better. This was a period when Westmoreland devoted much of his business and private conversation to the subject of challenges. "Many men can do fifty to one hundred per cent more than they think they can do if they have a challenge," he would say. Later he phrased this as his "theory of the stretch—stretching men more than they might otherwise think they could be stretched." Accordingly, since the battle group had moved to Puerto Rico faster than expected, he cut the required time between being notified and being airborne from six to two hours.

He kept prodding in search of other ways of improving the division's showing in the field. The 82nd Division and the XVIII Airborne Corps, parent headquarters for both the 82nd and 101st, often used supplies positioned in advance on the field of maneuvers, on the probably accurate assumption that in combat, the necessary airlift to put them there would be available. But Westmoreland insisted that the 101st use only what it could bring with it. He lightened his own command post—something he had learned about back at Remagen—by combining the G–2 and G–3 (intelligence and operations) sections into one work area under two connected tents. Individual battle groups under his command were using more spacious quarters for the same function. To add realism by having troops drop onto unfamiliar ground, Westmoreland worked out a cooperative plan whereby the 101st jumped at Fort Bragg and the 82nd at Campbell, and encouraged spirited performance by having officers of the host base act as maneuver umpires.

With his compulsion for detail, Westmoreland had to resist the temptation to act as his own division chief of staff, or his own G–3. Often, he would strain his staff's flexibility by assigning a battle plan, awaiting its completion, complimenting his staff on its work, then scrapping the whole idea and ordering another entirely different approach, just to test his command post's speed and adaptability.

He laid strong emphasis, as always, on physical readiness, both for himself and his paratroopers. He accumulated more and more credit for jumps, usually going with his division staff into the small Los Banos DZ, near the center of the post. Because the DZ was small, the commanding general and his colleagues often wound up in the top of a tall tree. Once, when he and the staff made a night drop, the G–3 and the general's aide landed and started looking for him. They were wandering through the woods, whispering, "Where is he? He ought to be around here somewhere . . ." when a voice came down from above,

"Dad gum it, Tiger, stop fooling around down there and get me out of this tree!" "Tiger" was the aide's nickname, and the young captain could not restrain a laugh. "I'll get you when I get down from here," the voice said, and "Tiger" quickly became sober and helpful. That time, Westmoreland descended by dropping his reserve chute, and the G–3 and aide were able to use it to swing him back and forth until he could grab the tree trunk and slide down. More often, the technique was to drop the reserve while still strapped into the entangled main chute, then to release and climb down it to the ground.

That G–3, Lieutenant Colonel John K. Singlaub, had been an instructor at the Ranger school at Fort Bragg, and kept in touch with his old friends there. He arranged that whenever the Infantry School did not fill its course quotas, the Ranger faculty would give the 101st a call on Saturday and enough paratroopers would show up Sunday to fill up the new class. Thus, the 101st had more men with Ranger training than most other divisions. Westmoreland found these men better NCO's, especially for patrol work and squad leading. If such a course could make that difference, he contended, then every NCO in the division should go through it. Thus he founded a division school at Campbell, which he named the "Recondo" school—combining "reconnaissance" with "commando."

To start the school, he chose a redheaded major with a handlebar mustache. Normally, Westmoreland frowned on mustaches in his commands, but this major happened to have won the Medal of Honor for leading a bayonet charge in Korea. His name was Lou Millet, and his all-out leadership and showmanship helped make Recondo school a much-desired assignment for soldiers of the division.

The course used "courage tests," such as climbing a tall

tree, sliding down a sloping rope some one hundred yards and dropping into water, all the while yelling some gung-ho paratrooper slogan. It called on its students to improvise means of crossing deep streams, imagining themselves on patrol in enemy territory, making night parachute drops, stretching the individual soldier's map-reading and small unit control ability. The students took turns acting as patrol leaders under these circumstances, and returned to their companies with new confidence immediately obvious to their platoons and squads. Westmoreland's aim was to run every NCO in his division, from squad leader up, through the school, and he did.

Unexpectedly, when the Lebanon crisis of the summer of 1958 threatened, Westmoreland was warned that his division might have to move by ship instead of by air. He ordered the division's engineers to start a twenty-four-hour school to teach loading for sea transportation, and scrounged in all directions for blocks and chocks for rigging equipment on flatcars. He sent Singlaub to the Middle East for briefings on the situation in case the division had to respond, but this emergency, too, faded before the 101st was needed.

The point is that whatever the crisis, wherever, his division had to assume it would be involved. Often, looking ahead to that indefinitely postponed "Army-Navy game," Westmoreland inspected the alert battle group himself. Once, he dug into soldiers' packs at the airfield and discovered several were stuffed with paper, which was lighter and made a neater appearance than socks and ponchos. To discourage this sort of shortcut, he often turned a supposedly routine inspection into an extensive exercise. Working closely with the Continental Air Command, he volunteered his jumpers for weekend drops by transport squadrons of the Air Force Reserve. His soldiers, who might think they were falling out for a Saturday morning inspection, would find themselves flown to Utah or California, Florida or New York, transferred into C–119's of the reserve units, dropped onto some nearby bombing range or abandoned airbase, then loaded aboard big C–124's for the trip back to Campbell.

There was no guarantee that a commanding general could be popular among his troops while running this kind of operation, week in and week out. It was hell on the family life of his officers and senior NCO's, and on the romantic aspirations of the younger soldiers. Still, those who served there insist that the paratroopers "idolized" Westmoreland. He jumped with them, set them an immaculate soldierly example and, perhaps most important, made them feel like more than parts of an impersonal machine by trying to inform them as fully as he could of the reasons behind their strict routine.

At Campbell, and today, he preferred to make the program of educating and propagandizing his organization one of "command information," rather than "troop information," with the implication that he himself wanted direct responsibility. When directives came from the Pentagon, he gave them a personal Westmoreland or 101st Airborne slant to impart more meaning to his troops, He made sure they understood why this inconvenience, that alert, this shortage of equipment took place. The 101st retained a high reenlistment rate, based partly on the paratroopers' feeling that their commanding general cared about them as men.

Westmoreland recalled later that "when I had the great privilege of commanding the 101st Airborne I attempted to be seen by the soldiers of that division, all of them, approximately once a month. Which means that I spent little time in my office. I felt that I should not only be seen during duty hours but I should be seen during off-duty hours.

"About once a month I would go down to the local towns and visit the bars and the bowling alleys and the skating rinks. I would meet the proprietors and I would talk to the soldiers while they were drinking beer and relaxing. It had a good effect.

"One time I was visiting a roadhouse which is about thirty miles from Fort Campbell. To my great surprise, I found the place filled with soldiers of the 101st, all drinking beer, and all of them wanted me to join them with a beer. Of course I refused, although I do like beer.

"I went over to the table and said, 'This doesn't make any sense at all. We have places on the post for you to buy beer, which is a much better environment for you. And look at all the money you'll save because you can get beer for twenty cents on the post.'

"One soldier looked up and said, 'Sir, the beer here is fifteen cents. The proprietor cut the price to attract the trade.'

"I said, 'Well, now, let's be realistic about this; you had to pay your cost of transportation, the wear and tear on your automobile, if you have one, and gasoline, et cetera, and when you added it all up, I think this is pretty expensive beer.'

"And this soldier looked me in the eye and said, 'Sir, don't worry about that. We just drink until we get a profit.' "

The story is more than a little joke told on the general by himself. If literally true, it also makes a point about his persistence in finding out how his troops felt, and another that he did not intend to make, one that might help to explain why he had to work so hard and consciously at creating a feeling of closeness to them. That was his apparent inability to understand that any soldier, even a cocky paratrooper, may want to drink beer off the post just because it is off the post. To Westmoreland, it seemed illogical for anybody to want to drink off post when he could buy beer at Campbell for just a nickel more.

Westmoreland's trips to the joints along the highways outside Campbell often were made with the provost marshal of the post, to check on how the military police were doing their job. Sometimes he tried to make friends with the proprietors, and often slipped in an implication that if they did not run honest places they might find them off limits to Army customers.

When he arrived at Campbell, there were openly grumpy relations between the post and the surrounding towns and counties, as well as between the post's military command and its civilian employees. Looking back, Westmoreland considers the command of the 101st Airborne, which included running Fort Campbell, one of the most satisfying jobs he ever had—because the particular military demands placed on the 101st were combined with a broader community relations challenge than any he had met before.

The merchants in the towns near the post objected to the existence of the post exchange in time of peace, considering it unfair competition. The constables of Montgomery County, Tennessee, south of Fort Campbell, picked on soldiers at every opportunity to fatten themselves on the fee system, under which they got a cut of every fine levied.

Westmoreland launched a public relations campaign reminiscent of the ones he had devised while with the 82nd Airborne at Fort Bragg and with the 187th RCT at Beppu, but bigger and more sustained. He went speaking, to every

Rotary, Exchange, Kiwanis and any other club that would have him, anywhere within range of the post. He brought groups of club members, teachers, businessmen to the post for tours, lunches and parades. Some of his propaganda was subtle, mentioning the post exchange as one of the fringe benefits in a soldier's hard life. Some was more direct, challenging the fee system and disputing the frequently voiced contention that it could not be changed without an unlikely act of the rurally dominated Tennessee legislature. He called on local editors, judges, and the sheriff to make sure he was on firm ground, then faced county officials and said fairness demanded a change. When they repeated the argument that the legislature had to act, he laid his facts before them and they changed the system. The general likes to recall that when he arrived, both Nashville newspapers were hostile to Fort Campbell, and when he departed their friendliness toward the post was the only thing the *Banner* and the *Tennesseean* ever agreed on.

When the 101st was re-formed, the civilian employees at Campbell had had no division to support since the 11th Airborne was shipped to Europe in 1956. When Westmoreland took over the post, many of them were more concerned with protecting their coffee breaks and anticipating quitting hour than with the relationship of their jobs to the division's mission. He set out first to motivate them, then to increase their efficiency. The motivation step was closely comparable to his external relations program with the outside public. He made talks to the civilians, visited them on the job in the laundry, the ordnance repair shop and elsewhere, trying to keep them informed. When he had an award to make, he went to the man on the job, to honor him among his colleagues, rather than calling the man into his office. He put out bumper stickers and posters, urging workers to "Back STRAC." STRAC, the Strategic Army Command, was senior headquarters for the readiness force of combined arms of which the 101st was a striking arm. All of the general's contacts with the civilian employees were not rah-rah, however. He could be subtle, as when he noted that the threat of movement in the Lebanon crisis had caused the post to spend more than its allotted funds that summer—and his accompanying hope that the work remaining to be done could be accomplished without any lay-offs.

For his efficiency campaign, Westmoreland took up many of his former classmates at Harvard Business School on their offers of "If there's ever any way I can help you, just let me know." He left them know, and some of them came individually, while others sent experts in specific fields to Campbell. Consultants arrived from General Electric, Union Carbide, Bell Telephone, Goodyear, Frosty Morn and other industries to study the post's way of doing things. One of their quickest findings had the ring of heresy to an inspection-oriented career soldier: "Your shops are too clean"—too much time was being spent on sweeping up, taking hands away from production and maintenance.

On their recommendations, plus his own notes from Harvard and experience at the Pentagon, plus his inherited "parsimonious background," Westmoreland based an ambitious effort he entitled "Operation Overdrive."

He began it by issuing a firm statement of purpose: "The operating budget has been reduced this year, and it is anticipated that there may be a further reduction during the next fiscal year. At the same time additional requirements have been imposed on the post. Our only solution to the problem is to increase productivity within each work area. By this I mean the productivity of each civilian employee

257

and military man involved in our industrial and administrative activities . . . In short, we must increase our efficiency and effect the fullest utilization of our available manpower, funds, and facilities.

"You are urged to evaluate your performance, review and analyze your responsibilities, take stock of your practices, and work with us to increase our manpower productivity. As a first step in increasing our efficiency, an immediate goal of ten per cent increase is established without increase in work force. I know I can depend upon you to play an effective role in attaining this objective."

If that prospectus sounded like a company's president addressing a meeting of plant managers, the detailed subprograms within Operation Overdrive could be compared to instructions issued by plant managers to shop foremen. They reached into not only blue-collar work areas, but into barracks repair, dependents' quarters maintenance, post exchange management, clerical procedures, stock controls, supply and mess ordering, and, on the military side, new forms of measuring troop unit performance.

The post had a three-man maintenance team, a carpenter, plumber and electrician, which toured housing areas on the lookout for signals from dependents that they needed help. If a wife needed a wire spliced, the plumber and carpenter stood by and watched the electrician perform the job. Westmoreland cross-trained the workmen so that one man could do the jobs previously handled by the three, and that one toured the post on a motorbike, with orders not to patrol slower than a prescribed speed. There was other cross-training. Shops were consolidated and relocated for efficiency's sake. The quartermaster parachute maintenance crew was shifted at slow periods to help the quartermaster clothing and equipment repair shop at its peak periods.

In reporting on Overdrive, Westmoreland relied on percentage figures—a tendency that drew criticism from some directions on a later, more publicized assignment. He announced an 18 per cent increase in overall production on the post in the first year of the program, a 420 per cent boost in valid suggestions from soldiers and civilian employees, a 24 per cent drop in the number of combat troops doing administrative work, a 12 per cent reduction in rations ordered for the same post population. Once rolling, Overdrive was successful.

This attention to administration did not manage to bind Westmoreland to his headquarters. As he related, he tried to move about as much as possible. He went home to South Carolina, where he addressed the student body of his alma mater, Spartanburg High School, telling them that when he had been graduated in 1931, "our military 'policy' was unpreparedness," while current military forces numbered a million and a half. He warned the students not to be "lulled into complacency" by the guile of the Soviet Union. That same night, he continued that theme before the local American Legion, declaring that the only sure way of dealing with Moscow was "unceasing and maximum military preparedness." To assume the situation will work itself out otherwise is "wishful thinking," he told the Legionnaires, adding that the Soviet Union has a "long-range blueprint for a creeping campaign of aggression, economically, politically and militarily . . ." He said the United States would have to maintain a large military force into the future, and he foresaw no end to the draft.

That was not his only trip back to South Carolina. On another, more strictly professional visit, he jumped in as part of Operation White Cloud, an exercise aimed at an imaginary guerrilla enemy—an exercise that seemed to look ahead, with talk of "restoring and neutralizing the border between Caroltenn and the neighboring aggressor satellite . . ."

For shorter hops, to surprise his own soldiers in the field, lessen his dependence on other trained men and learn the capabilities of equipment that would play an increasing role in warfare and his own career, Westmoreland took helicopter piloting lessons. For the would-be aviation cadet of 1936, it was fun. Westmoreland's coordination was good, and he became a passable pilot, although for a while his staff officers were concerned every time they heard the H–13 come to earth with a loud flop outside the division headquarters.

No flop was audible in Washington, however. As seen and heard from the Pentagon, Westmoreland had compiled a record as an outstanding division commander. The Army's chief of staff, again with Maxwell Taylor's recommendation, was conscious when he approved Westmoreland's next billet that he was placing the young major general in a line of succession that included some great names of American military history.

15

A Lasting Impression

1960–1963

All West Pointers, but few others, have heard of Colonel Sylvanus Thayer, the "father" of the United States Military Academy, who put it on a lasting academic footing between 1816 and 1833. Thayer, like Richard Delafield, Albert L. Mills, Hugh Scott and Samuel E. Tillman, earned his reputation primarily as superintendent at West Point. But his other successors include Robert E. Lee, Pierre G. T. Beauregard, Douglas A. MacArthur, and Maxwell D. Taylor, who passed through on their way to other wars.

When Westmoreland became the forty-fifth superintendent of the academy on July 1, 1960, he was but forty-six years old. Among all his predecessors, only MacArthur in his post–World War I glory had come to the job at an earlier age. Neither President Dwight D. Eisenhower, who appointed him, nor Taylor, who recommended him, nor Westmoreland himself expected this prestigious position to be the summit of his career. It was to be not capstone, but stepping stone. Yet, while realizing this, Westmoreland managed again to avoid the frequent failing of the ambitious—that of looking ahead so eagerly that the details of the job at hand lose their fascination. Although some of his assignments came as rewards, each also came as a test, and any one of them could turn into the job where finally his ability and determination merely matched, without surpassing, the challenge. That is the level where military careers lose their momentum, where officers make the decision to retire, honorably and with no implication of failure.

But a 160-year-old educational institution, built of stone and tradition, does not respond to mere forceful leadership as promptly as a battalion of cannon or a division of paratroopers. Before he ordered changes in curriculum or anything else affecting West Point's educational program, Westmoreland was obliged to convince the academic board that changes should be made. That board included the dean, heads of the academy's departments and the registrar. All of those officers were assigned on permanent tenure. They were aware that each superintendent, in modern times, stays in that position only about two years, usually not even seeing a single class through from plebe year to graduation. They are so situated that they can tell a new superintendent that many things he suggests already have been tried long ago, and found lacking.

It was not an unprecedented situation for Westmoreland. His dealings with senior generals when he was secretary of the General Staff had put him in a comparable situation, though at West Point the ultimate responsibility would lie with him. At the outset, he felt his way with the academic board, putting his energy into carrying out changes approved before his arrival, producing more immediate action in areas where he had more experience, where no deliberations by the board were necessary.

To begin with, he ordered the same kind of efficiency studies he had conducted on post operations at Fort Campbell. Within three months, he had introduced a point system, "identifying individual worker productivity, permitting comparison among employees and creating a competitive spirit among efficiency boards maintained at the work site." He plastered the area with posters: "West Point Points the Way in Post Efficiency." In his annual report, Westmoreland said, "It is intended that the program will increase efficiency by identifying and decreasing idle time, and provide a firmer basis for manpower requirements."

He shifted fifty separate logistical functions—storerooms, offices—from place to place, and moved the academy's post office and shipping terminal. He planned to bring in a computer to aid in post management and academy record-keeping, and serve as a modern educational and research tool for cadets. The rescheduling of much of the corps's field training into summer sessions allowed him to recommend reassignment of 204 troops from the academy's school troops unit, the 1st Battle Group, 1st Infantry. By the end of the 1960–1961 school year, he could report in the percentage figures he loved so well that overall output by post employees was up 10.8 per cent. Later similar reports were accompanied by examples: the laundry processed more pieces with six fewer employees, the dry cleaners did the same with one fewer; maintenance, motor pool and engineers followed their lead. Use of electricity was down. The furniture shop was put on an assembly line basis, which brought up its production figures and created an uncharitable opinion of Westmoreland which still can be elicited from old-time employees in the shop.

263

Officers who have devoted most of their careers to West Point believe that MacArthur as superintendent was remembered most for his emphasis on intensive physical training for all cadets, Taylor for instituting military psychology and leadership as a formal course, Garrison Davidson for the four-year study of curriculum revisions which was inherited by Westmoreland for implementation, and Westmoreland for his innovations in post and academy management.

But Westmoreland did not minimize those fields in which his predecessors will be better remembered. He outdid anything MacArthur would have dreamed of in physical training, for example, by working into the summer schedule of field work for yearlings a Recondo course like the one he had instituted at the 101st Airborne. *Pointer View,* the post newspaper, described Recondo from a cadet's impressions:

"The course lasts one week. During that time the cadet goes on day and night patrols with only a lensatic compass as his guide, climbs up and down a mountain, defends himself using only his hands as a weapon and takes the 'slide for life.' On a patrol, a platoon moves out into the woods and is split into two squads. Navigating by compass, each squad stalks an objective, takes it, then returns to a rendezvous point.

"The next day, with little rest, the cadets tackle their next objective, a craggy Hudson highlands mountain. Using knotted ropes, natural holes and hand holds, they scale a vertical mountain face and descend using climbing ropes. Encouraged by the 'friendly' NCO's the following day, they charge into a pit filled with wood chips for hand-to-hand combat. 'Don't touch that sandbag, Mister,' they hear as they defend themselves against their classmates armed with

264

bayonets or rifles. 'You touched that sandbag, Mister. Give me 20 pushups.' 'Yes, sergeant.'

"The last day they tackle the 'slide for life.' First, up one-by-one onto a 100-foot-high tower. Grab the pulley on a rope swinging over Lake Popolopen. Down he goes toward the water. He lets go only when an instructor signals with a flag. 'You splashed me, Mister. Give me ten.' 'Yes, sergeant. One, two, three . . .' Next up onto a 20-foot-high tower. Here they walk across a narrow log to another tower, stepping gingerly over stationary obstacles. 'Sergeant, Recondo (cadet's name) requests permission to step on your platform.' 'Do you want to mount my platform, Mister?' 'Yes, sergeant, Recondo ———— requests permission to mount your platform.' 'You may mount my platform, Recondo.'

"Then, down a ladder and the test is finished. The cadet now has a small idea of the skills needed for counter-insurgency. Those who complete all phases of this rigorous training are privileged to wear the Recondo patch, a silver and black arrowhead with USMA inscribed on it."

Staying in shape and in the eye of his charges, Westmoreland would turn up to join cadets on conditioning hikes in the mountains, and played tennis and squash regularly. But his interest in personal and intra-academy physical training was at least equaled by his attention to intercollegiate competition, for he knew that success there, however peripheral to education, had an important impact on the public's opinion of the Army, the cadets, their coaches, the academy and, not least, the academy's superintendent.

In his initial annual report, Westmoreland made a point of the fact that in 1960–1961, West Point varsity teams won 137 contests, lost sixty-seven and tied two, for a .671 percentage. But he did not single out the performance of the football squad, most noticed of all the varsity teams. He did not have to. All sports fans and academy alumni knew that the team that once ranked with the nation's best in the days of Coach Earl H. Blaik, fullback Felix Blanchard and half-back Glenn Davis had fallen on lean days. There had been a deemphasis of big-time sports since a cheating scandal in 1951 involving a group of football players. Under Coach Dale Hall, the former halfback and basketball star, the foot-ball team compiled a record of sixteen wins, eleven losses and five ties. What was much worse, it had developed a habit of losing to Navy. In November 1960, Westmoreland went down to Philadelphia and traditionally was joined on the Army side of Franklin Field for one half of the game by the President. He was embarrassed that his cadets lost again before that old Army man, Dwight Eisenhower.

The evening after that game, Army and Navy faced each other again, this time in the television quiz contest, the College Bowl. The producers had begun what they hoped would be a long series of confrontations between the two academies on the day when interest in any Army-Navy com-petition was at its height. Navy had won the first year. And that evening, Navy won again. Westmoreland's embarrass-ment was compounded, and he promptly announced that this could not go on.

Back at West Point, he called in the dean, Brigadier General William W. Bessell, Jr., and told him flatly that the Army was going to win next year's quiz. Bessell was for calling off the series immediately, on the basis that the con-test was purely a matter of chance and did not reflect the intellectual resources of the two academies. But Westmore-land said, "We will do it once more—and we will win."

While the Weight Lifting and Ordnance clubs were

being disbanded among the cadet corps that winter, a West Point College Bowl Organization was formed. The quickest-witted, most broadly informed cadets were picked, split into battalion teams and drilled on fast recall. The academic departments submitted long lists of questions in their specialties. The teams practiced, using buzzers as on the television show. Before the return match in 1961, the competitors were eliminated until two teams of four cadets each survived—one black team, one gold. At a final practice session, Westmoreland sat out in front and saw the gold (second) team win. But the black team was sent to the television studio, and it beat Navy. On that note, Westmoreland canceled further participation in the quiz series.

Army's performance on the football field was a stickier problem. To correct it was not a simple matter of organizing to try harder. It meant a change of personnel, and that implied a change in the deemphasis policy that had prevailed for more than a decade. Westmoreland pondered this for a long time, through two full football seasons, meeting with the Athletic Board in search of answers. Then he acted, releasing Hall from his contract.

Reporting to academy alumni, Westmoreland acknowledged that "the decision was solely mine and I assume full responsibility for it." Then, in typical tabular form, he explained it:

"1. It is my conviction that West Point should strive for excellence in every endeavor. This applies to academics, military duties, extra-curricular activities and athletics—not to exclude football.

"2. The highly selected young men that we have in the corps of cadets deserve the finest leadership, instruction and coaching that is practically obtainable.

"3. It is to the national interest, to the interest of the

Army, and of the academy that we, by our performance, create a public image of a winner. I do not presume to suggest that we expect to come out on top in all things, but I do have the firm conviction that we should more than hold our own with any institution competing with us on common ground. Our outstanding young men, esprit de corps, and concerted efforts should cause us, with understandable exceptions, to be habitually victorious.

"4. An atmosphere in which there is an absence of full confidence in a coaching staff is incompatible with the principles that guide this institution toward the attainment of its objectives."

Westmoreland added that he had not based his decision on any one game, but on the whole season. He complimented Hall for his "high character," and noted that the coach was being paid for the remaining year of his contract.

"I would like all graduates to understand that this decision does not presuppose that an imbalance will develop within this institution with respect to undue emphasis on athletics, to include football. It is my intention to maintain equilibrium among our programs. The fundamentals that we value will most assuredly be maintained. Excellence in all our activities will, however, be a salient objective," the superintendent concluded.

His move was noted, reported and discussed. But it was his second step that made news. He did not have to spread the word that Army needed a new coach, and given the circumstances of Hall's departure, it was widely assumed that the next one would arrive with a winning record behind him. Rumors of selections arose and drifted away until the first week of January 1962, when Westmoreland announced that he had hired Paul Dietzel, who had run up a record of forty-six wins, twenty-four losses and three ties as head coach at Louisiana State University.

The ensuing uproar came from several directions—from sportswriters, educators and others who chose to disregard Westmoreland's assurance that the shakeup "does not presuppose that an imbalance will develop within this institution with respect to undue emphasis on athletics . . ." But the loudest cry came from the Louisiana congressional delegation, which seemed to rank Army's acquisition of Dietzel with such outrages as the march north through Dixie by another West Pointer (and former president of LSU), William Tecumseh Sherman—especially since the coach's contract at LSU still had a year to run.

Again, Westmoreland used the West Point alumni magazine for a report defending his action. He recalled that Dietzel had been freshman coach at West Point, and later Blaik's assistant. He insisted that his move had been "ethical and aboveboard," with the advance knowledge and later concurrence of LSU. "Unfavorable publicity received by the academy is regretted," Westmoreland said. But as to the contract, "In this day it is one of the facts of life that every topflight coach is signed to a long-term contract. As a matter of fact, Paul Dietzel had a year to go on his contract when he was released to go to LSU. Although our actions were proper in every way, hiring an established coach carries with it the risk of censure." He said, "Dietzel did not agree to come for the money" (the salary was reportedly $18,500 at both schools), "but because of a desire to work with, and do his part in the training of, young men dedicated to a life of service to our country."

The Louisiana delegation made its fuss for the edification of its constituents, but alumni of West Point were interested in winning football games. (They could not know then that Dietzel's West Point record also would be so-so.) Those alumni also ran the United States Army, and had important influence on any executive or legislative changes at the United States Military Academy.

Westmoreland had been in close contact with prominent alumni since his arrival. He was pleased with his organization of a West Point Superintendent's Fund, a permanent system for soliciting major gifts from graduates and "friends" of the academy, each bequest earmarked for a specific project. He paved the way by submitting the idea to MacArthur, Eisenhower, Bradley and other famous names from the alumni register, and after they endorsed it he placed them on his board of honorary advisers. Among his active advisers were men from his past, Collins, Ridgway, Taylor and Gavin, and Lucius D. Clay served as chairman of the fund committee. He listed projects for which contributions would be encouraged: an electric chapel carillon, "a major sculptural project showing the contribution of West Point to American history," a new amphitheater, an activities center for first classmen, improved ski slope facilities, an expanded skating rink—all commendable works for which government funds would be unlikely. The program was promptly effective; many of these original target projects are in use today.

By the spring of 1962, as he approached what would be the end of an average superintendent's tour at the academy, Westmoreland had recorded these accomplishments around the edges of West Point's strictly educational function. And he also had achieved a comfortable working relationship with the academic board, whose members appreciated his willingness to listen patiently, his respect for their deeper educational backgrounds, and the firmness with which he stuck with a decision once he had made it.

He sped adoption of a math course applicable to economic allocation of military resources. He pressed ahead with the scheduled curriculum revisions, adding elective courses for the first time in the academy's history, and expanding the choice of electives each year. The board had resisted the proposal of his predecessor, Davidson, to curtail civil engineering, ordnance and perhaps military law to make room for the optional courses. It remained a tough problem. Westmoreland called meetings of the board, announcing in advance that no decision would be made on those particular days, to encourage the faculty to debate the question from all sides. Bringing in electives seemed a fine and modern idea, but reducing strictly military instruction to do it seemed self-defeating for a military academy. Finally, Westmoreland and the board reached agreement that a compromise way was to shift more of the academic load into the plebe year, clearing later time for electives.

Parallel to introduction of electives, Westmoreland put into effect a program of validating credit for courses, also approved before his arrival. It allowed cadets credit for courses taken at other colleges, or for proficiency tests in a subject, thus enabling them to take more advanced work during their academy years.

The board won him to its side on some questions, too. He came in with the belief that the permanent professors should do more classroom teaching, rather than relying heavily on officers assigned there for a single duty tour. He apparently got the idea from civilian educators who were publicly calling for more teaching by senior professors in their own schools. But the board convinced him that West

Point had an unusual situation, with department heads handling most of their own administration, selecting teaching staffs (often from officers they had known in their earlier careers), choosing textbooks and supervising. Again, there was an Air Force Academy suggestion that the service academies should begin granting masters' degrees. The board opposed it, expressing satisfaction with the existing system of sending academy graduates to civilian universities for advanced degrees. Westmoreland backed the board.

Another of Westmoreland's innovations was extension of the popular "third lieutenant" program overseas. Cadets already were being sent to Army units in the States for a month as platoon leaders or assistant platoon leaders, getting indoctrination into life in the real Army. Westmoreland gained permission for selected members of the first class to be assigned to similar duty with Seventh Army combat outfits in Europe.

As superintendent, Westmoreland had brought in two prominent consultants on the academic curriculum, one for mathematics, science and engineering, the other for humanities and social sciences. He endorsed and expanded the practice of inviting visiting professors for single courses, and had specialists in for lectures to the faculty. He supported Bessell's idea for creating permanent associate professors—permitting officers who previously had taught at the academy to return with tenure after a total of fifteen years Army duty.

Cadet morale was boosted by his approval of cooler, short-sleeved summer uniforms. Later, he allowed second classmen privileges formerly reserved for the first class—attendance at the theater, gymnasium, skating rink, lectures, seminars and clubs during evening call to quarters. First classmen were allowed in the officers' club on weekends. "As a result of this policy, a number of cadets have fallen by the wayside," he reported, "but it is apparent that these individuals would inevitably have run into trouble at a later date, perhaps as officers." No doubt remembering his own nights of cadet cramming, he permitted lights in barracks after taps—first desk lamps only, then overhead lights —and pronounced the experiment a success. Upperclassmen also were given a greater role in training their juniors.

Westmoreland not only kept his current cadets and their instructors alert by dropping in unannounced on every course offered during the year to all four classes; he also formalized the academy's interest in its past and future students. He ordered a "product evaluation" study of academy graduates' performance during their first years of commissioned service, to see where improvements might be needed. And he began a systematic search for outstanding high school students as potential cadets. In this connection, he tabulated the secondary school achievements of an arriving class. Of their number, 10.8 per cent had been valedictorians or salutatorians of their classes; 14.5 per cent were student body or class presidents; 28.9 per cent were athletic team captains, and so on—including, significantly for him, 12.6 per cent who were Eagle Scouts.

In that spring of 1962, what was happening in Southeast Asia demanded more and more of the attention of American professional soldiers. The Vietnam war was not new, but it was growing, and the administration in Washington foresaw the day when it might grow still more demanding.

Lyndon B. Johnson, then Vice President, had alluded to it when he spoke at West Point's commencement exercises the year before. "The Communists," he said, "will find that a nation which produced Davy Crockett, Daniel Boone and Jim Bowie is afraid of no forest, no swamp, no game of fighting, however toughly played." President John F. Kennedy ordered new orientation in the Army toward guerrilla warfare. The Special Forces School at Fort Bragg came into being; a counterinsurgency adviser to the Joint Chiefs of Staff was appointed. At West Point, the superintendent named a committee to see what part of the academy program already pertained to this kind of war, and recommend additions to it. Because counterinsurgency is not merely a matter of tactics, weapons and supplies, some courses in academic subjects such as history and social science were judged to be applicable, and a special eight-hour block of instruction in counterinsurgency as such was scheduled for first classmen. Colonel Richard L. Clutterbuck, of the British Army, came to lecture on how the Communist guerrilla effort in Malaya had been defeated.

The Vice President and visiting lecturers were among the dozens of guests entertained by Westmoreland and his wife at Quarters 100, the historic house alongside The Plain where the superintendents of the past had lived. When the Westmorelands arrived at West Point, that home was being renovated, so they lived for a while in a brick house among the colonels' families around Lusk Reservoir. Later, when they were in the spacious Quarters 100, they had cocktails or dinners for foreign generals, politicians, nobles—some who were promptly forgotten, others for whom Westmoreland had devout admiration.

Douglas A. MacArthur was one of the latter. Westmoreland had sent a delegation of cadets to wish him a happy birthday when he turned eighty-two, and MacArthur came back to the academy in May to accept the 1962 Sylvanus Thayer award.

Westmoreland and the cadet brigade commander

boarded a jeep with the old soldier as he reviewed the long gray line for the last time. Then MacArthur stood before the corps in Washington Hall and delivered, apparently without preparation, a forty-minute speech that stirred Westmoreland and had some of the cadets and staff struggling with their sentiments. Westmoreland introduced the five-star general as "one of America's most illustrious soldiers," and MacArthur eloquently spun a special West Point version of the "old soldiers never die" address he had made before Congress eleven years earlier. He dwelt on the academy's motto, "Duty, Honor, Country," as he told the cadets that "your mission is to win our wars," and concluded by acknowledging that "the shadows are lengthening for me . . . today marks my final roll call with you. I bid you farewell."

Less than a month later, the 1962 academic year ended with further eloquence, this time from Kennedy himself. When the President's helicopter alighted on the parade ground, Westmoreland was there to greet him and introduce him to his staff. Then he led Kennedy to his quarters where the President met Kitsy and their two daughters, and asked whether that was the whole family. Westmoreland had to tell the President, "No, sir, I have a seven-year-old son who was looking forward to meeting you till I told him he'd have to take off his baseball uniform and put on a suit and tie. He said, 'Under those conditions I'm not interested.' " Kennedy was tickled.

In his commencement address, Kennedy reflected that it often is hard to follow a military life in peacetime. "When there is a visible enemy to fight in open combat, the answer is not so difficult. But when there is a long, slow struggle, with no immediate visible foe, your choice will seem hard indeed. But you have one satisfaction, however difficult those days may be: when you are asked by a President of the United States or by any other American what you are doing for your country, no man's answer will be clearer than your own."

It was a spring of inspiration for West Pointers, with a yet uncertain anticipation that the foe would soon be more visible, and the combat more open. And in that spring, Westmoreland made a decision that an officer with less certainty of his own standing would not have ventured. He was eligible for transfer from West Point after two successful years. He also was eligible for promotion to lieutenant general. He chose instead to stay at West Point, in a billet that is specifically restricted to two-star generals. He knew he was not passing up a third star permanently; he and General George H. Decker, Army chief of staff, had a mutual understanding of that. But few would have had his confidence that he could make up for lost time after voluntarily remaining at the academy for another year because he wanted to attend to unfinished business. While he was preparing for his third year as superintendent, John H. Michaelis, highly decorated hero with the 101st Airborne in World War II and the 27th (Wolfhound) Infantry Regiment in Korea, became the first member of their West Point Class of 1936 to be promoted to lieutenant general.

The main unfinished business to which Westmoreland referred was the expansion of the cadet corps and the physical facilities in which it is housed and educated. Historically, the regiment of cadets had been a far smaller body than the brigade of midshipmen at Annapolis. Studies had concluded that the service academies ideally should provide half of each year's new officers in each branch, as a "benchmark of comparison" for those commissioned through the ROTC and officers candidate schools. West Point's board of visitors, made up largely of Congressmen, had approved the idea of expansion. Westmoreland had met with the superintendents of the other academies and won their agreement in principle that all should have the same enrollment. But formal congressional authorization still had been withheld.

Westmoreland went to work on this issue as the new school year began, appointing a committee to concentrate on expansion planning. And when he shared a box with the President that fall at Franklin Field, he scored some points even while Dietzel's Black Knights were losing to Navy again. At halftime, when the cadets marched onto the field, Kennedy asked Westmoreland why he had not brought the entire corps to the game. Westmoreland said he had, and that was it parading below. And, as if he had planned it that way, he followed up by noting to the President that he had submitted legislation to expand the corps to the size of the naval academy brigade. Kennedy was impressed, and the next Congress authorized a gradual increase in the corps's strength to 4,417, with matching expansion at the naval and Air Force academies.

For decades, there had been piecemeal expansion of the physical plant at West Point—a building there, a new residential section here. MacArthur, as superintendent, had proposed relocating Michie Stadium from the heights down next to the Hudson, where the railroad, river boats and other transportation could unload at its gates. He also wanted to move the cadet barracks onto Constitution Island, in the river. Since his time, there had been few suggestions so sweeping, but many for individual building projects. Westmoreland looked over all these ideas, compared them to the still broader needs for imminent expansion of the corps, and developed a single comprehensive plan.

In his survey, he had found that a major block to approval of some acutely required projects had been the assumption that the academy's noblest old grads—MacArthur, Eisenhower and others—would be insulted if their former barracks and classrooms were torn down for the sake of progress. So he went directly to those alumni for support. As one colleague tells it, he had just won Eisenhower's endorsement and was departing his Gettysburg farm when the former President called out, "Oh, by the way, I think you ought to go talk to MacArthur about it, too." Westmoreland had anticipated him, of course, and with the backing of those two, his plan was authorized by Congress with little further resistance. Today, construction cranes and masons are busy enlarging the cadet dining hall, adding new wings to the cadet barracks and starting other building projects, all in gray stone to match that which has weathered through the years on the Hudson highlands.

With these successes accompanying the further evolution of the academic curriculum and tightening of post management, Westmoreland was satisfied that his business at West Point finally was finished. He was leaving a tangible, granite impression. In June 1963, he asked his old friend Maxwell Taylor to address his last graduating class. Later that same month he loaded Kitsy, Stevie, Margaret and Rip in a Ford station wagon and drove south, back to Fort Bragg, where a new command and that delayed third star awaited him.

16

"They Want Above All Things a Leader . . ."

1963–1964

At bright midmorning, Westmoreland stood at attention on the parade field at Fort Bragg and took a major general's thirteen-gun salute from Battery A of the 319th Field Artillery. Fifty state flags stirred in a light summer breeze as he trooped the line of the honor guard, soldiers picked from the 187th Airborne. Briskly, he was briefed then on his new command and forthcoming maneuvers.

At 5:30 that afternoon, Westmoreland led a stick of paratroopers who had served under him in other units as they dived from a C–130 Hercules over Drop Zone Sicily, named for the objective onto which the 82nd Airborne Division had made its first combat jump.

That is how he took over XVIII Airborne Corps and Fort Bragg on July 15, 1963. It was his third tour of duty at Bragg—first as an artillery battalion commander in 1941–1942, then as a regimental commander and division chief of staff from 1946 to 1950, now as senior officer of the entire post. His command of XVIII Corps stretched far beyond Bragg, giving him control not only of the 82nd Airborne and the eighty thousand soldiers, employees and dependents at the North Carolina base, but also of the 101st Airborne, still stationed at Fort Campbell; other Army divisions available for specific missions; and supporting units scattered at fifty-three posts around the country.

XVIII Corps was the striking arm of STRAC, the Strategic Army Corps, and Westmoreland already was closely attuned to its mission of readiness. He had lived with it for two years as commanding general of the 101st, and was dealing with familiar problems and people as he moved into the next higher level within what he called "freedom's fire brigade."

His responsibility for the fastest-moving element of STRAC gave him a particular concern for logistics—for the readiness not only of men, but of supplies and equipment, and of the means to move them. He was authorized to maintain direct interservice liaison with the Military Air Transport Service, which would lift his troops wherever they were needed. This was, in his case, a formality that legalized the passing of paper back and forth with MATS; in Korea and Japan, then later at Campbell, he already had made a strong point of developing informal friendships with the air officers on whom he had to depend. Westmoreland also conducted thorough logistics readiness inspections of the units under his control. One officer said the general and his staff would move through an outfit under inspection "like a plague of locusts." Another, a former logistics deputy of the Continental Army Command, noted that STRAC had "units to operate ports or to unload in the stream if ports are not available . . . and to operate railroads. We have long-haul units for highway transport and units to build roads behind the advance of our combat units . . . We can maintain our equipment, thousands of tons of everything so essential for sustained combat."

It was a field of experience that would be invaluable to Westmoreland in the near future. The first field exercise held by the corps under his command, which began less than a week after his arrival, also had a close pertinence to what lay ahead.

That was Swift Strike III, the largest peacetime maneuvers in the nation's history. The exercises were conceived as an example of the type of limited war situation in which the modern Army, and especially STRAC, might find itself involved overnight. A background scenario was prepared, setting the hypothetical stage. It imagined a conflict between "Blue Homeland, a strong country and a constitutional federal republic," and "Red Homeland," another strong country which was exerting such unwanted influence over a small third nation, neutral Columbia, that "maintenance of internal order would be a problem." Tension mounted as Red Homeland sent in "volunteers," and Blue Homeland sent in guerrilla organizers. Step by step, the two major countries approached war over little Columbia. One hundred thousand men, airborne and surface-bound, aviators and cannoneers, were assigned to the maneuvers. They covered a broad South Carolina area over which Westmoreland had practiced war twenty-one years earlier. The names of the rivers were Pee Dee and Savannah, the air bases Donaldson and Myrtle Beach, among others. Their relationship to what was happening in the real world could hardly have been more obvious had they been code-named Mekong and Bassac, Da Nang and Bien Hoa.

Westmoreland hesitated no more in assuming working

command in the field than he had in making his first parachute jump with the corps a few days earlier. His staff
quickly became aware that he functioned to a large extent
as his own operations officer. During the day, he would tour
his units, making small talk with privates, chatting with
commanders to give them a clearer idea of what he had
assigned them in written orders. Back at his command post,
he would call in his principal staff officers and discuss the
corps's next moves, giving his aides an opportunity to pick
holes in his plans before they were hardened. After the
evening meal, he would have a "brainstorming" session
with the entire staff group on logistical, intelligence, communications and other aspects of the forthcoming action.
One of those who took part called those evenings "crash
feasibility studies." They lasted until close to midnight, and
Westmoreland was up early the next day, back in the field,
supervising the orders thus formulated.

Swift Strike III was still under way when the third star
Westmoreland had passed up the year before by remaining
at West Point finally came through. Lieutenant General
Albert Watson II, commanding general of the Third Army,
came to Westmoreland's office at Bragg to pin on the added
star. One of the newly created lieutenant general's first
duties in that rank was to congratulate his corps for its
performance in the mass maneuvers. He told the troops that
they had operated "at a tempo at least twice as fast as we
would encounter in combat. We extended ourselves almost
to the limit." The personnel and other payloads dropped
and flown into the exercise exceeded those brought into
Normandy by the 82nd and 101st divisions, he added.

One of the few functions at Fort Bragg which did not
fall under Westmoreland's jurisdiction was the Special Warfare School, created by President Kennedy's order. But his

lack of authority there did not prevent his taking a particular interest in the counterinsurgency tactics being taught at the school. It was run by his West Point classmate Major General William P. Yarborough, and Westmoreland worked closely with him, observing Special Forces training and demonstrations, bringing Green Beret students into his corps's exercises. In addition, the 82nd Airborne had organized a Ranger-style school patterned after the Recondo course Westmoreland had set up with the 101st, and the general frequently rode out to check on its activities.

Fort Bragg did not escape the kind of efficiency drive Westmoreland had imposed on Fort Campbell and West Point, either. With those campaigns behind him, he rocked Bragg by setting a goal of a 20 per cent increase in employee productivity. Labeling Bragg, with its $148,000,000 annual payroll, as "both a city and big business," he elevated his deputy chief of staff to deputy post commander, and designated him "city manager" to preside over the efficiency program. It was beginning to take effect in the fall of 1963 when two events took place that eventually were to pull Westmoreland into the headlines read by a shaken world.

On November 1, in Saigon, Premier Ngo Dinh Diem was deposed by a military coup, and later slain. Three weeks later in Dallas, President Kennedy was killed by an assassin's bullets.

Diem had been hard for Americans to deal with. Politically, and hopefully militarily, his fall was considered by most in the administration as a positive development. But if his successors were to be dealt with any more easily, the dealing would have to be done by someone who had not been tied tightly to Diem. Henry Cabot Lodge, on the diplomatic side, had arrived after Diem's decline in Washington's favor had accelerated, and he had been stern with the premier from the start. General Paul D. Harkins, on the military side, was so closely identified with Diem that his influence on the premier's successors could not be great. He had to be replaced, and for such a sensitive assignment, the new man in the White House would give meticulous attention to the replacement.

President Lyndon B. Johnson; Robert S. McNamara, Secretary of Defense; Cyrus R. Vance, Secretary of the Army; General Maxwell D. Taylor, off the retired list for duty as chairman of the Joint Chiefs of Staff, and General Earle G. Wheeler, chief of staff of the Army, all realized that the selection of a new American military chief for Vietnam could mean failure or success in a venture to which the United States already had made heavy commitments of prestige, though not yet of personnel.

When they began their search in the final weeks of 1963, they did not restrict it to the Army. While the Army played the primary role in the advisory program, the senior American officer in Saigon would be concerned with a combined arms effort. His personal qualities, as much as his strictly military experience, would be considered. They wanted an officer who could handle surprises, one who would not arrive in Saigon with the assumption that he was bringing with him all the answers, one who would be receptive to learning on the job.

At the Pentagon, the records of thirty to forty officers were examined, their individual traits discussed. Gradually, their number was reduced. So were the service branches involved: by the time a handful of generals were selected for consideration at the White House, all of them were from the Army. The President was presented with the names of four men, and told that they were all so capable that the choice might be settled fairly by the flip of a coin.

The senior man among them was Lieutenant General Harold K. Johnson, then serving as the Army's deputy chief of staff for military operations. The junior nominee was Major General Bruce Palmer, Jr., assigned as Harold Johnson's assistant for plans and operations. The other two had been promoted to lieutenant general on the same day. They were Creighton W. Abrams, Jr., commanding general of V Corps, and Westmoreland.

Johnson, commissioned from West Point in the Class of 1933, was captured at Bataan as a battalion commander in the Philippine Scouts, and survived the Bataan death march and three and a half years as a prisoner of war. His postwar career had been heavy with staff assignments, including outstanding service with the G–3 section of the General Staff at the Pentagon during Westmoreland's duty there in the mid-1950's.

Palmer, Abrams and Westmoreland were classmates, graduating from the military academy together in 1936.

Palmer was a brilliant student, placing sixth in the class. While Westmoreland was serving as chief of staff with the 9th Infantry Division in Europe, he held the same billet with the 6th Infantry Division in the Pacific. Since then, his career also had been weighted toward staff work. When Westmoreland was secretary of the General Staff, Palmer had been his assistant, with the enlightening assignment of liaison officer to the White House. Interestingly for purposes of this search for a Vietnam replacement, he was a native of Austin, Texas.

Abrams placed far down in the Class of 1936, but starred on the West Point football team. He won a wide reputation and a series of decorations as a battalion and combat command leader with the 4th Armored Divison in Patton's Third Army. Much of his time since 1945 had been in armored units, interrupted by three successive assignments as corps chief of staff during and after the Korean War.

On January 7, Wheeler called Westmoreland to Washington and told him he was being sent to Saigon as Harkins's deputy. That he would later take over from Harkins did not need to be stated.

President Johnson and McNamara believed Westmoreland's experience as West Point superintendent showed he could take a scholarly, rather than dogmatic, approach. They felt his recent familiarity with teaching methods could help him in upgrading training in the Vietnamese Army, that his personal example might make an impression on the ruling generals, who made boodling and intrigue a way of life, and that his direct, by-the-numbers approach might produce accurate assessments and reports on the progress of the war.

Taylor recommended Westmoreland strongly, on the basis of his own long familiarity with Westmoreland's character and record, and additionally because he considered an airborne background valuable for an adviser—or commander—involved in an antiguerrilla war, where battalions operating independently without relation to front lines are the rule.

The President had been Westmoreland's guest when he addressed the graduating Class of 1961 at West Point, and had liked him. One of the things he found most likable was Westmoreland's lingering Southern accent, which was not strong but made Johnson feel comfortable with the general, gave him the feeling that here was a man he could trust. At the turn of 1963–1964, a few weeks after moving into a

White House staffed by men he had not selected, most of them with Boston or Ivy League accents, this was important to the President. He chose Westmoreland, and four years later he maintained that he had never regretted that decision for one second.

The selection of Westmoreland did not imply that there was anything lacking in the three other generals recommended for the Vietnam job. The fact that the sifting process had produced their names marked them for new responsibilities. Six months after Westmoreland's assignment, Harold Johnson was made chief of staff of the Army, and shortly afterwards Abrams became vice chief. Palmer succeeded Johnson as deputy chief for military operations. Later, he and Abrams both would join Westmoreland in Vietnam, and the President would be able to tell himself that if the whole effort should fail, it would not be because he had not used his best men—the four most highly recommended generals all were in position to bear down on the war.

Westmoreland had less than three weeks to prepare himself, turn over his command at Fort Bragg, and report for duty in Saigon. He sought all the information he could get at the Pentagon. One of those who briefed him was Marine Lieutenant General Victor H. Krulak, counterinsurgency adviser to the Joint Chiefs of Staff. Krulak long had made a specialty of antiguerrilla tactics, and later his and Westmoreland's notions of how to conduct the Vietnam war were to differ widely. Within ten days, Westmoreland found himself "saturated" with briefings, with listening hour after hour. He decided, before departure, to make a sentimental trip back to West Point.

There, he gathered the Class of 1964, the cadets he

called "my classmates" because they had arrived together in the summer of 1961. To them, he delivered a highly revealing lecture, one he must have compared privately to MacArthur's farewell address there two years before. He summarized for the cadets his pride in being a soldier, his principles and methods of leadership, what he called his "philosophy," in terms that confirmed the full-time consciousness that his friends always had assumed guided his career. For those who know him primarily through his meticulously prepared public speeches and his guarded response at press conferences, it is an enlightening dissertation, as close as Westmoreland has come to disclosing what motivates him, and thus deserves extensive quotation in any study of the moral and intellectual equipment with which he approached his new assignment.

He was departing for that job, he told the cadets, "with a great deal of pleasure and anticipation," but without underestimating its challenge. He disclosed then that he felt a sense of mission in heading for Vietnam, and that he considered himself and his fellow West Pointers a special breed, with a calling perhaps comparable to the ministry.

West Pointers, he said, "have a sacred trust to provide the dedicated leadership and service to our nation which is so essential to our national security. I certainly view this, and I'm sure you view it, as a very high calling and a noble cause. I feel it's up to a West Pointer to dedicate his personal life and his conscience to this idea. This has been the West Point tradition over the years. I must say that the country can be thankful if this is the case."

Leaving the academy, "you're going to be dealing with just ordinary people . . . all people aren't honest. Many have low, if any, sense of duty . . . many citizens go to extremes to avoid any type of military service or any type of service to their country. I feel that West Pointers must be different, and that is why as a group they have been universally and uniquely successful throughout history."

Westmoreland must have thought of some of the civilian offers he had turned down during and after Harvard when he told the class he hoped they would not "be lured away by superficial considerations. I hope you will make a commitment to service for better or for worse, and I am confident that in the long run you'll be happier. It's been my observation over the years that the unhappy and discontented man is that man who is undecided and who's undedicated. He's the man who's restless. He's the man who's looking across the hill to contemplate greener pastures."

Relating how he had thought at twenty-two that he would make a better regimental commander than platoon leader, he adjured any budding lieutenant, "Don't be a meathead . . . It's a man with an inflexible mentality. Try to see all sides of the question. Don't fall into the trap by thinking you know all the answers." This flexibility was a quality Johnson and McNamara thought they saw in Westmoreland himself, and what confronted him in Vietnam seemed relevant to his further advice: "Now realize, gentlemen, that many problems defy full solution and must be lived with. Despite the fact that you might strive to solve these problems, some of them defy solution. We just don't deal nowadays, or at any time, I think, in the history of civilization, with blacks and whites, with complete rights and complete wrongs . . ."

Much about his own personality could be read into his assertion that "in my view the positive approach is the key to success . . . And it's the one that has a strong influence over people. Men welcome leadership. They like action, and they relish accomplishment . . . Speculation, knowledge, is not the chief aim of man—it is action . . . All mankind feel themselves weak, beset with infirmities, and surrounded with danger. The acutest minds are the most conscious of difficulties and dangers. They want above all things a leader with the boldness, decision and energy that, with shame, they do not find in themselves. He, then, who would command among his fellows must tell them more in energy of will than in power of intellect. He has to have both . . . but energy of will is more important . . ."

There, dropped in among a rambling collection of hints to aspiring second lieutenants, was an apt explanation of the Westmoreland manner and of what had guided his career. In school, at The Citadel, at West Point, he had not been a top student, one of the "acutest minds" to which he referred. But he had a straight back, a strong chin, a direct gaze and an eagerness to lead, and he inexorably passed the men who won the highest grades in his classes. It is less likely that he discovered this theory of men and leadership and then adapted himself to it than that, with his constant habit of self-examination, he assessed himself realistically and later, when he came across the theory, adopted it for his own because it fit him so well. Either way, he exemplified it.

Westmoreland proceeded in the same direction, telling the cadets that "as an officer in the service, the important thing is to get the job done. The how is not as important as the objective . . . Needless to say, the means must be proper, must be honest and ethical. But they do not necessarily have to be moderate . . . Stern action does have its place. It's been my experience that after a commander takes appropriate action to get results . . . the means are forgotten, but morale soars . . ."

He told them that a figurative kick in the pants often

was a good leadership technique; that a leader should always be constantly seen by his men because "this tells them without saying so in words that you have a sincere interest in them"; that officers should never lend money or sign notes for their men; that they should avoid criticizing their seniors but be alert to learn more from poor leaders than from good ones. "One fortunate thing about the service that doesn't apply to civilian life is if you don't like your boss, wait six months or a year and you'll get another one . . ."

Then he brought the cadets back to the reason for his visit, when he told them to "beware of snow jobs." Describing Catherine the Great's gullibility in the case of the fake progress displayed by Potemkin, he said, "You will find many Potemkin demonstrations in the service and in any other walk of life, for people try to deceive you as to their standards, their qualities, their accomplishments . . . In connection with my forthcoming assignment, that is one of the real problem areas—to get the facts from the Vietnamese as to what is going on in that strife-torn country. Because the Vietnamese, as soldiers under your command, are inclined to tell you what you want to hear, and not what the actual facts are. This is a human failing . . . don't be naïve about it."

The general approached his summing up, and pounded home to the Class of 1964 that "the best motivator I know is desire by the commander to do a superior job. This attitude by the commander or the leader will inevitably rub off on the troops . . . Gentlemen, concentrate on the job at hand. Give it your full energy and your best effort. The first principle of war is that of the objective. This is a good personal philosophy."

Digressing again, Westmoreland pointed to his new aide as an example for the cadets. That captain, of the Class of

1956, had been summoned by the general from the Special Warfare School at Bragg and asked whether he would be interested in becoming his aide. The captain assumed Westmoreland intended to remain as commanding general of XVIII Airborne Corps, a job he had had barely six months. He did not know of the general's Vietnam orders, and at that time Westmoreland could not tell him. The young officer said no thanks, and when asked why, said he wanted to go to Vietnam. A few days later, when he was told the general was going there, the captain accepted. Westmoreland expressed his admiration for the captain's attitude, and this led him again to declare that "the men of West Point have a very high calling and a patriotic trust . . ."

"Now," Westmoreland said, "in conclusion, I very much agree with the philosophy of Rudyard Kipling, which I think is very profound, and has always been one of my favorites . . ." And, to no one's amazement, he recited seriously for the Class of 1964 lines that are framed and hung on the walls of more than one Boy Scout troop room, verse that might have gotten another speaker tittered off the stage had he offered it to a class of the "acutest minds" graduating from another university:

> *If you can talk with crowds and keep your virtue,*
> *Or walk with Kings—nor lose the common touch,*
> *If neither foes nor loving friends can hurt you,*
> *If all men count with you, but none too much;*
> *If you can fill the unforgiving minute*
> *With sixty seconds' worth of distance run,*
> *Yours is the Earth and everything that's in it,*
> *And—which is more—you'll be a Man, my son!*

There was one other aim of Westmoreland's trip to New York. In Manhattan, he took the elevator at the Waldorf

Towers to pay his respects to MacArthur. The old man was much weaker than when he had visited West Point in 1962; Westmoreland was aware that he might not see him again. MacArthur had spent much of a long career in the Far East, Westmoreland only one year. As usual, the old soldier drew on his rhetoric, telling the younger general, "I am sure you realize that your new assignment is filled with opportunities . . ." He paused, then added, "and saturated with hazards."

17

COMUSMACV

1964–1965

Harkins was waiting at Tansonnhut airport when Westmoreland, wearing a civilian suit and flying Pan American
instead of a special Air Force jet, arrived in Saigon January
27, 1964.

In many ways, the older general was a victim of the
political circumstances under which he had to work. When
he had been assigned to Vietnam two years earlier, he, too,
had been carefully chosen on Taylor's recommendation. A
newspaper reporter's son who quit high school, he had become a National Guard sergeant, then entered West Point
via exams. After graduating in 1929, he spent the 1930's in
the cavalry before becoming George S. Patton's deputy
chief of staff for the North African landing. He remained
the "ramrod" of Patton's staff through Africa, Sicily, Italy,
France and Germany, winning a reputation for a tact and
diplomacy that offset Patton's bluffness. After the war, he

held a variety of command and staff positions, including a tour in the G–3 section of the general staff which over-lapped Westmoreland's time there. He was at Honolulu as deputy commander and chief of staff of United States Army Forces in the Pacific when Taylor and Decker, then Army chief of staff, submitted his name to Kennedy as the man to organize the new Military Assistance Command in Vietnam.

That new command, MACV, symbolized the beginning of the shift of the American role from merely giving advice to helping fight the war. It closely followed Taylor's fact-finding expedition to Vietnam in October 1961, when the former Army chief of staff, later chairman of the Joint Chiefs and ambassador to Saigon, was serving as military adviser to Kennedy. The Taylor mission had extracted from Ngo Dinh Diem promises of reforms, both political and military, and in return the United States would deepen its commitment to back the premier. The original American detachment in Vietnam, MAAG (for Military Assistance Advisory Group), continued to grow but was subordinated to Harkins's MACV as the senior command brought in helicopters, attack aircraft and men to fly them.

Diem was glad to have the financial, logistical and combat support, but loath to use it. He defaulted on his promises of reform, and while Harkins pushed organization of the strategic hamlet program, moving the peasants into fortified villages, Diem's army continued to fight a parallel static, defensive war—when it fought at all. Diem, one reporter observed, considered his army "like a shiny new Cadillac," and did not want it dented. Thus his officers avoided contact with the Viet Cong, which might produce casualties and reprimands from Saigon. Accordingly, the military situation ran farther downhill.

Harkins, whose tact was one of the reasons for his assignment, steadfastly refused to offend Diem by conceding this military decline. His line was, "We've got them off balance—they can't take this much longer." The Americans in the field knew better, and reported same to him, but he never acknowledged it publicly. There were many incidents like the one in a Mekong Delta province where Harkins was briefed by the Vietnamese province chief, who knew of Harkins's close contact with Diem, and who maintained that some four hundred strategic hamlets were working smoothly within his jurisdiction. The Vietnamese hosts did not give the United States sector adviser a chance to brief the general, so the American major insisted on taking Harkins aside. He told him the province chief's figures were "a lot of crap," that perhaps forty strategic hamlets, at the most, were viable. Harkins blew up, chastised the major for backbiting and told him to accept the Vietnamese statistics.

The major told the story to reporters. So did many other majors and colonels who felt their efforts were useless unless the truth were known back home. Relations between Harkins and the press deteriorated. Relations between Diem and the American press, progressively worse, struck bottom when the premier's government used force to crack down on Buddhist opposition. Although the new ambassador, Henry Cabot Lodge, took a tough line with the government after that, Harkins was still supporting Diem and voicing military optimism when a group of officers deposed the premier November 1, 1963.

After the coup, correspondents in Saigon reported accurately that Harkins's identification with Diem meant he would not have the confidence of the anti-Diem clique newly in power. Shortly before his assassination, Kennedy, angered by this, ordered the general's tour extended beyond the two years that might have ended it in January. But he knew the facts by then. The search for a replacement, which gradually narrowed down to Westmoreland, already was underway.

Thus, when Westmoreland shook hands with Harkins on the hot tarmac at Tansonnhut, he was stepping into a delicate relationship. He was clearly labeled "deputy," and this had been underlined when Washington had Harkins make the first announcement of Westmoreland's assignment. But he, Harkins and the Vietnamese generals who were distrustful of Harkins all understood that his deputy status was temporary. It was Westmoreland's turn for tact. This situation was much too public and sensitive for the brashness with which he had handled difficult relations with his seniors in France and Korea.

He spent many of the days during his five-month overlap in the field, while Harkins was in Saigon. His commanding presence, his businesslike attitude helped buck up many American advisers at a time when they needed it. He made it clear that he wanted to hear the full story, not only the part that conformed to the line that progress was steady and victory certain. He took a mission to Malaysia to study the tactics of the successful antiguerrilla war there, guided by Sir Robert Thompson, who had run that war and was assigned as head of the British advisory group in Saigon. The British in Kuala Lumpur laid heavy emphasis on the need for a coordinated civil-military effort, including the meshing of army and police operations. As he traveled about Vietnam, Westmoreland demonstrated his own growing awareness of the dual nature of the problem by taking along not only such military officers as Major General Joseph H. Moore, his high school classmate from Spartanburg, newly assigned to head the Air Force's Vietnam effort; he also invited officials from the Agency for International Development and the United States Information Service, intending to impress the Vietnamese as well as junior Americans with the many-sidedness of the war.

On April 25 in Washington, President Johnson ended whatever suspense had remained about command relationships in Saigon. He announced that Westmoreland would succeed Harkins, but at the same time attempted to show that Harkins was leaving in good standing by extending his retirement date from mid-May to August 1.

Almost simultaneously with Johnson's announcement, MACV issued an order that would eliminate any later possibility of doubt about who was in charge of the American military commitment on the scene. Soon after his arrival, Westmoreland had asked that MACV be changed from a joint command to a specified command, in which one service—the Army—would be superior. The Air Force and Navy headed it off. But the Pentagon did back his later effort to merge MAAG, the strictly advisory American operation, with MACV. His success happened to throw an old friend out of a job. He was the enthusiastic Major General Charles J. Timmes, the MAAG commander, senior American general in Vietnam in length of service there, who had worked with Westmoreland in the 82nd Airborne Division. In what some of the press called "Westmoreland's coup," Timmes's group was merged out of existence and he was transferred back to the States.

There was nothing personal in it. It was intended to "eliminate duplication of functions and improve responsiveness," according to the directive that put it into effect. It also gave Westmoreland, who did not yet have formal command, assurance that he would inherit machinery capable of handling a much larger combat, rather than advisory, force—if and when that change should be ordered.

By June, the facts Westmoreland had gathered in his field trips and behind his Saigon desk had produced what seemed to be, at that stage of the conflict, an orderly approach to winning it. Westmoreland and Lodge took it to Honolulu and proposed it to McNamara, Taylor and others at a conference called to review the war. They called it *hop tac*, which is Vietnamese for "cooperation." Its thesis was that the provinces surrounding Saigon should have first priority, and that when they were cleared of the enemy, control of other major population centers should be expanded outward until the country was pacified. It was the "oil spot" theory, and they sold it to McNamara and Taylor. One reporter, who could not know then how long Westmoreland would remain in Saigon, and how quickly events could change, wrote that the general was "gambling his reputation and future career" on *hop tac*.

When he headed back from Honolulu, Westmoreland was acting commander, although his title remained "deputy." Harkins returned to Washington to serve out his active duty as an adviser at the Pentagon. Only on August 1, the date of Harkins's retirement, did Westmoreland officially become COMUSMACV.

It was a dual ceremony. With the removal of the qualifying prefixes before his title came the addition of a fourth star to his rank. His promotion to full general came a year and a day after he acquired his third star at Fort Bragg. It made him the first man in the West Point Class of 1936 to achieve that goal of all ambitious cadets. He closed his eyes tight under his black brows, threw back his head and grinned with delight as a familiar team affixed the new stars to his collar. It was the same pair who had pinned on his

major general's stars in Washington nearly eight years before—on the left, his wife, Kitsy, and on the right, Maxwell
D. Taylor.

Kitsy flew into Saigon soon after her husband, bringing
all three children. Stevie, the oldest girl, was fifteen; Rip
was ten; and Margaret nine. They moved into an unreal
situation. The children went to American schools and softball games, and Stevie's teen-age boy friends roared in and
out the drive of the Westmoreland villa on motorbikes as if
it were a home in Chevy Chase or Arlington. Once a week,
perhaps a hundred dependents of the military and civilian
Americans overran the villa to watch a movie imported
from home. Fathers went to work earlier and came back
later, but otherwise most of them, as viewed by their families, might as well have been doing a tour at the Pentagon.

The unreality was in what went on behind the villas, the
dependents' schools and post exchanges. When Westmoreland departed each morning, he might be headed for a day
in his office or a day in the field. There were many days
when he flew to government outposts demolished by the
Viet Cong, and somberly inspected the ruins while questioning the survivors or their American advisers. There
were others when he welcomed arriving United States servicemen, telling incoming officers that this was what their
professional lives had prepared them for, and while they
were here he expected them to put in a minimum of sixty
working hours every week. Increasingly often, he said farewell to departing soldiers, leaving for the States in gray
metal boxes draped with the American flag. There were
days like the one when enemy slugs ripped through the
Caribou he was riding, and wounded both pilots and several
Vietnamese soldiers as the plane lifted off the steel matting

of the runway at the ill-fated A Shau Special Forces camp. Kitsy was never certain when her husband left for work in the morning that he would come home to the villa in the evening.

She and the children did not have to accompany Westmoreland into the field to feel the war's closeness. Kitsy spent many evenings in Red Cross work, which included time in hospital wards with the wounded. Going to and from school, American children looked through steel screens on the windows of their buses at dirty orphans, beggars, bar girls, Vietnamese soldiers and draft-dodgers, one-legged men who had not dodged the draft, and at barbed wire about palaces and embassies. The bus windows were screened to prevent anyone's dropping in a hand grenade as he slipped past on a bicycle. The stands at the American softball field, the American-attended movie theater, the American embassy were bombed. Yet Kitsy and eighteen hundred other dependents stayed, to be near their husbands and fathers.

Taylor had not known, when he saw Westmoreland at Honolulu, that he soon would be joining him on duty in Saigon. It was not until July began that Lodge, a liberal Republican, decided to exercise his option to leave the ambassadorship after almost a year, and flew back to join the belated effort to deny his party's presidential nomination to Barry Goldwater. Taylor was tough-minded about Vietnam, and familiar with it; he had the military prestige to give his opinions weight with the generals who were taking turns running the Saigon government; he had behind him years of working smoothly with Westmoreland, and he was available. Johnson shifted him from chairman of the Joint Chiefs of Staff to ambassador to South Vietnam.

Westmoreland automatically deferred to Taylor, not merely because of his military seniority and because it was a habit he had developed when he was secretary of the General Staff under him at the Pentagon. Despite the growing American military involvement, the ambassador remained the head of the American mission in Vietnam. Westmoreland, who renders and expects to be rendered every courtesy in the lexicon of protocol, saluted and said sir to Lodge, and did so with particular enthusiasm to Taylor.

Except for that brief time between his retirement and reactivation by Kennedy, Taylor's whole adult life had been military. He was the author of the American commitment in Vietnam at that stage. He had known Westmoreland since COMUSMACV was a twenty-nine-year-old battalion commander. But he did not attempt to exert his senior position or his expertise to diminish Westmoreland's authority. Knowing that the responsibility for the success or failure of the military effort would fall on Westmoreland, and perhaps reflecting that his own reputation for evaluating and recommending men was involved, he kept his hands off Westmoreland's role. Yet both of them understood that their jobs were bonded together as if by epoxy. That was acknowledged true in any counterinsurgency effort, where, as that already old cliché phrased it, "the hearts and minds of the people" are such a major factor in military success. But in Saigon, it was more so because Taylor's job was to deal with the government, and the government was the military; Westmoreland's job was to advise the military, and the military was the government.

In either of those roles, the series of military men who played musical chairs in Saigon in 1964 did an abysmal job. The first lift in morale after Diem's removal was short-lived.

302

The men who succeeded him demonstrated that their motives had been negative, merely to rid the country of Diem's rule, and personal, merely to seat themselves in his place. They brought with them no concept of how to improve on his performance, either governmental or military.

But the Viet Cong had a concept, and it stepped up its efforts to impose it on the country amid the mass firings of provincial leaders who had the taint of Diem, then the firings of their replacements because they had the taint of Diem's successors. As 1964 wore on, the war news was consistently bad. And after the long insistence on optimism during Diem's rule, those in the field were reporting this bad news almost with a feeling of revenge. The prospect seemed bleak.

The job of Westmoreland's advisers was for each to attach himself to his "counterpart"—the man he advised. A captain usually advised a Vietnamese battalion commander, a major advised a regiment, a colonel a division. Westmoreland, too, had a counterpart in the head of the government's armed forces, and his duty was to inspire and instruct that officer to rally his forces, reform his tactics and reverse the pattern of defeat. But his first problem, amid the constantly shifting cast in Saigon, was merely to know from day to day who his counterpart would be. McNamara, Taylor and to a lesser extent Westmoreland, too, greeted the leader of each new coup with such enthusiasm that onlookers wondered how that country could have so many saviors and still be sinking into defeat. One of them, a goateed general named Nguyen Khanh, regularly came and went from power, and the visiting McNamara went through the motions of building him up as a hero. Westmoreland was restrained in his attachment to any of the in-and-out regimes. He did not want to appear to be meddling in politics, and he had the recent example of Harkins to remind him of how a man in his assignment could lose his effectiveness by too-close identification with a ruler who might be a has-been tomorrow. He tried to keep his relations with the generals on a professional military basis. This did not, in 1964, assure that they would thus be simple, or productive.

In mid-December of that year, Westmoreland flew quickly back to South Carolina to attend his father's funeral. Vigorous until his death at eighty-eight, James R. Westmoreland had spent his later years in Columbia, haunting the halls of the capitol for gossip with his political friends while the legislature was in session, spending most afternoons at the local stockbroker's offices. His acumen had remained sharp; he left an estate of more than $1,200,000, almost all in stocks and bonds, half of it to his widow and the other half, after taxes and expenses, to be split between the general and his sister. Jimmy Byrnes and others were at the rites, and Westmoreland attended in uniform. As his father was lowered into his grave, he rendered him a final, sad salute, and hurried back to Saigon.

The demonstrations of American backing for Khanh and others who passed on and off the Saigon stage were made in the hope that the next group of coup planners thus would be discouraged. But the imminent successors to each general knew that, politically, the United States could not withdraw its support from any non-Communist regime, lest the whole set come toppling down atop Americans and Vietnamese alike.

As the military situation deteriorated, it became ever clearer that the show of Washington's backing, supplemented by advice and airplanes, would not be enough to prevent collapse. Desertions from the South Vietnamese army mounted, and its overall size decreased rather than grew at the time of the country's greatest need. When its battalions fought, too often they blundered into ambushes, stubbornly refusing to post flank security and take other routine precautions for which their advisers pleaded. Outposts and district towns were hit and overrun, making the rural population more cynical than ever about government protection and yielding the enemy crops of American-made weapons. In Saigon, riotous demonstrations, some encouraged by the Viet Cong, kept each regime nervous about which riot might bring in its successor. In Washington, President Johnson was beset by advice that only large-scale United States intervention could save South Vietnam.

Just before Westmoreland got his fourth star and formal command of MACV, an added five thousand American troops were ordered to Vietnam, still as advisers, and accompanied by more material support. Three days after he took over, the President directed American bombers to strike North Vietnamese naval installations to retaliate for enemy torpedo boat runs at United States destroyers in the Gulf of Tonkin. Both were tokens, the latter intended as a warning of what the Seventh Fleet and the Air Force could do if Hanoi persisted. During the election campaign of 1964, Johnson rejected the counsel to intervene massively, and contrasted this policy of restraint with Goldwater's desire to let the generals run the war. He hoped, but could not guarantee, that events would allow him to stick to the line he had laid down during the campaign.

They did not. Three months after Johnson overwhelmingly defeated Goldwater, largely on the issue of "Whose finger do you want on the button?," the military picture was darker than ever. Viet Cong strength was up; South Vietnamese was further down. The enemy carried out a series of attacks on American billets and installations. When they dropped mortar rounds on the United States compound at Pleiku, on the plateau of the central highlands, Johnson decided he had to strike back. He ordered air raids against the north and dispatch of a battalion of United States Marines to Da Nang. He also ordered all American government dependents evacuated from Vietnam.

At the White House, the President issued a statement repeating that "we seek no wider war," but that in the face of the enemy provocations, "we have no choice but to clear the decks and make absolutely clear our continued determination to back South Vietnam in its fight to maintain its independence."

In Saigon, Westmoreland said, "Now the rules of war have changed, and the policy makers in Hanoi are confronted with the necessity of balancing their resources against the damage they may suffer. They've got to take a look down that long road and decide whether they really want what lies ahead for them if they persist in past policies."

At Tansonnhut airport, dependents were shuttled out by the planeload. Both Taylor and Westmoreland had opposed evacuation of civilians for months, until the decision to bomb the north caused Johnson to fear heavy reprisal terrorism against American dependents. Kitsy wore a dark suit with a lace collar, and carried a bouquet given her by Vietnamese saying farewell. She climbed the plane's ladder and threw a kiss back toward her husband, who was smiling. Joe Moore, beside him, bit his lip as he waved to his wife.

Stevie Westmoreland was sixteen by then. As she started toward the ramp, one of her friends said, "We only have to go because of your father. It's his fault, you know."

"It is not," said Stevie. "It's the fault of Lynda Bird's father, not mine."

To "clear the decks" verbally, as the President had done, is dramatic. But its effect on a determined enemy is more psychological than military, even when it is accompanied by a limited bombing campaign. The Viet Cong, its strength and morale built up during the months of confusion and indirection in Saigon, mounted increasingly larger attacks against the government, from one end of South Vietnam to the other. It mauled battalions of the Thanh, or Quat, or whichever regime happened to occupy Saigon's Gia Long palace during a given offensive. The government's forces were being slaughtered steadily in the first half of 1965, and both Americans and Vietnamese in Saigon feared they would not be able to prevent the enemy's accomplishment of one or both of two politico-military objectives: cutting the country in half along Highway 19, from Qui Nhon through Pleiku, or capturing a provincial town and holding it as the capital of "liberated," Viet-Cong-controlled South Vietnam—two degrees of disaster.

Westmoreland still could do little more than advise, and advice was not enough. American airpower under his command was growing, the Marines who came into Da Nang were reinforced by more, assigned to protect coastal bases while still other units came ashore. The number of American servicemen in South Vietnam went up from 3,164 on Harkins's arrival in 1962 to 16,000 when Westmoreland came to Saigon in January 1964. It was 27,000 when the American dependents were sent home in February 1965, and their departure was a signal for the inflow of thousands more soldiers, Marines and airmen. But those thousands still were a trickle compared to what was needed, for the South Vietnamese government, accompanied by the Allied military forces supporting it, was slipping fast toward outright, irrevocable defeat.

The cables from Saigon to Washington hammered home the seriousness of the situation, and the flat fact that only American intervention, fast and massive, could save it. President Johnson could not argue the military necessity, but the domestic and foreign political aspects of major intervention related closely to the speed and size of Washington's response. American ground units were sent, in battalions and brigades at first. Their stated role was defensive —the protection of United States installations. This did not involve them at the outset with the Viet Cong, which was ambushing convoys between the central coast and highlands, besieging outposts from the rice plains of Quang Ngai to the Cambodian border. The war was still being lost. As spring turned to summer, another military junta assumed power in Saigon, this one headed by a general named Nguyen Van Thieu and a flamboyant young air vice marshal, Nguyen Cao Ky. Taylor stepped out at the embassy after the year he had promised, and Lodge volunteered to come back to replace him. And Westmoreland authorized American ground units to fight alongside their Vietnamese allies.

The sequence of steps by which the first United States combat units were brought into the country, then eased into combat was at the heart of the debate over Johnson's "credibility gap." At each step, the administration was asked whether this was a new stage of the war, whether it signified a change in American policy. They were in fact unnecessary questions, because the thickest observer could comprehend that the introduction of American units, and their assignment to action, were important departures from what had gone before. But despite the obviousness of the answers, the White House, the Pentagon and the State Department repeatedly said there was nothing new about what was happening. Later, when those troops had tiptoed into full-scale combat, the administration's critics were to assert that the President had intentionally misled them for domestic political purposes, because he did not want the country to know how deeply it was becoming involved. The administration's explanation, while and after it minimized each degree of intervention, was that it did not want to excite the enemy, including the Soviet Union and especially China, into drastic reaction. With concern over the oriental phobia about loss of face, the thesis held that inserting troops and bombing bridges was evident enough to both friend and foe, but that if Washington blew its trumpet challengingly each time it made another move, the Chinese might be provoked into doing something to preserve their prestige. To those who wished to be charitable toward the administration, this explanation made sense. But many people, including most reporters in Washington and Saigon, did not have that desire. Westmoreland, charged with organizing the growing American presence, had the further task of pretending it was just a more emphatic way of advising Saigon's armed forces.

Neither the pretense of the buildup's innocuousness nor the fact of its gradualness could go on long if American forces were to save South Vietnam from military collapse. The President faced this fact soon after the Viet Cong attacked Dong Xoai, a village and military outpost sixty miles north of Saigon, slashing apart defenders and rescuers. On July 28, 1965, Johnson called a press conference in the East Room of the White House, and there before live television cameras he in effect took back his administration's repeated assurances that nothing was new. He sketched the situation somberly, outlined the necessity of American involvement, and told the country, "This is really war."

The man in charge of that war was Westmoreland. But until the President gave it the label it deserved, the general had very little control over it. At last, with Johnson's public acknowledgment, he was to be allowed to subordinate the role of adviser to that of commander. Within carefully prescribed policy limits, Westmoreland had been presented a blank check, to be filled out with whatever was necessary to prevent defeat, and perhaps later, to shape some form of victory. But if that sounds simple, it was not. Neither bombs nor rifles, ballots nor propaganda leaflets, napalm nor cholera shots can win such a war alone. All are involved. To prosecute a war of such complexity demands leadership of rare breadth, to match the Mao who devised and the Giap who applied the techniques of insurgency which brought South Vietnam halfway to her knees.

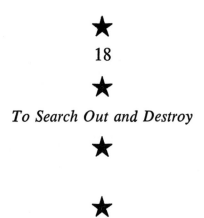

18

To Search Out and Destroy

With Kitsy gone, Westmoreland lived in his Saigon villa with two of his staff. For many months after evacuation, his wife lived in Honolulu, among friends, but that became too public. Every time Westmoreland had an opportunity to visit them he was obliged to undergo involuntary press conferences at the airport. Stevie, a dark, blossoming beauty, began to find scurrilities scrawled on her school desk, because she was her father's daughter. So Kitsy moved back west, to Clark Field, outside Manila. There, she was little more than two jet hours from Saigon, and her husband could fly over for an occasional weekend or less without fanfare. Stevie was sent to college in the States, Rip later enrolled in school on the big island of Hawaii, and Margaret kept Kitsy company. The general's wife busied herself with Red Cross work in the hospital at Clark, often visiting the wards during the day, then going back in the evening when a new flight of casualties arrived after a sharp battle.

After two, three, then four years, Westmoreland's eighty-four-hour work week was so much a matter of habit that he had trouble remembering there had ever been a shorter one. He rose between 6 and 6:30 A.M. for breakfast on the villa porch—one soft-boiled egg, two slices of toast, ginseng tea. Sometimes wearing his bathrobe to avoid wrinkles in that day's uniform, often donning tropicals or fatigues before eating, he would read the Saigon English-language papers and *Stars & Stripes* except when his colleagues were present. If they were, they could expect a foreign affairs quiz from COMUSMACV. Joined by his aide, Westmoreland headed for the office in time for a 7:30 arrival.

Cables were waiting. Then daily briefings, quick ceremonies, reception of visitors. Three times a week there were staff conferences, covering the events of that day and those since the previous gathering. Twice daily, he had briefings from his combat operations center. There were meetings of the American mission council, headed by the ambassador, and sessions with his own counterpart, the Vietnamese chairman of the Joint General Staff. For more than three years, there was thrice-weekly tennis at the Cercle Sportif Club, played doggedly under Saigon's noonday sun to keep in shape for marathon hours of work; but after a crotchety Senator back in Washington complained that the general was playing while his troops were fighting, Westmoreland stopped. Regularly, there were helicopter and jet trips to the field, and back in time for dinner, or diplomatic functions when they could not be skipped.

As Westmoreland changed out of his uniform at 8:15 or later, his houseboy would bring him a beer or a light

Scotch. With dinner, he would have wine if there were guests, although rosé gives him headaches, and if there were no guests, he was likely to let himself go and have a dish of chocolate ice cream. Newspapers, clippings from the States and official reading sometimes kept him busy until lights out about eleven o'clock. Other evenings, there were long conversations with the brigadier generals, colonels or other officers who came and went as residents of the villa during his extended tour. One of those talks explored the question of how the generals of World War II would fit into the Vietnam war. The early consensus was that they would not fit at all, because Vietnam was so different from anything in their experience. Then gradually, as the officers discussed individuals, they concluded that the smartest ones would be successful anywhere, but the full-speed-ahead types like Patton would be hopeless in a war like that in Vietnam. The implication of Westmoreland's agreement was that he did not class himself in the latter group.

Whether he belonged there or not posed a vital question to a non-Communist world committed to resist the steady encroachments Khrushchev had misnamed "wars of national liberation." The President of the United States and his ablest advisers had searched meticulously for the one general best qualified to conduct a war unlike any their country had ever fought before. If Westmoreland was that man, then his performance would say much about whether modern America could breed, educate and train military leaders who could prevail in the indefinite decades of challenge promised by its adversaries.

Of all the traits Westmoreland displayed in the years from The Citadel to Saigon, none was more conspicuous than his personal bearing and conduct. Before a newcomer can guess whether the general is dull or bright, he is certain that he is in the presence of a soldier. It is a characteristic scoffed at by some as superficial. But it is hard to overestimate its importance among soldiers who, from platoon to field army, reflect the example set for them. Nor was Westmoreland's example one of appearance alone. His long hours of work in Vietnam were not merely to stay on top of the cable traffic, situation reports and intelligence estimates that might otherwise have overflowed his office. He wanted every American in the country to know that the same kind of devotion was expected from him. Its effect was visible among civilians as well as military men. In his earliest days, when his effect on South Vietnam's fortunes was not via the battalions he commanded, because he had none, his personal force and directness were a reassuring constant amid the shifting regimes and dwindling fortunes of Saigon.

His habit of flitting about the country was only partly to remind his forces of his presence and his attitude. He felt it essential to see the ground where operations were forthcoming, to understand local situations through the words of the commanders on the scene, rather than merely his own staff officers. While looking and listening, he made decisions in conversation without a time-consuming exchange of bureaucratic paper. Some of his sharpest staff officers thought for a while that this was a dangerously untidy way of doing business, but the system involved follow-up memoranda from each command on any decisions made in the field, and these were put before Westmoreland for corroboration or slight alteration. The result was not messy but methodical and time-saving, and in the process Westmoreland became more familiar with operational details in each province than most other officers at division level.

His own un-Pattonlike approach to his subordinates was demonstrated again one day when he was stoking that knowledge of operations and terrain. He had invited General Cao Van Vien, his counterpart as chairman of the Joint General Staff, along with two of his staff to fly in a twin-engined U–8 and watch the 173rd Airborne Brigade make a combat jump into the Viet Cong's Zone C stronghold. Westmoreland brought along the map coordinates as written down by his aide. Circling over the spot, they found no action. One of the officers lifted his binoculars, found the transports far off to one side, and the U–8 arrived in time for its passengers to witness only the last sticks of jumpers. Westmoreland, somewhat discomfited before Vien, merely said softly, "Later my aide will probably be embarrassed about this." Nothing else was ever heard about it in public.

Being soft-spoken never denoted any slippage in Westmoreland's own self-esteem or the increasing importance of his command in Vietnam. He occupied only one seat in the mission council, outnumbered by the ambassador, the deputy ambassador, the heads of AID, CIA, USIS and others on the civilian side. But in that circle, he was the one who spoke for the increasing hundreds of thousands of military men, and the billions of dollars committed to their support. He resisted any efforts to chip away at his MACV. When the civilian side wanted to shift the Vietnamese regional and popular forces out of Army control and tie them together with the national police, it would have meant taking them out of Westmoreland's advisory jurisdiction. He pigeonholed the suggestion. When Washington sent out his classmate, General Creighton W. Abrams, it did so partly to prepare a successor for Westmoreland, but also to straighten out a situation in which the second senior American in uniform there was an Air Force lieutenant general who fell into acting command of a field army whenever Westmoreland was absent. When it sent Robert W. Komer from the White House to specialize in pacification, it meant him to take off Westmoreland's shoulders part of the extra load imposed when that effort was made a military responsibility. Komer assumed the title of ambassador, but this met no enthusiasm in MACV. On Westmoreland's charts Komer's position was shown by a dotted line opposite that of Abrams. Komer was listed as deputy *to* COMUSMACV, while Abrams rated the title of deputy COMUSMACV. But Westmoreland had asked for neither of them.

Nowhere was Westmoreland's assertion of his position more firm than in dealings with the press. He was conscious that reporters had been the vehicle of his predecessor's disfavor, whether Harkins deserved it or not. Westmoreland did not block the access of individual reporters to the news. But he had a firm rule that no other officer in the country would be allowed to brief the entire press corps on policy at one sitting. The Marine generals in I Corps had a degree of independence from this control. But he wanted to keep the flow of high-level opinion tightly in his own grasp, to avoid contradictions, retain coherence and hopefully to promote a favorable perspective even in times of depressing news by preventing an atmosphere of personal vendetta like that which grew during Harkins's tenure.

MACV's most frequent relationship with the press, however, came each day in Saigon when field-grade information officers briefed reporters on the day's military events. Westmoreland's efforts at mutual confidence often were frustrated by some of these officers, whose open dislike of the press and their assignment was compounded by the accusatory tone of some of their questioners. The resulting distrust and grumbling died down only slightly when COMUSMACV himself had regular background briefings for the established American correspondents and a few non-Americans. Westmoreland would display his encyclopedic knowledge of what his troops and the enemy were doing in every corner of the country, and try to place the daily communiqués and the battles the reporters had witnessed themselves into the context of a year or a monsoon season. Seldom was the information any more highly classified than what individual correspondents could obtain from the general's subordinates in Saigon or the field. But there was satisfaction for them in being able to place their questions directly to the man in charge, even if normally they were restricted to attributing what he said to a "military spokesman." Westmoreland supplemented these sessions by inviting senior correspondents, one at a time, to accompany him on most of his flying trips about the country. They were not expected to write about the secret conversations they sat in on; the object was to familiarize them with Westmoreland and his view of the war.

The other side of the general's information policy was transmitting the word to his troops, which he had described in earlier years as "command information." It was just as carefully thought out as his dealings with the press. He has told how, in early 1946, he flew back from Europe ahead of the 71st Infantry Division, which he was bringing home to inactivation. Aloft, he thought to himself: If ever I am in charge of a war in the future, what would I do differently on the basis of what I have learned in Africa and Europe in the past thirty-nine months? He wrote down his answers. He would emphasize troop orientation so they would understand why they were fighting and what their concrete objectives were. He would set up an inspector general system, responsive to troops' complaints, where appropriate to correct abuses and at other times simply to show the private that someone cared about his problems. Third, he would create a corps of professional investigators to stay ahead of the black marketeers, thieves and others who prosper on war.

Somewhere over the Atlantic, Westmoreland folded those neat conclusions and stuck them in a pocket. Two decades later, he produced them and put them into effect in Vietnam. And in executing the first of them, he used that same one-two-three style in publishing troop information on small cards, intended to be instantly available memory joggers for captains and corporals in tight spots.

When he arrived, and long thereafter, the monotonous success of Viet Cong ambushes was one of the most depressing facts of combat life. He issued a card that included the elementary precautions against ambush. He borrowed from the Marines a sheet of more than 150 Vietnamese phrases like "booby trap" and "Will you help us make a loudspeaker appeal?" and issued them under the MACV imprimatur, complete with dotted lines for folding to pocket size. Perhaps consciously imitating Mao's listed principles for guerrillas, he ordered distribution to every American serviceman in Vietnam of a card bearing nine rules for getting along with mutual respect with the people among whom the war had to be fought. They began with, "Remember we are guests here; we make no demands and we seek no special treatment," and ended with "Above all else you are members of the U.S. Military Forces on a difficult mission, responsible for all your official and personal actions. Reflect honor upon yourself and the United States of America."

How Westmoreland commanded was less important than how he believed the war should be fought when he was in the policy-making role of COMUSMACV. His leadership techniques illustrated again his methodicalness, the habitual foresight with which he laid the ground before proceeding step by considered step. These characteristics gradually gave his recommendations more weight at the White House than those of any other military leader, and sometimes more than those of McNamara himself. As his tour extended, he often bypassed the Commander in Chief, Pacific, who was Admiral Ulysses S. Grant Sharp, and his messages flew over both Pearl Harbor and the Pentagon, directly to the President. But neither his dominant position within the Saigon mission council nor the respect with which his advice was treated by Johnson meant that he always prevailed.

For many months, the IV Corps zone, the rice-rich Mekong Delta, was the one section of the country where American ground troops were not active. The Vietnamese IV Corps commander was a proud man, and he did not want to concede that the Americans would be much help there. After he was transferred, the political roadblock was cleared, but still there was hesitation because, among other reasons, heavy American firepower was too likely to cause accidental civilian casualties in the populous delta. Then Westmoreland arrived one day at a mission council meeting with a formal proposal for moving his troops into the delta, a proposal so thoroughly staffed in advance that none of those ready to argue against it stood a chance. Westmoreland even was able to say that he already had a base building at My Tho, "just in case" it was needed. A civilian official said the general consistently was able to "run circles around the rest of us" on staff work. Westmoreland even came to those council sessions with his speeches prepared ahead, leaving nothing to chance.

Yet, at the other end of the country and along its western borders, he did not have his way so consistently. When an officer at one of the artillery positions just below the demilitarized zone suggested that maybe they could use some of the long-range 280-mm. guns designed for either nuclear or conventional shells in the late 1940's, Westmoreland was willing to investigate. He found out the only remaining 280's were museum pieces at Fort Sill. Again, remembering the extensive though unsuccessful feint his paratroopers had planned with Eighth Army in Korea, the general floated the idea of a fake amphibious invasion of North Vietnam, just above the DMZ. The purpose would be to pull the enemy guns and divisions above the dividing line into the open, where they could be cut up by United States planes and artillery. The President vetoed the suggestion, on the grounds that Hanoi could and certainly would claim the invasion move had been real, and had been victoriously repulsed by its forces.

Westmoreland shifted Army brigades to the I Corps area to take over some of the Marines' area of responsibility, freeing more Marine battalions to combat the North Vietnamese invading directly through the DMZ. He won permission for Marine battalions to sweep through the southern half of the zone, though for years he was unable to gain approval for anything more than secret small-scale patrol missions into enemy sanctuaries in Laos and Cambodia. When Washington wanted to build a static barrier across the country just south of the DMZ, Westmoreland was reluctant. He thought it would be too costly, that its sophisticated radar and listening devices would be frustrated by the jungle and rough terrain, and that no emplacement or line could be effective unless it were fully manned by troops who could be used better as mobile forces. He suspected that it would be called the "Westmoreland line," and that when it leaked he would be held responsible for what was sure to be labeled a failure. It also is true that the barrier was considered by some as a physical infiltration stopper on which Washington could fall back as an excuse if it wanted to halt bombing of the north for political or diplomatic reasons—and Westmoreland strongly supported continued bombing there. The barrier was built anyway, and since McNamara announced it, his name, not Westmoreland's, was attached to it by reporters.

The most emotional debate about Vietnam in newspaper columns and congressional committee rooms has concerned whether the war is worth fighting at all. The most realistic, among those who acknowledge that the war is there and must be fought, is not over whether, but how. Among them, the three broad subjects of most frequent disagreement over the conflict within South Vietnam are closely related, and Westmoreland is at their center. They are the buildup of American forces, its management and how far it should proceed; the employment of those forces; and the preparation of the South Vietnamese Army to take over eventually the defense of the country's borders and internal order.

Westmoreland's nature and background make it certain that he would have preferred to go about the buildup gradually, first constructing ports and bases, then amassing supply backlogs, then bringing in combat troops to operate from those facilities. But when the President signaled the expanded American commitment in 1965, there was no time to lay such groundwork. Washington could not make the decision; it had to be Westmoreland's. He knew it was a calculated risk, but he called for combat forces to be deployed even before they had logistical backup, to prevent the country's collapse. The 1st Infantry Division, the 173rd Airborne Brigade, the 1st Air Cavalry Division, a brigade of the 101st Airborne Division, more Marines arrived. A brigade of the 25th Division was airlifted across the clogged Vietnamese ports directly into Pleiku. While those troops fought major battles on the Van Tuong peninsula, at Plei Me, the Ia Drang valley, the Bong Son plain, most of their food and ammunition was being flown in or transferred by lighter from ships offshore. From July through December 1965, Westmoreland brought in 121,000 added troops, and in the following six months, another 96,000. As they were fighting, more than 40,000 civilian construction workers were turned loose dredging, grading and laying airstrips; military engineers, communicators and paper-pushers, less quickly mobilized than combat divisions, arrived in multiplying thousands, starting to outweigh the line troops who had preceded them.

Westmoreland's calculated risk paid off. The country was dragged back from the edge of defeat. Westmoreland believed he took the initiative away from the enemy between the low point of mid-1965 and a year later. He said the Allies had stopped losing and started winning. He had nearly 300,000 troops in mid-1966, about 60 per cent of them in combat units if not carrying rifles or flying Phantoms. He threw them into the strategy which is most clearly identifiable as the Westmoreland concept of war in Vietnam. Not content with holding the South Vietnamese population then in friendly hands, he ordered his forces to search and destroy the enemy in his swamp and mountain hiding places.

He called it a "two-fisted strategy," and illustrated it many times with a shadowboxing act. He showed how a boxer uses his right hand to protect his body and his left hand to keep punching, always on the offensive. The right hand was compared to the troops, mostly Vietnamese, assigned to protect the pacification effort in the villages within Allied control. The left was troops on search-and-destroy missions, mostly Americans, taking the fight to the enemy. Those troops were interchangeable, as when the boxer shoots his right into an opening. But when the defensive troops, the right hand, are away from their primary mission, the opponent has an opening, so they cannot safely be away long. The crashing truth of this reservation was underscored when the enemy attacked cities the length of South Vietnam while Westmoreland was concentrating his forces around Khe Sanh, near the demilitarized zone, in early 1968. But he insisted that he would not "button up," because then the enemy "can whale you with both hands and all you can do is sit there and take it. If you take all your troops and pull them back to support revolutionary development, to secure, the enemy is going to move in. He'll operate with impunity in the countryside, in the jungles, and in the mountains, and he will, in due time, surround you, and you will find that you have very little freedom of action, just like the boxer who loses his full initiative."

There were many, not only civilians but generals, who disagreed with the search-and-destroy strategy. Their case was strengthened by the enemy offensive against the cities. Prominent professionals in the Marine Corps, Westmore-

323

land's old friend Gavin, Israel's Moshe Dayan were among them. McNamara began to have his doubts about the extent of it. One of the most voluble of these men felt that Westmoreland's concept was a product of his traditional Army education and experience, based on war against a visible enemy who can be found, fixed and fought. He and others thought Westmoreland had too strong a tendency to strike out at what was tangible while giving too little attention to the "national cancer" of enemy propaganda, extortion, night terror and taxation. He decried the general's effort to "quantify the essentially unmeasurable." These military leaders felt that men and money were wasted chasing the enemy into unpopulated wastelands where he had the advantage. Let him alone until he comes out where you have the firepower and the short lines of supply, they advised, and then kill him.

Westmoreland heard but did not hold back. He did not believe the population could be ringed so securely that the Viet Cong, sliding through the darkness, could be denied access. He felt that much of his effort depended on the psychological effect of denying both sanctuary and success to the enemy. He made his commanders understand that he wanted to win every engagement, large and small, and that he was unhappy if enemy main forces were known to be resting anywhere unharassed. Stretching his troops' mobility remarkably with helicopters, he sent them whirling into base areas held by the Viet Cong for years. Zone D, Zone C, the Iron Triangle, the Ho Bo woods, the Rung Sat special zone, the mountains of Kontum and Pleiku provinces, the jungles along the DMZ were no longer undisputed enemy territory. Bulldozers followed the choppers and infantrymen, slicing out roads and airstrips so brigades could respond quickly if the enemy returned. Operations White

Wing, Masher, Hastings, Paul Revere, Cedar Falls, Attle-
boro and more ripped apart Viet Cong battalions and ran-
sacked caches of weapons and provisions that represented
years of hard labor.

The war against the enemy's main forces went well, as
reported in casualty figures and intelligence estimates.
Westmoreland could say at the end of 1967 that the enemy
had suffered eighty thousand killed in that year alone. He
also could speak in terms of roads opened, rice harvested,
defectors rehabilitated, and especially of South Vietnamese
presidential elections, which he termed a "mortal blow" to
the enemy. All these are symptoms of success in what has
been called "the other war" but in fact is the most important part of the entire struggle to make South Vietnam
viable and demonstrate that guerrilla-style "wars of national liberation" are not magically certain to succeed. In
South Vietnam, however, the statistic that would mean
most is elusive, clouded by the unreliability of census figures
and the seesaw nature of the contest for domination of
hamlets on the fringe of the mountains and jungles. That is
the proportion of the country's population under control of
the Saigon government, both militarily and politically. Even
before the enemy offensive of early 1968, Westmoreland's
and Komer's figures indicated that this proportion was
growing very slowly, and not meeting their hopes.

In Westmoreland's mind, the answer was more troops.
When North Vietnamese regular regiments and Viet Cong
units rejuvenated by fillers from the North mounted attacks
against outposts and towns along the edge of their sanctuaries in the DMZ, in Laos and Cambodia, they had to be
fought, and when they withdrew they had to be searched
out and destroyed. This meant concentrating manpower in
the left fist of the Westmoreland shadow-boxing act, the

offensive hand, and inevitably thinning out the forces remaining to defend the cities and villages and expand the population under friendly control. Each time Westmoreland conferred with the President, McNamara and the Joint Chiefs, at each meeting at Honolulu, the LBJ Ranch, Manila, Guam or Washington, his desires for more men were heard and weighed. McNamara, on another of his inspection trips to Vietnam while Westmoreland's request for a step-up to some 620,000 men was under consideration, surprised reporters, Vietnamese and Westmoreland himself when questioned about another manpower increase. It might help, he said in Saigon and on his return to Washington, if the men already in Vietnam were used more efficiently. A prompt clamor arose, about a falling-out between the Secretary of Defense and COMUSMACV. It was not as simple as that. McNamara gave Westmoreland credit for understanding the problems created at home and in Vietnam by the American buildup. Once the general even suggested delaying an increase already approved because of its potential addition to Vietnamese inflation. Westmoreland had stuck to the one-year limit on soldiers' Vietnam tours, and argued against calling out the reserves, preferring an all-active force with higher morale. On this trip, the secretary had seen the vast United States logistical overhead, true, but he also had been impressed more than ever by the hordes of draft-age Vietnamese riding motorbikes around Saigon while American casualty rates grew. He came home and recommended against a new inflow of the size Westmoreland wanted, but he placed simultaneous pressure on Saigon to lower the conscription age of its youth.

When Westmoreland's mother died in July 1967, he returned to her funeral and later joined the President, Mc-

Namara and Wheeler at the White House. There, Johnson declared that "we have reached a meeting of minds" on troop needs, and at the same time praised Westmoreland highly. COMUSMACV told how the logistical foundation in the combat zone was complete, and new troop shipments could be used for fighting instead of support. The underlying fact, it turned out a few weeks later, was that Westmoreland for the time being would be allowed up to 525,000 troops. The general himself was the first to predict that the American commitment might start to decline before that level was exceeded. Satisfactorily or not, the question of American troop strength was answered.

Increasingly more persistent was the parallel question of the Vietnamese Army's strength and performance. Even Westmoreland's well-wishers maintain that this is the area of his greatest shortcoming, that once he was armed with well-trained, mobile, responsive American divisions he forgot his original role of adviser and became so engrossed with assimilating and deploying his own troops that he allowed deterioration of the forces on whom long-range success depended. Westmoreland would not, could not deny that he had concentrated on fighting the war with the best equipment he was given. He saw the 1965–1967 period as an emergency during which United States forces had to carry the principal combat role while the Saigon government's units rebuilt and tried to recover from the low point to which they had stumbled. Yet, even as the American battalions were doing most of the fighting with the enemy main forces, South Vietnamese casualties continued to exceed those among American troops. Most of these losses were in the regional and popular forces, the small, ill-trained militia units whose lonesome duty it is to guard villages and outposts in marginal territory.

While the Americans bore the combat load, the Vietnamese Army (ARVN) grew by 50 per cent between 1964 and 1967, and the regional and popular forces and national police by 65 per cent. This growth stretched thin and cracked the veneer of already inferior leadership in the government's units. Westmoreland advised Ky, Thieu and Vien to put a ceiling on their forces' numerical strength and to concentrate on improving their quality. To reduce desertion, a major plague in Vietnamese units, he convinced the Vietnamese to start using names instead of merely numbers in troop records, to organize personal files on soldiers like the American serviceman's record jacket, to use data processing machinery to handle all this material. This not only made it more difficult for an individual to abandon his unit, but tightened up on a corrupt commander's opportunities to draw the pay of men who had deserted. He urged creation of labor battalions for first-time deserters, and adoption of the death penalty for the third offense—and the new rules were made retroactive. Complete officer selection lists, rather than just the names of those promoted, were published. Thus pride's role in performance and promotion was increased. To improve the soldiers' relations with the population they were supposed to protect and convert, Westmoreland had the Vietnamese issue memoranda much like his own lists of behavior rules for Americans. They underscored the importance of the troops' personal appearance, an entirely new idea except in certain elite government units, and laid down the law against "pillaging, rape, corruption and bribery."

Westmoreland gave Abrams overall cognizance of the government's military effort and the pacification program in which the Vietnamese forces were supposed to specialize. He assigned such hand-picked men as Brigadier General

Edward M. Flanagan, who had served with him in the 82nd Airborne and in Korea, to the full-time job of training director, operating in the headquarters of the Joint General Staff. They worked hard on leadership, especially among younger officers. For the first time, officers' career management was begun. This meant alternation between staff and command, between Saigon and the field, instead of an individual's being condemned to combat without end or living the good life without having to prepare for a fighting assignment. They pushed promotion of NCO's to officer ranks, raising sergeants' morale and breaking into the tradition of reserving commissions for youths from upper-class families. A battalion commanders' school came into being. The military academy at Dalat was upgraded from a two-year curriculum to four years. A National Defense College was organized for senior officers, who study there the broader economic, political and international implications of their careers. This last, so reminiscent of the Army War College in Pennsylvania, only emphasizes Westmoreland's personal involvement in each of these steps.

In late 1967, the expansion, training and tightening up of the armed forces had brought them to a higher state of readiness than they had ever known. But this did not guarantee their immediate eagerness to take on the lean, stubborn regiments of the North Vietnamese Army. In November, for example, when the enemy swept out of Laos to fall on the highlands town of Dak To, American forces engaged them and called on Saigon for ARVN reinforcements. But Westmoreland's operations officer encountered Vietnamese reluctance to go dashing into such a bloody fray. He had to buck the question up to Westmoreland, who took it directly to Cao Van Vien with the argument that this was going to be an important victory and the Vietnamese themselves should have a part in it. Only after that did Saigon send its paratrooper battalions, and they fought well. The initial success of the enemy's onslaught against the cities was attributable in large part to the absence of troops on Tet holiday leave despite intelligence hints that the offensive was coming. Still, Westmoreland aimed at bringing the Vietnamese into more and more combined operations against the North Vietnamese along the edges of the country. He started rearming them with the M–16 rifle, a status symbol among troops in Vietnam despite its controversial performance, in place of the old M–1's and carbines with which they had slogged through the paddies for so long. He tried to prepare them, in short, for eventually shouldering the brunt of the war—main-force and guerrilla.

Out of his past, the general had summoned the boldness with which he raced his guns into battle west of Kasserine, with which he packed men and tanks into the Remagen bridgehead before the bridge collapsed, and applied it in amassing a war machine without a logistical base in Vietnam, then ordering it onto the offensive before an army and a government collapsed. In employing the Vietnamese Army thus saved, he was reverting to the care with which he drilled his artillerymen at Fort Bragg, his paratroopers at Beppu and Fort Campbell. To retain his balance during the political winds, both Vietnamese and American, which blew throughout this controversial war, he needed tact like that which had brought him unscarred and unlabeled through the conflicts of policy and personality in Washington during the 1950's.

The caution with which Westmoreland operated alongside the military juntas which ran Saigon in his early days there enabled him to hold the confidence of the Thieu-Ky group when it took power in June 1965. While the regime endured, he did not relax his restraint. Another in his position might have asked Vietnamese generals in for drinks in the evening, or made a habit of tennis or cards with them to cultivate their trust and learn what they were thinking. Westmoreland stuck to a strict personal policy of having no Vietnamese guests at home, in order to preserve his neutrality—or at least the appearance of it. In fact, he was as aware as Ky and Thieu were that the success of the climactic effort of his career to date depended almost as surely on governmental stability in Saigon as the government's continuance depended on his military success. According to some American civilian officials who served alongside him, his assessments of character and motivation among the Vietnamese occasionally were naïve, perhaps reflecting imperfect understanding of the fact that all generals are not as straightforward as he is. But when the ouster of Lieutenant General Nguyen Chanh Thi as commander of I Corps in early 1966 brought on a new crisis that caused the government to teeter, there was no naïveté in Westmoreland's understanding of what that disaster would mean.

Working closely with the embassy and in touch with Washington, he endorsed the repeated dispatch of Colonel Sam Wilson, the mission coordinator, to Hue to try to convince Thi to call an end to the disorder that followed his removal. When Ky declared that he was going to Da Nang to put down resistance there, Westmoreland ordered in C–130's off missions in all directions to transport the Vietnamese Marine battalions with which Ky wanted to enforce his threat. But at the same time he was counseling the Saigon generals not to carry their countermoves so far that they would precipitate, rather than prevent, the spread of

331

violence. When Ky wanted planes to take troops to Da Nang a second time, he had to use his own creaky C–47's. In July, as the crisis moved toward either resolution or revolution, Westmoreland flew at Ky's request to meet Thi, and repeated his urging for the soldierly Thi to place his country ahead of righting any purported wrongs to himself. When Westmoreland asked him to sit down and talk with Ky, the ousted general agreed. Out of that and subsequent conversations grew Thi's third period of political exile— from French Indochina, from Diem's Saigon, this time from Ky's directorate. The crisis waned, and the government survived.

In the Washington to which Thi was banished, and in concentric waves across the country from the Senate Foreign Relations Committee and Walter Lippmann's column in the *Post*, there was active uncertainty about the regime Westmoreland had helped to preserve, and the war he had to fight. Willy-nilly, as the congressional campaigns of 1966 came and went, and with heat as presidential campaigns accelerated in 1968, Vietnam took a central role in American politics. Westmoreland could not help but be dragged in, too, and opinion of him varied with the individual citizen's attitude toward the war.

Lyndon Johnson admitted to no doubts about either the war or the general. As he had made the decision to go into Vietnam on a large scale, so he had picked the general to direct the move. Over four years, he came to look forward to the weekly reports Westmoreland sent him, which he considered frank and candid, enclosing bad with good. He respected Westmoreland's breadth of view, which he felt was comparable to that of George C. Marshall. When asked in topmost councils his opinion about bombing the docks of

Haiphong, Westmoreland would spell out the military desirability of the move, then add, "But if I were you, Mr. President, I'd do a lot of thinking before I did it," and go on to remind him of the Russian ships in the harbor, and of what the United States had felt obliged to do following the sinking of the *Maine* and the *Lusitania*. To Johnson, this made Westmoreland a far bigger man than other military advisers who would advocate the air strikes but reserve judgment on their political aspects, saying that was not in their field. It was Westmoreland's urging that convinced Johnson he should fly from the Manila conference to Cam Ranh Bay, and there on two separate occasions the President personally awarded him the Distinguished Service Medal. Westmoreland's steadiness and reliability caused Johnson gradually to consider the general as close as a member of his family, and to invite him to live at the White House whenever he reported back to Washington. The President told people the general had more and bigger things in his future.

Some other people had the same idea, although they happened to be of the opposite political persuasion from the President. In the early precampaign stages of maneuvering for 1968, some Republicans looked at the selections available to them and feared another defeat ahead. They thought back to the last winner their party had produced, a handsome, politically unpretentious amateur who happened to be a military hero. On the apparent assumption that all generals are Republicans, they thought Westmoreland would make a good presidential candidate. But Westmoreland gave them no encouragement. The clues to his party politics, if he had any, were skimpy. He was born in South Carolina of a conservative Democratic father. He was friends with Jimmy Byrnes, another conservative Democrat, and Strom Thurmond, who was so conservative he switched to the Goldwater GOP in 1964. By South Carolina standards, however, Westmoreland was unusual in his attitude about matters of race, and he underlined this when he went home and told the legislature in Columbia in 1967 about how bravely Negro soldiers were doing their duty in Vietnam. The general's frequently stated pride in the economies he had ordered at Fort Campbell and West Point, and in his use of time-and-motion studies and other devices inimical to unions, testified to his orientation toward business more than toward labor. He openly admired MacArthur, a hero to the political right. Long before he was committed to duty in Vietnam, he was making speeches about the Communist threat abroad. He had been embraced by a President who in campaign years was the most partisan of Democrats. But he had never worn a party pin, only an Army uniform, and he made it clear to all who asked that he had no plans beyond fulfilling his assignment in Saigon.

There were still other people who had quite different ideas about the general. Predictably, these included congressional critics who refuse to believe anything said by anyone identified with the war. Also predictably, pickets against the war, the bomb and the draft found him a convenient symbol of all they opposed—though, presumably because the President's omnipresence and hyperbole made him such a lightning rod, Westmoreland attracted remarkably little derision from protesters who were not objecting directly to his appearances. They seemed to feel that he was a professional, and what he did, even what he said, should be blamed on Johnson rather than the general himself. Only

after the enemy's widespread Tet offensive did Congressmen and columnists start to debate actively the wisdom of
his strategy, in his name rather than the President's.

The pickets were present, perhaps two hundred of them,
across Park Avenue from the Waldorf-Astoria the day
Westmoreland spoke to the annual meeting of the Associated Press in April 1967. They yelled, and a few scuffled
with police, but they made no trouble for the general. Westmoreland stood to deliver a speech prepared before he left
Saigon, seeking to touch on all the points that seemed to
bother the people back home. Its drafters had sought words
easy to pronounce, to allow for the acknowledged stubbornness of Westmoreland's tongue. It dealt with why
America was fighting, the extent of Hanoi's direction of the
enemy effort, the quality of South Vietnamese and United
States troops, and the relationship of support at home to the
war 12,500 miles away. Into that last section, the general
had slipped a phrase that seemed to him a perfectly fair
description of events. He told the editors that he and his
men in Vietnam were "dismayed by recent unpatriotic acts
here at home," that those acts were handing the enemy
success "which he cannot match on the battlefield," and
that they "inevitably will cost lives" of American and Allied
troops. Westmoreland was amazed by the uproar that followed. His audience gave him a long ovation, but antiwar
legislators, commentators and others across the country had
been insulted personally by his comment about "unpatriotic
acts." Westmoreland's intended target was much narrower:
he was speaking a few blocks from United Nations Plaza,
where demonstrators had burned the American flag and
destroyed draft cards earlier the same month. It seemed to
him, as he spoke the day after a visit to the West Point he so

335

revered, that he was making a statement with which any American would agree. Stung by what he read afterward, he left out any such references later that week when he became the first general since MacArthur to address a joint session of Congress.

Neither his assurances nor the President's quieted dissent. It grew, and concern about the war's progress broadened to many among the general public who did not argue with the administration's position that it was being fought in a good cause. They were perturbed by enemy successes, by reports that the war was in a stalemate, that it might turn out to be unwinnable. Alarmed by the consistency with which the weekly casualty count reported more than one hundred American dead, often two hundred, infrequently five hundred, they began to ask, how long must this go on?

From his arrival in Saigon, Westmoreland had resisted the temptation to read the future and predict how long the war would go on. He had seen the result of Harkins's public optimism, and heard how hollow McNamara's 1963 prediction that United States troops could start home by the end of 1965 turned out to be. Privately, even while reciting his statistics of progress, he never pretended that it would be won soon. He stood at the President's elbow outside the LBJ ranch house in August 1966 when Johnson said, "The single most important factor now is our will to prosecute the war until the Communists, recognizing the futility of their ambitions, either end the war or seek a peaceful settlement. No one can say when this will be, or how many men will be needed, or how long we must persevere." In his Associated Press speech in New York, the general had described the Vietnam conflict as a war of attrition, which by definition is a long war. On no other subject, neither his own politics nor Saigon's, neither press relations nor diplomatic relations, had he so unremittingly exercised the caution that was bred into him and reinforced in a military lifetime.

But the pressure of public opinion was on the administration, and on him. If he could, and did, describe his progress in Vietnam as "tremendous," then why was he unwilling to project that progress toward a date when American soldiers would have completed their job? Under that pressure, delicately, perhaps reluctantly, when he came back to Washington yet again in November 1967, he made his first public estimate of the war's duration.

The first hint of it came after he testified behind closed doors to the House Armed Services Committee. One of its members emerged to tell reporters the general had said that in another two years, the United States might be able to start "phasing out" its troops from Vietnam. Then Westmoreland stood before the National Press Club and spelled out his assessment of what had gone before and was yet to come, imposing on the war the same sort of retrospective order he had given the Remagen bridgehead when he described that chaos afterward as a well-organized arch and keystone.

He divided the war into four phases, two of which were nearing completion—the initial rescue of Saigon's tottering army and installation of American combat and support elements, followed by assumption of the offensive and stabilizing the government to the point at which national elections could be held. He could not foresee the enemy's Tet attacks when he said that with 1968, "we have reached an important point when the end begins to come into view," and in that third phase American forces would continue the offensive, including a larger move into the delta, but would start gradually to turn operations over to Vietnamese units.

Phase Four would "see the conclusion of our plan to weaken the enemy and strengthen our friends until we become progressively superfluous . . . U.S. units can begin to phase down as the Vietnamese Army is modernized and develops its capacity to the fullest. . . The Vietnamese will take charge of the final mopping up of the Viet Cong [which will probably last several years]." Questioned, Westmoreland estimated that Phase Four could start in late 1969.

There it was, flat on the record, a plan, a prediction, a date. If he was accurate, he would have proved that a product of a cotton mill town in South Carolina, of Boy Scout Troop 1 and West Point, who learned warfare in Tunisian deserts, Normandy hedgerows, German forests, Carlisle seminars, Korean paddies and Pentagon conferences, a soldier whose personal immaculateness reflected his orderly mind, could wield American power effectively against an enemy whose unorthodoxy persuaded millions that it was invincible. He would have taught a lesson that could cause historic reappraisals in Hanoi, Peking, Havana and Moscow. But if he was wrong, opponents of his President and his war would try to bury the name of Westmoreland in the Vietnamese graveyard of reputations beside those of his predecessors.

Although he would move on before the war's final resolution, it would be his hundreds of eighty-four-hour weeks, the pattern he imposed with his boldness and stubbornness, that would determine its outcome. And its outcome would influence directly the question of whether a divided world would resign itself to settling its differences by economics and diplomacy, or resort yet again to arms and blood.

SOURCE NOTES

Research for a book about a living man turns more to conversation with his contemporaries than to written documentation. When it deals with a general whose career is continuing and sometimes controversial, many of those interviewed prefer not to have specific bits of information attributed to them. For that reason, I wish to acknowledge the help of the dozens who have contributed to this book by mentioning them under broad periods of Westmoreland's career, rather than under individual chapters. To start, I will note that for general background about the years and events involved, I have relied on the files of the Baltimore *Sun* and the *New York Times*, especially on the perceptive pre- and postwar reporting of the late Mark S. Watson in *The Sun*.

The Reverend Hiram K. Douglass, of Florence, Alabama, kindly made available his genealogical research on the Westmoreland family. The general's late mother, Mrs. J. R. Westmoreland, and his sister, Mrs. N. Heyward Clarkson, Jr., were helpful on ancestry, boyhood and later periods. Among others interviewed about the boyhood section were the Reverend William L. Ball, Jr., Dr. Wardlaw Hammond, Dr. Boykin Lyles, E. W. Marshall and especially Conrad P. Cleveland in Spartanburg; and Lieutenant General Joseph H. Moore in Honolulu. I used *History of Spartanburg County* by Dr. John Belton O'Neall Landrum; *The Scribbler* (Spartanburg High School yearbook), 1931; the files of the Spartanburg *Herald* and *Journal*; and "General Westmoreland's Scouting Days" by Sam Traughber in *Scouting Magazine*, May 1966.

Cleveland and Hammond also were involved in the cadet period, as were James F. Byrnes and W. D. Workman, Jr., in Columbia, South Carolina; Colonel Richard Ripple (Ret.) in Honolulu; Lieutenant General Leonard C. Shea in Washington and Colonel Charles P. Nicholas at West Point. *The Sphinx* (Citadel yearbook), 1935; *West Point Today* by A. C. M. Azoy and Kendall Banning; *Official Register of Officers and Cadets, U.S.M.A.,* 1933–1936; and *The Howitzer* (West Point yearbook), 1933–1936 were useful.

The general's wife and her parents, Colonel and Mrs. Frederick Van Deusen (Ret.) of Fayetteville, contributed to the prewar section, and of course Mrs. Westmoreland's help covered all the postwar period. Also, for Fort Sill and Schofield Barracks, I interviewed Lieutenant General Charles D. Herron (Ret.), Colonel and Mrs. Ripple, Nicholas and Shea. Hawaiian Division and 8th Field Artillery records were examined at Schofield, and 18th Field Artillery records in the National Archives.

Most of those who helped with the 9th Infantry Division period, from 1941 to 1946, contributed to several successive chapters. They included the Reverend Edward T. Connors and Manuel Brum, who prepared a valuable, admiring memoir of Westmoreland; Orlando Bruno, Richard W. Black, John Clemmey, Thomas Collins and Thomas Delmore, all like Father Connors from the Boston area. Major General Louis A. Craig (Ret.), Governor Otto Kerner, Brigadier General Justin W.

Stoll (Ret.), General Maxwell D. Taylor (Ret.), General Williston B. Palmer (Ret.) and Lieutenant General James M.
Gavin (Ret.) all were interviewed in Washington, and Colonel
John W. MacIndoe in Saigon. Throughout Westmoreland's association with the 9th Division, I relied heavily for setting and
chronology on the official division history *Eight Stars to Victory* by Joseph B. Mittelman. Particularly useful also were
volumes of the United States Army in World War II series,
among them *Northwest Africa: Seizing the Initiative in the West*
by George F. Howe; *Sicily and the Surrender of Italy* by Lieutenant Colonel Albert N. Garland and Howard McGaw Smith,
assisted by Martin Blumenson; *Cross-Channel Attack* by G. A.
Harrison; *Breakout and Pursuit* by Blumenson; and *The Siegfried Line Campaign* by Charles B. MacDonald. Other references included *Kasserine Pass* by Blumenson; *A Soldier's Story*
by Omar N. Bradley; *The Bridge at Remagen* by Ken Hechler;
and records of the 9th Division and the 34th Field Artillery
Battalion in the National Archives.

For the postwar and Korean War period, I interviewed
Brigadier General Edward M. Flanagan in Saigon, Colonel
Nicholas Psaki at Bien Hoa, Colonel George S. Pappas and
Mrs. Carmen Mitchell at Carlisle, Brigadier General George S.
Beatty and Major General Joseph R. Russ in Washington, and
Brigadier General Elvy B. Roberts at Fort Jackson, as well as
Cleveland, Gavin, MacIndoe, Palmer, Stoll and Flanagan. *Army
War College: A Brief Narrative* and records of the War College
at Carlisle were used, along with one volume of the United States
Army in the Korean War series, *Truce Tent and Fighting Front*
by Walter G. Hermes; *History of the 187th Airborne R.C.T.*;
and command reports of the 187th in the National Archives.

Interviews covering the Stateside period between Korea and
Vietnam were with Karl N. Carter of Roanoke; President Lyn-
don B. Johnson, Secretary Robert S. McNamara, Major General
William C. Garrison, Major General Elias Townsend, Major
General Paul F. Smith and General George H. Decker (Ret.)
in Washington; J. G. McDonnell and Mrs. Marie F. Warren of

Fort Campbell; Colonel John K. Singlaub, Colonel Robert A. Cuzick and Colonel Robert M. Piper in Saigon; Brigadier General William W. Bessell, Jr., at West Point, in addition to Flanagan, Nicholas, Palmer, Roberts, Taylor and Shea. I referred to *The Uncertain Trumpet* by Taylor; *War and Peace in the Space Age* by Gavin; "Airborne Minutemen" by Westmoreland in *Ordnance,* January–February 1959; "Management Analysis: Not a Comptroller's Toy," Parts 1 and 2, by Westmoreland in *Armed Forces Management,* September and October 1960; *Annual Report of the Superintendent, U.S.M.A.,* 1961–1963; files of *Pointer View,* the West Point newspaper, and *Assembly,* the alumni magazine; files of *Paraglide,* the Fort Bragg newspaper; "STRAC—the Army's Capabilities for Limited War," including "The How of STRAC," by Westmoreland in *Army,* December 1958; the transcript of Westmoreland's speech to the West Point Class of 1964, which also produced excerpts in earlier chapters; and Tom Scanlan's column in *Army Times,* January 19, 1966.

The opening chapter about Vietnam obviously is based on personal observation, supplemented by conversations with my colleagues, whose help in the final two chapters was essential. They include Wendell S. Merick, Ward Just, William Tuohy and Ronald Ross in Saigon; Peter J. Kumpa and Charles Mohr in Hong Kong, and Philip Potter and Tae Yun Chung in Washington. The nonjournalists interviewed for these chapters included Brigadier General J. W. Chaisson, Barry Zorthian, Flanagan and officers of other services who have asked not to be identified, in Saigon and elsewhere; President Johnson, McNamara, Taylor, Peter Tarnoff, Robert Don Levine, Harold Kaplan, Lieutenant General Nguyen Chanh Thi and others in Washington. Among the written sources were *Mission in Torment* by John Mecklin; *The Making of a Quagmire* by David Halberstam; "Inheritor of a Wretched War" by Jack Langguth in the *New York Times Magazine,* November 15, 1964; and "The Westmoreland Coup" by Beverly Deepe in the New York *Herald Tribune,* June 12, 1964.

INDEX

ABRAMS, CREIGHTON, 14, 285–287, 315–316, 328
African campaign, 102–122
Allen, Terry, 127
Army War College, 198–201

BALL, WILLIAM L., JR., 48
Barnwell, Virginia, 46
Barriger, William L., 220–221
Bayerlein, Fritz, 161–162
Beebe, Joseph E., 117
Bessell, William W., Jr., 266
Blumenson, Martin, 113
Boatner, Haydon L., 204–205
Boy Scouts of America, 38–44
Bradley, Omar N., 60, 71, 119, 124, 135–136, 150, 159, 196
Buckner, Simon Bolivar, 63, 70–71
Budge, Larry, 14–15
Byers, Clovis E., 193
Byrnes, James F., 37, 46, 57, 304, 334

CHILDS, EUGENIA TALLEY. See Westmoreland, Eugenia Talley Childs
Childs, W. G., 33–34
Chu Lai, 24–25
Churchill, Winston, 135–136
Citadel, The, 48–49, 50–57
Clark, Mark W., 212, 219
Clemmey, John, 110, 116
Cleveland, Conrad, 189
Collins, J. Lawton, 135–136, 194
Command and General Staff College, 197–198
COMUSMACV. See Westmoreland, William C.
Connors, Edward T., 133
Craig, Louis A.: advises W on career, 173–174; appoints W as his chief of staff, 147; in Western Europe, 140–167 *passim*, 169–174

DAVIDSON, GARRISON, 264
Davis, Benjamin O., Jr., 66
Dayan, Moshe, 324

343

Decker, George H., 276
Di An, 11–12
Diem, Ngo Dinh, 283, 295–296, 302–303
Dietzel, Paul, 268–270, 277
Dobson, Hubert R., 41, 62
Dong, Pham Van, 23
Dulles, John Foster, 227
Dunphie, Charles A. L., 106–107, 109, 111–112

EDDY, MANTON S., 100–101, 118, 132–133, 140
XVIII Airborne Corps, 279–280
18th Field Artillery, 77
8th Field Artillery, 81–82
82nd Airborne Division, 182–184, 192, 194–196; Sicilian campaign, 123–127
Eisenhower, Dwight D., 105–106, 135–136, 150, 159, 170, 238, 261, 278
Employees Savings Bank, 37–38
Evans, Emma, 47

FERGUSSON, ROBERT, 58
504th Parachute Infantry Regiment, 182, 184, 186
Flanagan, Edward M., 328–329
Fort Benning, 183–184
Fort Bragg, 87–88, 89–101 passim, 279, 282–283
Fort Campbell, 243–260 passim
Fort Sill, 74, 76–80
Freiherr von Broich, Fritz, 112
Fuller, Belle, 36

GAVIN, JAMES M., 126, 182–183, 186, 192–193, 226, 324
Glover, Hayne, 52
Goering, Hermann, 127
Goldwater, Barry, 301, 305
Gulf of Tonkin, 305

HALL, DALE, 266, 268
Hammond, Lester, 209–210

Hammond, Wardlaw, 40, 47, 49, 52
Harkins, Paul D., 284, 286, 294–298, 304, 307, 316, 336
Harvard Graduate School of Business, 229–232
Hatch, Melly, 80, 85
Hatterson, Corporal, 19
Hawaii, 80–87
Hay, John H., Jr., 12
Herron, Charles D., 82, 86
Herron, Jimmie, 82, 84, 93
Hitler, Adolph, 140, 162, 170
Hitt, Robert M., Jr., 56
Hodges, Courtney H., 154–155
Hoge, William M., 158–159
Holderness, Stephen, 69–70
House Armed Services Committee, 337–338
Howell, Reese M., 132, 141–143
Huebner, Clarence R., 154–157

IRWIN, S. LEROY, 99, 107, 109, 111, 117, 122, 186

JENNINGS, ELISABETH, 46, 48
Johnson, Harold K., 285, 287
Johnson, Lyndon B., 326–327; conduct of Vietnam war, 305–310, 332–336; names Taylor ambassador to South Vietnam, 301; West Point commencement address, 273–274; and W's assignment to Vietnam, 284–287, 298

KENNEDY, JOHN F., 274–277, 282–283, 295–297
Kerner, Otto, Jr., 96, 99; African campaign, 103–104, 110–111, 116, 121; Sicilian campaign, 125–126
Kesselring, Albert, 113
Khanh, Nguyen, 303
Komer, Robert W., 316
Korea, 203–224
Krulak, Victor H., 287
Ky, Nguyen Cao, 308, 331–332

LANG, JOHN W., 53–54
Leviero, Anthony, 239
Lodge, Henry Cabot, 283–284, 296, 299, 301
Long, Talton W., 245
Lyles, Elizabeth, 46, 48

MAAG. *See* Military Assistance Advisory Group
MacArthur, Douglas A., 59–60, 261, 264, 274–275, 277–278, 293, 334
McAuliffe, Anthony J., 201
McCoy, Harold L., 14
MacCullough, Bullhead, 78
MacDonald, Charles B., 147
McNamara, Robert S., 299, 303, 319, 321, 336; and W's assignment to Vietnam, 284–287; and W's conduct of war, 324, 326–327
MACV. *See* Military Assistance Command, Vietnam
Manfredi, Giuseppe, 127
Marshall, George C., 147, 332
MATS. *See* Military Air Transport Service
Michaelis, John H., 276
Military Air Transport Service (MATS), 280
Military Assistance Advisory Group, 295, 298
Military Assistance Command, Vietnam, 295, 298, 315–318
Military College of South Carolina. *See* Citadel, The
Millet, Lou, 251
Mittelman, Joseph B., 133
Mo Duc, 22–24
Montgomery, Bernard, 105, 114, 118, 135, 158, 164–165
Montgomery, Victor, 35–36
Moore, Joseph H., 41, 297–298, 306

NATIONAL POLICE FIELD FORCE, 17
9th Infantry Division, 88–89, 126, 128, 131, 133, 140–141, 143; African campaign, 105–122 *passim*; Elbe River, 168–172; Fort Bragg, 90–101 *passim*; Normandy, 135–139; Western Europe, 144–167 *passim*, 179–180
Nixon, Richard M., 248–249

OITA PARACHUTE TRAGEDY, 217–218
187th Airborne Regimental Combat Team, 12, 203–224 *passim*
101st Airborne Division, 240–242, 243–260 *passim*
Operation Overdrive, 257–259

PACOLET MILLS, 35–37
Palmer, Bruce, Jr., 285, 287
Palmer, Williston B., 193–197, 201, 232, 234–236, 238
Patton, George S., Jr., 114, 116, 176, 294, 313
Payne, Sally, 93–94
Pearce, Sergeant Major, 18–19
Pegler, Westbrook, 90
Pershing, John J., 73

RCT. *See* 187th Airborne Regimental Combat Team
Radford, Arthur W., 226, 236, 239
Recondo, 251–252, 264–265
Rencken, Donald A., 114
Rich, Charles, 247
Ridgway, Matthew B., 123–124, 236
Ripple, Richard, 84, 93
Rommel, Erwin, 105–107, 109–110, 112–113
Roosevelt, Franklin D., 57, 64–65, 90
Rosson, William B., 22–25

SA HUYNH, 20
71st Infantry Division, 179–180, 181
Sharp, Ulysses S. Grant, 319
Shea, Leonard, 69–70
Sicily, 123–131

Singlaub, John K., 251

60th Infantry Regiment, 174–179, 181

Sokhonov, Major General, 170

South Vietnam, 302–303, 305–308, 325; army, 327–330; increased part in war, 331, 338

Spartanburg, S.C., 29–49 *passim*

Spartanburg *Journal*, 34–35

Stoll, Justin, 112, 117–118, 130, 151–152, 160–161, 172

Strategic Army Corps (STRAC), 280–281

Summerall, Charles P., 54–55

Swift Strike III, 281–282

TAYLOR, MAXWELL, 125–126, 132–133, 219, 223, 264, 294–295; recommends W as COMUS-MACV, 284, 286; recommends W as superintendent of West Point, 260, 261; and Vietnam war, 299–303, 306, 308; and W as his secretary of the General Staff, 232–241 *passim*; selects W as commander of 101st Airborne Division, 241–242

Tet offensive, 335, 337

Thi, Nguyen Chanh, 331–332

Thieu, Nguyen Van, 308, 328, 331

34th Field Artillery Battalion, 131–133; African campaign, 103–122 *passim*; citation for African battle heroism, 113–114; at Fort Bragg, 91–101 *passim*; Sicilian campaign, 125–129

39th Infantry Regiment, 100, 114, 123–124, 127, 131

Thompson, Sir Robert, 297

Thurmond, Strom, 334

Timmes, Charles J., 298

Tolson, John J., 14–16

Trapnell, Thomas J. H., 205

Truman, Harry S, 98, 187

Tucker, Reuben H., 184, 244

Twining, Nathan F., 226–227, 236

VANCE, CYRUS R., 284

Van Deusen, Frederick, 80, 86

Van Deusen, Katherine. *See* West-moreland, Katherine Van Deusen

Van Fleet, James A., 212

Vien, Cao Van, 315, 328–329

Viet Cong, 324, 325, 338; increased activity, 1965, 307–310; political and military concept, 303

Vietnam war: "credibility gap," 308–309; Diem's conduct of, 1962–1963, 295–296; disagreement on conduct of, in U.S., 321, 323–324, 326; increase in U.S. troops, 307–308, 322; "oil spot" theory for winning, 299; "search and destroy" tactics, 322–323; W's conduct of, 314–333 *passim*

WATSON, ALBERT II, 282

Watson, Mark S., 238

West Point: W as cadet, 57–74; W as superintendent, 261–278; W's address to Class of 1964, 287–292

Westmoreland, Eugenia Talley Childs, 33–49 *passim*, 182, 326

Westmoreland, James Ripley, 32–49 *passim*, 51–52, 56–57, 183, 304

Westmoreland, James Ripley II, 229, 275, 278, 300–301, 311

Westmoreland, Katherine Stevens, 193, 275, 278, 300–301, 307, 311

Westmoreland, Katherine Van Deusen, 79–80, 86, 198–199, 202, 214–215, 224, 231, 275, 278, 300–301, 306, 311–312; children born to, 193, 229, 235; marriage to W, 187–190

Westmoreland, Margaret Childs, 235, 275, 278, 300–301, 311

Westmoreland, Margaret Rush, 37–39, 41, 45, 49, 73, 84–85, 182, 304

Westmoreland, Thomas, 30–31
Westmoreland, William C.: appointed 9th Div. chief of staff, 145–147; birth, 35; Boy Scout activities, 38–44; children born to, 193, 229, 235; at Citadel, 51–57; citations, 130, 164, 333; as COMUSMACV, 284–286, 294 *ff.*; congressional and newspaper criticism of, 334–337; fails Air Force physical, 72, 87; genealogy, 29–32; Hawaiian service, 80–87; leadership, tactics and views on, 96–98, 208–209, 218–219, 289–292; marriage, 189; parachute training, 183–185; Pentagon assignment, 225–241; political affiliations, clues to, 333–334; promotions, 82, 94, 100, 138, 152, 214, 235, 282, 299; relations with Vietnamese, 303–304, 318, 330–331; secretary of the General Staff, 232–241; testimony to House Armed Services Committee, 337–338; transfer to infantry, 174; at West Point, 57–74, 261–278; address to West Point class of 1964, 287–292; youth, 36–48
Wheeler, Earle G., 284, 286, 327
Wilson, Charles E., 227–228, 236, 238–239
Wilson, Sam, 331
World War II: African campaign, 102–122; Normandy invasion, 136–139; Sicilian campaign, 123–131; Western Europe, 135–143, 144–167, 168–179

YARBOROUGH, WILLIAM P., 283